T0322374

Sixteen Stormy Days

Sixteen Stormy Days

The Story of the First Amendment to the Constitution of India

Tripurdaman Singh

BLOOMSBURY ACADEMIC

LONDON • NEW YORK • OXFORD • NEW DELHI • SYDNEY

BLOOMSBURY ACADEMIC
Bloomsbury Publishing Plc
50 Bedford Square, London, WC1B 3DP, UK
1385 Broadway, New York, NY 10018, USA
29 Earlsfort Terrace, Dublin 2, Ireland

BLOOMSBURY, BLOOMSBURY ACADEMIC and the Diana logo
are trademarks of Bloomsbury Publishing Plc

First published in Great Britain 2024
First published in India in 2020 by Vintage Books, an
imprint of Penguin Random House India

Copyright © Tripurdaman Singh, 2020, 2024

Tripurdaman Singh has asserted his right under the Copyright,
Designs and Patents Act, 1988, to be identified as Author of this work.

For legal purposes the Acknowledgements on pp. viii–ix constitute an
extension of this copyright page.

Cover image © Rawpixel, iStock/Getty Images Plus

All rights reserved. No part of this publication may be reproduced or transmitted
in any form or by any means, electronic or mechanical, including photocopying,
recording, or any information storage or retrieval system, without prior
permission in writing from the publishers.

Bloomsbury Publishing Plc does not have any control over, or responsibility for,
any third-party websites referred to or in this book. All internet addresses given
in this book were correct at the time of going to press. The author and publisher
regret any inconvenience caused if addresses have changed or sites have ceased
to exist, but can accept no responsibility for any such changes.

A catalogue record for this book is available from the British Library.

A catalog record for this book is available from the Library of Congress.

ISBN: HB: 978-1-3503-8438-5
        ePDF: 978-1-3503-8440-8
        eBook: 978-1-3503-8439-2

Typeset by Integra Software Services Pvt. Ltd.
Printed and bound in Great Britain

To find out more about our authors and books visit www.bloomsbury.com
and sign up for our newsletters.

CONTENTS

List of Plates vi
Acknowledgements viii

Introduction 1

1   The Build-up 15

2   Will the People Wait? 35

3   The Deepening Crisis 61

4   The Gathering Storm 87

5   The Clouds Burst 111

6   The Battle Rages 141

7   The Aftermath 175

*Appendix 1: Articles 15, 19, 31 of the Constitution: 1950
    v. 1951* 195
Appendix 2: Timeline of Major Events 201
Notes 204
Index 246

PLATES

1 A Constituent Assembly meeting, 1949. B. R. Ambedkar, chairman of the Drafting Committee, sat in the centre.
2 B. R. Ambedkar presenting the final draft of the Constitution to Rajendra Prasad, chairman of the Constituent Assembly, 25 November 1949.
3 Legal luminaries, later cabinet colleagues: B. R. Ambedkar and C. Rajagopalachari, 1948.
4 The Constituent Assembly in session, 1948.
5 Signatories to the Constitution: a page from the Constitution bearing the signatures of (among others) J. B. Kripalani, Purushottam Das Tandon, Hriday Nath Kunzru, Govind Malaviya, Begum Aizaz Rasul, Sucheta Kripalani, Shibban Lal Saksena, Mahavir Tyagi, Mohanlal Gautam and Algu Rai Shastri.
6 The first Cabinet of the Republic of India with the president, 31 January 1950. Seated L to R: B. R. Ambedkar, Rafi Ahmed Kidwai, Baldev Singh, Abul Kalam Azad, Jawaharlal Nehru, Rajendra Prasad, Sardar Patel, John Matthai, Jagjivan Ram, Amrit Kaur and Shyama Prasad Mookerji. Standing L to R: Khurshed Lal, R. R. Diwakar, Mohan Lal Saksena, N. Gopalaswami Ayyangar, N. V. Gadgil, K. C. Neogy, Jairamdas Daulatram, K. Santhanam, Satya Narayan Sinha and B. V. Keskar.
7 A stamp bearing the portrait of the Anglo-Indian leader and educationist Frank Anthony.
8 A stamp bearing the portrait of the liberal leader Hriday Nath Kunzru.
9 Jawaharlal Nehru addresses a committee meeting, 1949. Rajendra Prasad and Sardar Patel are seated to his left.

10   Jawaharlal Nehru addresses the Constituent Assembly, 1946.

11   Jawaharlal Nehru signing the Constitution, 1950.

12   Colleagues and competitors: (L to R) Shyama Prasad Mookerji, Jairamdas Daulatram, Govind Ballabh Pant, Jagjivan Ram and Jawaharlal Nehru.

13   Founders of the Republic – Members of the Constituent Assembly, 1950. Among the figures in the front row: Baldev Singh (first from left), John Matthai (second from left), Amrit Kaur (fourth from left), Jawaharlal Nehru (fifth from left), Rajendra Prasad (seventh from left), Shyama Prasad Mookerji (first from right), Jagjivan Ram (third from right) and Sardar Patel (fourth from right).

All images courtesy of Wikimedia Commons.

ACKNOWLEDGEMENTS

To borrow rather freely from an oft-quoted proverb, it takes a village to create a book and bring it past the finishing line. It has been no different with this one. The founder of that village in my case was the late C. A. Bayly, who first introduced me to the pleasures and pitfalls of historical research as a graduate student in Cambridge, and to whom I owe a great debt of gratitude. A similar debt of gratitude is owed to Mushtaq Qureshi, who has been a pillar of strength throughout.

Many rewarding conversations with Meghnad Desai, James Manor, Swapan Dasgupta, Tahir Kamran, Gopalan Balachandran, Fali Nariman and Philip Murphy have informed my writing, and I am deeply grateful to them for their generosity and encouragement. I have been extremely fortunate in having had the intellectual companionship of friends and colleagues who have helped me refine and sharpen my ideas: Adeel Hussain, Harshan Kumarasingham, Ali Khan Mahmudabad, Amir Khan, Parul Bhandari, Nicolas Blarel, Narayani Basu, Anshul Avijit, Shruti Kapila, Zareer Masani, Kanishka Gupta, Aditya Balasubramaniam and Simon Wolf.

The School of Advanced Study, University of London, has provided me with an invigorating academic home in which to pursue my intellectual interests. I'd particularly like to thank the Institute of Commonwealth Studies (ICwS) and its former director Sue Onslow, as well as Chloe Pieters and Kay Musonda for their support. Thanks are also due to the British Academy for their generous funding of my research and my time at ICwS.

I am exceptionally grateful for the love and support of my friends and family, who have provided much of the scaffolding that keeps my literary and academic ambitions propped up. Special thanks in this regard to Digvijay Singh Deo, Nadia Cavalletto, Aviv Fonea, Plum Schrager, Alessandro Malusa, William Marks, Kathryn Santner,

Siddhartha Chaturvedi, Kitty Brandon-James, Imran Jumabhoy, Lucy Jacobsen, Catherine Katz, Casra Labelle, Rina Kuusipalo, Abhijit Iyer, Karolina Adamkiewicz, Cleo Roberts, Papatya Sutcliffe and Francesca Andrews.

And finally, a special word of thanks to Maddie Holder, who has been a kind, patient and considerate editor, and has championed this book throughout.

Introduction

'Somehow, we have found that this magnificent constitution that we had framed was later kidnapped and purloined by lawyers,' thundered Prime Minister Jawaharlal Nehru as he moved the Constitution (First Amendment) Bill to be referred to a standing committee in Parliament on 16 May 1951.[1] Fundamental rights, individual liberty and freedom had been the dominating ideas of the nineteenth century, he declared, relics of a static age trying to preserve existing social relationships and social inequalities. These ideas were now passé, overtaken by the bigger and better ideas of the twentieth century, dynamic ideas of social reform and social engineering, enshrined in the Directive Principles of State Policy as guidelines for the newly independent state, and embodied in the grand programmes of the Congress party.[2]

Nehru had every reason to be angry. Land reform, zamindari abolition,[a] nationalization of industry, reservations for 'backward classes' in employment and education, a pliant press – these were the shining new schemes of social engineering that were going to remake the social and political fabric of the new nation.[3] Zamindari abolition and land reform had been a part of the Congress programme for close to twenty years at the time. Nationalization and a planned economy had been the driving force behind the creation of the first National Planning Committee in 1938, presided over by Nehru himself. The social and economic framework of the newly independent society was to be transfigured, with the prime minister himself leading the charge.[4]

And yet, three-and-a-half years since independence, when the Congress party held unchallenged sway over the state, these flagship schemes had almost ground to a halt. The government's entire social and economic policy was in danger of failing. Armed with Part III of the new Constitution – guaranteeing the fundamental rights of citizens – zamindars, businessmen, editors and concerned individuals had repeatedly taken he Central and state governments to court over their attempts to curtail civil liberties, regulate the press, limit upper-caste students in universities and acquire zamindari property. Over the fourteen months the Constitution had been in force, the courts had come down heavily on the side of the citizens and struck mighty blows against the government.

In Delhi, the government's attempt to censor the *Organiser*, a Rashtriya Swayamsevak Sangh (RSS) newspaper,[a] had been countermanded.[5] In Bombay, the government's order banning *Cross Roads*, a left-leaning weekly critical of Nehru and the Congress government, had been quashed.[6] In the resultant case, laws used to censor and punish the press under the tropes of 'public order' and 'public safety' – the relevant sections of the Madras Maintenance of Public Order Act and the East Punjab Public Safety Act – had been declared void by the Supreme Court on account of their violation of the freedom of speech. Zamindari abolition had met a similar fate. In Uttar Pradesh, the Allahabad High Court had passed a series of injunctions restraining the government from taking any action under the newly passed Zamindari Abolition Act while it examined its constitutional validity. In Bihar, the State Management of Estates and Tenures Act had been declared ultra vires of the Constitution by the Patna High Court, violating Article 31 (the right to property) and Article 14 (the right to equality).[7]

In Madhya Pradesh, the Central Provinces and Berar Regulation of Manufacture of Bidis Act, which controlled and regulated the production of bidis, was held void and declared inoperative by the Supreme Court because it violated the right to carry on any trade or profession.[8] Nationalization of road transport in Bombay survived by a whisker after parliamentary intervention. In Madras,

---

[a]Zamindaris were large landed estates, controlled by a 'zamindar' or semi-feudal chief who served as a revenue intermediary between the cultivators and the state. Zamindari holdings ranged in size from a few dozen acres for small zamindars to thousands of square kilometres for large ones such as the Maharajas of Darbhanga. Zamindari abolition was the Congress government's programme to acquire these estates with minimum compensation and redistribute the land to peasant cultivators.

the infamous 'Communal Government Order' granting caste-based reservations in educational institutions had been struck down by the Madras High Court, which pointedly observed that Article 15(1) preventing discrimination on caste, communal, racial and linguistic grounds would become an 'empty bubble' if such orders were held to be legal and constitutional.[9] The decision was upheld by the Supreme Court, which then went on to also strike down communal reservations in government jobs.[10] In the courts and in the press, the government had repeatedly come in for withering criticism.

The entire Congress programme to remake India and consolidate its position had encountered formidable roadblocks: fundamental rights guaranteed by the Constitution, tenacious citizens, a belligerent press and a resolute judiciary determined to vigorously uphold fundamental freedoms. By early 1951, with elections looming and major initiatives continuing to run afoul of constitutional provisions, Prime Minister Nehru had grown increasingly exasperated with his plans being thwarted. Impatient and stubborn at the best of times, he chafed at the temerity of those that stood in his way. The situation, in his own words, was intolerable.[11] 'It is impossible to hang up urgent social changes because the Constitution comes in the way' he wrote to his chief ministers. 'We shall have to find a remedy, even though this might involve a change in the Constitution.'[12]

The very same Constitution that the Congress had championed barely twelve months before now became its bugbear. The very freedoms so ceremoniously granted on 26 January 1950 were now major stumbling blocks on the road to progress. The very makers of the Constitution now railed against too much liberty. Nehru's solution was straightforward – to bend the Constitution to the government's will, overcome the courts and pre-empt any further judicial challenges. In his view, wider social policy had to be determined by the government, and neither the courts nor the Constitution could be allowed to stand in the way.[13]

Declaring that the courts stressing fundamental rights over the Directive Principles of State Policy and resultant social changes was hindering the 'whole purpose' of the Constitution itself,[14] the prime minister introduced the Constitution (First Amendment) Bill in Parliament on 12 May 1951 to remove the constitutional roadblocks that held back his grand plans. The changes envisaged turned out to be more profound and pervasive than anyone had anticipated, went further than anyone had expected. In fact, so far did they stray from the original that India's pre-eminent legal scholar Prof. Upendra Baxi called it 'the second constitution' or 'the Nehruvian constitution'.[15]

In a nutshell, the bill proposed several major modifications. It sought to introduce new grounds on which freedom of speech could be curbed – public order, the interests of the security of the state and relations with foreign states. In the original Constitution, these had been limited to libel, slander, defamation, contempt of court and anything that undermined the security of the state or tended to overthrow it. With the addition of the three nebulous new provisos, left to the government of the day to define, the right to freedom of speech and expression was to be drastically curtailed.

The bill sought to enable caste-based reservations by restricting the right to freedom against discrimination from applying to government provisions for the advancement of backward classes.

Nothing would now prevent Parliament from creating special measures for backward communities, and none of these measures would be legally challengeable even if they breached any of the fundamental rights provisions. The bill sought to circumscribe the right to property and validate zamindari abolition by adding two new Articles empowering the state to acquire estates without paying equitable compensation and ensuring that any law providing for such acquisition could not be deemed void even if it abridged this right. And finally, it sought to introduce a special schedule where laws could be placed to make them immune to judicial challenge even if they violated fundamental rights – a veritable repository of unconstitutional laws beyond the court's purview, a schedule described by the jurist A. G. Noorani as an 'obscenity created by wilful resolve'.[16]

The amendment proved to be a lightning rod for criticism and galvanized opposition to the Congress regime. 'Cutting at the very root of the fundamental principles of the constitution', charged the leader of the Opposition, S. P. Mookerji,[17] as he led the counter-attack against the bill, calling it 'the beginning of the encroachment of the liberty of the people of Free India'.[18] 'Further curbs on freedom', blared the headline in a prominent newspaper.[19] 'Improper, unjustified and highly undemocratic', declared the Nagpur High Court Bar Association.[20] And these were only the opening salvos. What unfolded over the next two weeks, as Parliament debated and then passed the bill, can only be described as the first battle of

Indian liberalism, as a disparate band of forces took up the fight to preserve the expansive freedoms the Constitution had originally granted.

Outside Parliament, the press, the intelligentsia, traders, constitutionalists and lawyers joined the battle. Newspapers sharply criticized the government. Opinion pages bristled with indignation. The All India Newspaper Editors' Conference and the Federation of Indian Chambers of Commerce and Industry protested against the move, passing resolutions and sending delegations to meet the prime minister. Across the country, bar associations and the legal fraternity came together to oppose any amendments to civil liberties, and retired judges organized and attended protest meetings. An outraged young lawyer (and future judge), Rajinder Sachar,[21] angrily wrote to the editor of the *Times of India*, calling the amendment a move to 'literally stifle all genuine criticism of the Government'.[22]

Inside Parliament, a small and scattered but vocal and spirited Opposition took up the challenge of defending civil liberties. Luminaries of the freedom movement and the original Constituent Assembly, such as Shyama Prasad Mookerji,[b] Acharya Jivatram Kripalani,[c] Hari Vishnu Kamath,[d] Naziruddin Ahmed and Hriday

---

[b]Shyama Prasad Mookerji (1901–53) was a barrister, academic and politician from Bengal, widely considered a promoter of Hindu nationalism. President of the All India Hindu Mahasabha from 1940 to 1946, he was a member of the Constituent Assembly from 1946 to 1950 and Minister for Industry and Supply in the Nehru Cabinet. He fell out with Nehru over the Nehru–Liaquat Pact in 1950, resigned from the government, and became the unofficial leader of the Opposition. In October 1951 he formed a new political party, the Bharatiya Jana Sangh, that would eventually evolve into today's Bharatiya Janata Party.

[c]Jivatram Kripalani (1888–1982) – popularly referred to as 'Acharya' or teacher – was a former schoolteacher and a close associate of Gandhi. Kripalani became general secretary of the Congress in 1928, serving in that position for twelve years, and was the president of the party from 1946 to 1948, during the crucial years of independence and Partition. A trenchant critic of Nehru, he quit the Congress in 1951 and became one of the founders of the 'Kisan Mazdoor Praja Party' (The Farmers and Workers Party).

[d]Hari Vishnu Kamath (1907–82) was a former civil servant turned independence activist and politician. He was elected to the Constituent Assembly in 1946 on a Congress ticket but left the party in 1950 to join the Praja Socialist Party, on whose symbol he was elected to the Lok Sabha in 1952 and 1962.

Nath Kunzru,[c] savaged the bill when it was presented and launched blistering attacks on the government. Nehru challenged them to 'combat here, in the marketplaces, in the country, everywhere and at any level'.[23] In fiery exchanges, Nehru accused Mookerji of being a liar, while Mookerji called Nehru a dictator. Tempers ran high. Debate was heated and impassioned, and furious oratory was witnessed in a parliamentary session described by a major newspaper as being at 'the lowest level of parliamentary dignity'.[24]

Lest anyone be deceived, this was no storm in a teacup.

Several Congress parliamentarians took the government to task. Others pointed out that it was inappropriate for an unelected provisional parliament to amend the Constitution. Initially, even Nehru was daunted. 'The Bill for the amendment of the Constitution is meeting with a good deal of opposition in the press and elsewhere,' he wrote to his chief ministers, 'but we hope to get it through, even though it requires a two-third majority.'[25] 'Until the last moment, I shall not know whether we can have the requisite two-thirds majority,' he worriedly confessed to Bidhan Roy, the chief minister of West Bengal.[26] Congress whips were pressed into action to try and shepherd their flock, and prevent the bill from being criticized in the House. Despite the strong pressure, however, several conscientious objectors refused to budge. Still others criticized the government in Parliament, but eventually chose to abstain when the House voted.

The battle raged for two weeks, in Parliament and outside, across the columns and opinion pages of newspapers, in bar associations and courtrooms, through protest meetings and angry letters to editors. The bill was eventually passed after a bitterly acrimonious debate on 2 June 1951, with 228 ayes, twenty noes and a large number of abstentions, the final numbers obscuring the intensity of the battle. The storm blew over just as quickly as it had gathered. Things returned to normal. Parliament moved on to debating the Representation of the People Bill. The brevity of the whole event partially masked the gravity of its implications. But no one was fooled.

---

[c]Hriday Nath Kunzru (1887–1978) was a prominent Liberal politician and a vigorous proponent of limiting executive power. Starting out with the Congress, he later founded the National Liberal Federation – a loose collection of moderate political figures. He was a member of the Central Legislative Assembly (the legislature for British India) from 1926 to 1930, the Council of State from 1936 to 1942, the Constituent Assembly from 1946 to 1950 and the Rajya Sabha from 1952 to 1964.

What had come to pass was nothing short of a radical rewriting of Part III of the Constitution. The original constitutional provisions on fundamental rights were effectively ripped apart. The relationship between the state and the citizen was altered for all time. A precedent was set for the easy, almost casual amending of the Constitution and the passing of retrospective legislation. A mechanism for bypassing judicial review was created. Sedition had been retrospectively validated. A host of public safety and press control laws had been made operational again. Free speech was curtailed – no longer would it be necessary for the security of the state to be seriously undermined for it to proscribe free expression; it merely had to be in its interests to now do so. The subservience of the Constitution to government policy was demonstrated. The constitutional groundwork was laid for a host of repressive legislation to follow. A vital, cardinal change had occurred, which would have immense long-term consequences for India, its people and its politics.[27]

In the case of the Madras Communal General Order, a full bench of the Supreme Court had confirmed: '[The] chapter of Fundamental Rights is sacrosanct and not liable to be abridged by any Legislative or Executive Act or Order, except to the extent provided in the appropriate article in Part III. The directive principles of State policy have to conform to and run as subsidiary to the Chapter of Fundamental Rights.'[28] This entire system of reasoning, the bedrock of the constitutional order of things, was overturned as a denial of democracy.[29]

'Without adequate reasons,' as Shyama Prasad Mookerji accused Nehru, 'you have sought to curtail rights and liberties deliberately given only sixteen months ago.'[30] We have yet to realize, let alone fully appreciate, the profound consequences that have flowed from the First Amendment, the legislative powers it has conferred and the legal instruments it has enabled.[31] Since then, activists, human rights figures, intellectuals, writers, historians, politicians, journalists and even comedians have often faced the brunt of a repressive state and onerous laws, for which the enabling constitutional infrastructure was built by this amendment in 1951.

Yet, this view of the Constitution and of the fundamental rights to which the Nehru government subscribed was exceedingly new. The right to frame a constitution for India and defend the personal liberties of individual Indians had been a pivotal demand of the

nationalist struggle for independence. From the time the demand
was first articulated in 1895 through the Constitution of India
Bill (popularly called the Swaraj Bill and rumoured to have been
authored by Bal Gangadhar Tilak), through the Commonwealth of
India Bill in 1925,[32] the Motilal Nehru Report in 1928[33] and the
purna swaraj resolution of 1930,[34] the journey had been long and
arduous.

The Constitution was thus seen as the culmination of the efforts
of several generations of nationalists, and the fulfilment of the
Congress pledge to achieve complete freedom for the Indian people.
'The coming of the Republic is a very big landmark in our history
and the beginning of a new era,' wrote Jawaharlal Nehru. 'It brings
fulfilment on the political side at least of the dream of vast numbers
of Indians for generations past. It is the fulfilment of our pledge.'[35]
In his message to the nation, he called it 'the consummation of one
important phase of our national struggle'.[36]

From the outset, when the new Constituent Assembly first
convened at 11.00 am on 9 December 1946, no one had been in
doubt as to the momentous nature of the task at hand. 'We are
here to guarantee the rights of the people,' Mahavir Tyagi,[37] future
minister in the Nehru government, had argued.[38] On his election as
the permanent chairman of the Constituent Assembly, Dr Rajendra
Prasad had proudly declared its intent to 'place before the world a
model of a constitution that will satisfy all our people, all groups,
all communities, all religions inhabiting this vast land, and which
will ensure to everyone freedom of action, freedom of thought,
freedom of belief and freedom of worship'.[39]

The chairman of the Drafting Committee and the minister of
law, Bhim Rao Ambedkar, described individual rights, and the
constitutional remedies designed to enforce and safeguard them,
as the 'very soul of the Constitution and the very heart of it'.[40] He
exhorted the government and the people to observe constitutional
morality, noting that 'if parliamentary government was to succeed,
both the people and the government should observe certain morals
or conventions of the constitution'.[41] 'Indeed, if I may say so,' he
had emphatically asserted in the Constituent Assembly, 'if things
go wrong under the new Constitution, the reason will not be that
we had a bad Constitution. What we will have to say is that man
was vile.'[42]

On 26 January 1950, when the new Sovereign Democratic Republic of India was proclaimed, the Constitution was called 'a formidable document embracing in its range the structure of government, fundamental rights, the legal framework and the directive principles of State policy'.[43] 'India enters into her new existence as a Republic under the best constitutional auspices,' gushed the *Times of India*.[44] It was, as the leading headline in the *Hindustan Times* called it, 'a day of great significance and fulfilment',[45] and, in the words of the noted lawyer C. P. Ramaswamy Iyer, the beginning of 'the most far-reaching and significant experiment in human history'.[46]

One of the Constitution's authors, the great educationist and writer K. M. Munshi, proudly called it 'a remarkable achievement of the Indian nation ... the first free act of Free India'.[47] 'If this constitution endures,' he wrote, 'we will emerge as one of the most powerful countries on earth.'[48] Another author, H. N. Kunzru, weighed in and 'called the chapter on fundamental rights and assurances of the greatest value'.[49] A third author (and future minister), K. Santhanam, wanted to 'develop the idea of the sanctity of our Constitution' and make the people firmly believe in its sacredness.[50] Prime Minister Nehru himself described it as the foundation of the country's republican freedom.[51]

How, then, did 'this magnificent Constitution', in Nehru's words, 'the most elaborate declaration of human rights yet framed by any state', as the editors of the *Times of India* called it,[52] 'the biggest liberal experiment in democratic government', as the Oxford don and the world's leading professor of constitutional law, Sir Kenneth Wheare, described it,[53] go from being a charter of freedom for India's people and the fulfilment of their dreams in 1950 to being an impediment in the way of the will of the same people by 1951?

How did fundamental rights – the heart and soul of the Constitution, so ceremoniously and pointedly given in 1950 – become lacunae in the same Constitution and the cause of grave difficulties by 1951? What led to the leading framers of the Constitution turning on their own creation within fifteen months, to the Government of India and the Congress party taking the extraordinary step of radically amending the Constitution they themselves had piloted in 1950? Who got up to defend the newly granted fundamental rights when the moment came, and how did this climactic battle unfold? And finally, what were the consequences? Were there lacunae in the Constitution, as Nehru believed, or was man (and the government) vile, as Ambedkar had asserted before the Constituent Assembly? These are the questions this book seeks to explore, and within them lies the story it seeks to tell.

It is the story of how the Government of India discovered that mouthing platitudes to civil liberties was one thing, and upholding them as principles was quite another. It is the story of how the primacy of a government's social agenda over the Constitution and individual freedom was affirmed. It is the story of how the entire chapter on fundamental rights was vandalized and the courts emasculated – and the long shadow this has cast over Indian politics ever since. It is the story of how this amendment came to be and how it was passed. It is the story of how the great liberal promise of the Constitution was belied. But more than anything else, this is the story of the great but ultimately futile – and now forgotten – battle that was waged to preserve the original Constitution and the individual freedoms and civil liberties it had granted.

The battle over the First Amendment was the first battle of Indian liberalism, and its intrepid warriors the first great defenders of our individual rights and freedoms. They included the unlikeliest of characters – Hindu nationalists like S. P. Mookerji and M. R. Jayakar, Gandhian stalwarts like Acharya Kripalani, committed socialists like Shibban Lal Saksena and Jayaprakash Narayan,[f] conscientious Congress rebels like H. V. Kamath, Syamnandan Sahay[g] and K. K. Bhattacharya, jurists like Pran Nath Mehta and M. C. Chagla, press associations, editors, lawyers and businessmen; men whose ideological and editorial successors today might scarcely believe (but would do well to remember) they held the views they

---

[f]Jayprakash Narayan or JP (1902–79) – popularly referred to as 'Lok Nayak' or 'People's Leader' – was one of India's greatest socialist politicians. He joined the Congress in 1929 on Nehru's invitation and later formed the 'Congress Socialist Party', a left wing grouping within the Congress fold that would eventually split from the parent organization and become the 'Socialist Party'. In the 1970s he led a movement against the government of Nehru's daughter Indira Gandhi that triggered the imposition of the Emergency.

[g]Rai Bahadur Shyamnandan Sahay (1900–57) was a zamindar, educationist and politician from Bihar. He served as the vice-chancellor of Patna University and was the founding vice-chancellor of Bihar University, Muzaffarpur. He was elected to the Constituent Assembly in 1946, and to the first Lok Sabha in 1952 as a Congress candidate.

did. Nehru and the Congress bent on pruning fundamental rights, Mookerji and the RSS batting for individual freedom and civil liberties – it was a truly dramatic period in Indian history.

Even as memory of those fateful events has receded, their relevance to contemporary politics, legislation and public discourse in India has only grown. As governments across the board have shown themselves only too eager to both create and utilize repressive and coercive legislation, it has grown ever more important to identify and understand how constitutional support for such legislation was created through the First Amendment. This was acknowledged as late as 2018, when India's then finance minister, the legal luminary Arun Jaitley, hinted that he thought the First Amendment almost a 'paradox in our jurisprudential evolution' and vulnerable to challenge[54] – a contention now likely to be tested in the Supreme Court, which in October 2022, in a rather strange turn of events, agreed to hear a petition challenging the validity of the First Amendment.[55]

This book, then, is an attempt to shine a spotlight on this paradox, the events that led up to it, the people who created it, the people who resisted it and fought against it, and the debate it generated. This is a story that deserves to be told, not only because it has been all but forgotten,[56] not only because the First Amendment holds the key to understanding the position of civil liberties and freedoms today and has had immense consequences for India, but also because it is a cautionary tale about the precarity of individual rights from which there is much to learn. Not least, that the easy dichotomies that have traditionally been drawn, more so in recent times, between liberal and authoritarian visions of India, between Nehru and Mookerji, between the Congress and the RSS, between progressive and reactionary politics, are more than blurred when taken up for closer examination.

In the current political climate in India, constitutionalism, sedition and fundamental rights have come to dominate public discourse. As political conflicts over fundamental precepts such as freedom of speech, the right to dissent, the laws of sedition and the role of reservations have escalated, the Constitution has been firmly brought to the centre of Indian political life. Hawks within the current establishment often demand an amendment to the Constitution to bring it in line with their own political inclinations, prompting fears about the constitutional order itself.[57] On the other side, the idea of an existential threat to the Constitution from the BJP and the RSS animates the Opposition. Figures such as Shashi Tharoor have often accused the Modi-led government of 'orchestrating a deliberate and strategic assault on the Constitution and fundamental rights'.[58]

This is now a frequent lament: that freedom of speech and expression and the right to dissent are under threat, that critical and oppositional voices are being silenced and that the constitutional foundations of the republic are being eroded.[59] Nevertheless, even in all this cacophony, the furious exchange of allegations and counter-allegations, it is forgotten that these questions go back to a single moment in Indian political and constitutional history: the First Amendment, when the political and constitutional relationship between the state and the citizen was remade, and the gateway opened to the progressive encroachment of civil liberties. The constitutionally and legally sanctioned ability of the government to censor and prosecute dissenting voices wasn't born overnight. Often attributed to a disavowal of the liberal democratic spirit by post-Nehruvian India,[60] this is actually a story with its roots in 1951.

For example, Section 124A of the Indian Penal Code, which deals with sedition, is today cited as a remnant of British colonialism, now misused as a means of silencing dissent.[61] Yet, not even its most prominent critics ever note that the founding fathers of the Constitution of India did not intend for it to remain on the statute books. It had found no constitutional support in the original Constitution. It was revalidated in 1951, despite intense opposition, by the introduction of new grounds under which free speech could be curtailed – 'the interests of the security of the state', rather than undermining the security of the state or overthrowing it. Far from being a simple remnant of colonialism, sedition is an outcome of the First Amendment to the Constitution, and the Nehru government's desire to clamp down on critical voices and hasten its planned social revolution, unencumbered by constitutional obligations – a truly 'deliberate and strategic assault on the constitution and fundamental rights'.

One does not excuse the other, of course, and it is not the purpose of this book to provide an evidentiary cloak to ratify one political position or its opposite. History is the site of an ongoing struggle in India's fractious and polarized political scene,[62] making historical questions difficult to divorce from present concerns and anxieties. Nevertheless, this book seeks to tread the ground of historical scholarship – not contemporary debate. While it is in one sense responding to the pull of the present – after all, the questions historians ask are in some way prompted by the world we inhabit[63] – this story of the First Amendment is neither defined by present-day concerns nor meant to provide historical justification for contemporary egregiousness. It does, however, relativize the present, placing it within a broader historical trajectory and a constitutional context that have made things the way they are, providing a perspective that makes us aware of how current arrangements – to quote the intellectual historian David Armitage – 'are not only not inevitable but as much the outcome of good and bad choices, and greater and lesser accidents'.[64] More importantly, it provides fertile territory on which to interrogate interpretations of India's early constitutional history.

Whereas older scholars like Granville Austin had seen individual liberty as one of the key goals of the Constitution's framers,[65] recent legal scholarship has stressed that the chapter on fundamental rights was, the framers' assertions to the contrary notwithstanding, never intended as a bulwark in the service of liberal individualism.[66] Progressive voices argue, and with some justification, that the Constitution, written up amid the violence and upheaval of Partition as an answer to Indian society's perceived lack of democratic values and incapacity for social reform, had already privileged the state and the social revolution right at the outset.[67] Such views tend to not only gloss over the intensity of the struggle over constitutional norms that characterized the incipient republic; they also carry about them a whiff of inevitability – suggesting that Nehruvian statism appeared as a fait accompli at the republic's founding. But as the story of the First Amendment demonstrates, this was anything but obvious at the time. Nehruvian statism was far from a done deal. Large swathes of legal, political and social opinion thought otherwise. Other options and configurations were available. The First Amendment was a critical juncture.[68]

The sixteen months between the promulgation of the Constitution of India in January 1950 and its amendment in June 1951 constitute one of the most significant periods in Indian political and constitutional history. The relationship between state and society and the balance of power between the great organs of state – the entire social, political and constitutional fabric of the nation, the basic social contract – was decisively altered. This is the story of that alteration.[69]

1

The Build-up

The Background

Fundamental rights and individual freedom had been the basic and essential foundation for the entire constitutional enterprise from the minute the Constituent Assembly had begun its work. The idea, and indeed, the intent, to frame the Constitution of India as a charter of freedom had been affirmed from the moment President Rajendra Prasad declared the assembly's resolve to:

> place before the world a model of a constitution that will satisfy all our people, all groups, all communities, all religions inhabiting this vast land, and which will ensure to everyone freedom of action, freedom of thought, freedom of belief and freedom of worship, which will guarantee to everyone opportunities for rising to his highest, and which will guarantee to everyone freedom in all respects.[1]

The Constitution, specifically the provisions for civil liberties and their enforcement, was thought to be a crucial factor that was to distinguish the newly independent government from its colonial predecessor. It was going to certify that the nature of post-independence government rule would be fundamentally different from its colonial past; that the British Raj was not going to be replaced by Congress Raj; that the white sahibs were not simply going to be replaced by brown sahibs. This difference was going to be illustrated by the government's desire to uphold individual freedoms rather than encroach on them. Independence and the

Constitution were thus imagined as representing a clear dividing line between a repressive colonial past and a liberal new present.[2] This was the majority belief, at any rate.

As a Constituent Assembly member from West Bengal, P. L. K. Maitra stated, 'Now that we have got our own state, our own government elected by the people, with a President elected by the people and of the people ... there is no danger of civil liberties being trampled under ruthlessly and carelessly as it has been done in the past under British rule.'[3] Most members professed similar confidence in their government when it came to the protection of fundamental rights, even while expressing concern for the misuse of provisions such as preventive detention. It simply could not, in their eyes, be an engine of repression like its colonial predecessor.[4] Durgabai Deshmukh[5] was only echoing majority sentiment when, in a moment of rhetorical flourish while discussing preventive detention, she forcefully asked, 'Can there be a greater advocate and champion of personal freedom than our government, our Prime Minister, and our Deputy Prime Minister who always are here to give relief to the poor, and the needy and those who suffer?'[6] Personal freedom, civil liberties and individual rights had thus been a constant theme running through the tenure of the Constituent Assembly, at the back of every member's mind and the backdrop to a great many debates over the specific forms of their manifestation in the Constitution. The appointment of the redoubtable Sardar Vallabhbhai Patel as the chairman of the Advisory Committee on Fundamental Rights, Minorities and Tribal and Excluded Areas demonstrated the importance that the assembly attached to these subjects. Despite his own ambivalence towards expansive personal freedoms and his desire to subject them to grounds of public order, morality and grave emergencies,[7] the Sardar still very much acknowledged the all-encompassing nature of fundamental rights as a concept.

He was fully conscious that they represented a break from the colonial past and placed major restrictions on the formidable powers that the colonial state had granted itself under the Government of India Act, 1935. The supremacy of the Constitution was noted and definitively asserted by Patel when he presented the interim report of the Advisory Committee to the assembly in April 1947. Fundamental rights were to be justiciable – enforced by the courts of the land. They were to stand above all other legislation, previously enacted laws and regulations, which would have to comply with them under all circumstances. This was the crux of Clause 2 in the interim report Patel presented, which basically stated that all laws and regulations inconsistent with the rights guaranteed by the Constitution would stand abrogated. This indeed was to be critical to the new independent republic shedding the baggage of its colonial antecedents.

Everything considered, the very purpose of having fundamental rights in the Constitution was to safeguard individual freedom from executive fiat and legislative overreach and bad regulation as well as repressive legislation. This was the position that Patel supported and endorsed when he encouraged the assembly to adopt this clause. He declared:

> It is essential that this clause should be passed if these rights are considered justiciable and fundamental. If they are not justiciable then they are not consistent. But if it is considered that those clauses which confer rights on citizens which could be enforced in law, then it is necessary that any act, custom, regulation or notification which takes away or abridges this right must be abrogated. Otherwise it is meaningless.[8]

When the clause was put to vote by President Rajendra Prasad, the principle 'that all existing laws, notifications, regulations, customs or usages in force within the territories of the Union inconsistent with the rights guaranteed under this part of the Constitution shall stand abrogated to the extent of such inconsistency' was unanimously accepted by the Constituent Assembly, to loud and persistent applause.[9]

Thus, as early as April 1947, even before the provisions on fundamental rights were given concrete shape or inserted into the Constitution, the centrality of fundamental rights, and the principle that all existing and future laws inconsistent with them would stand invalidated, was accepted and confirmed by the founding fathers. So was the principle that they were justiciable – that ordinary citizens would move the courts to protect those rights, and the courts would judge whether laws or regulations contravened the rights that the Constitution would guarantee. Even more importantly, these fundamental rights were not thought of as expedients to be junked at momentary difficulties but as enduring and permanent guarantees to citizens, as Nehru himself argued before the assembly. 'A fundamental right should be looked upon, not from the point of view of any particular difficulty of the moment,' he surmised, 'but as something you want to make permanent in the Constitution.'[10]

These principles – that fundamental rights were permanent guarantees to be upheld even when it was inexpedient, that laws and regulations inconsistent with constitutional provisions would be abrogated and that the extent of inconsistency would be judged by the courts – formed a clear dividing line between colonial and independent India. They became Article 13 of the new Constitution. This conception of fundamental rights and their position in the political, institutional and legal framework of the new republic was the foundation of the Constitution and the constitutional order. It undergirded the lengthy debates over the wordings and insertion of specific Articles. It was accepted across political divides, even when limitations to fundamental rights were written into the Constitution itself.

In this way, when the Constitution came into force on 26 January 1950, it was not only the result of endless study and discussion in the Constituent Assembly and an endless search for compromise, as K. M. Munshi wrote, but also a broad acceptance of the principles that underlined the whole enterprise.[11] Everyone – the press, concerned citizens, legal experts and assembly members themselves – understood, accepted and loudly proclaimed the implications of the fundamental rights (and their limitations) enshrined in the Constitution. This included proponents of limitations on fundamental rights who wished to prioritize the needs of the state, like Munshi himself.

Highlighting the features of the new Constitution, the *Times of India* boldly wrote, 'Laws inconsistent with the provisions of the part on fundamental rights shall to the extent of such inconsistency, be void.'[12] It noted that there were no exceptions, that any law in contravention would automatically stand nullified.[13] That the courts were to judge the extent of such inconsistency was also not lost on anyone. 'These articles are primarily intended to warn the legislatures that they should be careful in legislating in this field,' wrote K. Santhanam, assembly member and future minister, 'and that the Supreme Court has the final, if an indeterminate, voice in these matters.'[14] 'The judiciary is, and always will be, the guardian of the people's liberties,' added M. C. Chagla, the chief justice of Bombay (and another future Cabinet minister).[15]

These were precisely the implications that gave the chapter on fundamental rights its elemental importance. It was no surprise that Ambedkar proudly described individual rights and constitutional remedies to enforce and safeguard them as 'the heart and soul of the whole Constitution'.[16] It was for these reasons that on its inauguration, analysts of the new Constitution called it 'the most elaborate declaration of human rights yet framed by any state',[17] the foundation of India's republican freedom,[18] fulfilment of the Congress party's pledge of *purna swaraj* to the people[19] and the 'biggest liberal experiment in democratic government'.[20]

Despite the fact that limitations on these rights and the grounds for circumscribing them were written into the Constitution itself, such overarching praise was more than justified for the simple principles that Patel had emphasized as far back as 1947, principles that underpinned the entire constitutional edifice – fundamental rights as permanent guarantees that were judged and enforced by the courts, and which no ordinary laws could contravene. This explicit, unambiguous principle was the line that set the new republic apart from its colonial predecessor. It signified, in Nehru's own words, 'the beginning of a new era'.[21]

Yet, when the new era dawned on 26 January 1950, it roused profoundly ambivalent feelings within the government and the establishment. 'Few of us, I suppose, are satisfied or feel happy about conditions in the country,' wrote Nehru.[22] Now that the last remaining tie with the erstwhile colonial masters was broken, it was as if nationalist stalwarts who had seamlessly transitioned from colonial prisons to the mansions of Lutyens' Delhi, with all the trappings of power and paraphernalia of authority, finally awoke to the enormity of the change that had been wrought. Their own commitment to the freedom of their fellow citizens was about to be tested.

Ambedkar had openly expressed his anxiety before the Constituent Assembly that India might lose both its Constitution and its democratic freedoms in the future. Given the lack of a democratic tradition, the rampant presence of 'bhakti' or political 'hero worship' and the wide disparity between the republican promises of the Constitution and rampant socio-economic inequality, he thought this a distinct and ever-present possibility.[23] As the new republic was announced, Patel weighed in with cryptic pragmatism, telling the people, 'We worked hard to achieve our freedom. We shall have to strive harder to justify it.'[24] Santhanam struck a note of caution: 'If the people of India are not imbued with the principles of individual liberty and their representatives in the Central Parliament and State Legislatures are inclined to be tyrannical,' he warned, 'the constitutional provisions will give the citizen only a very limited protection.'[25]

In the end, it was left to Chakravarti Rajagopalachari, the outgoing governor-general, to express just how uncomfortable the establishment was with the kind of freedom it was granting its own citizens. 'We must restore the unqualified reverence for the state that our ancients cultivated, reverence for law and discipline', he insisted with remarkable candour. 'In fact, we want a revival of feudal manners and chivalry but in terms of modern democracy.'[26] The last official representative of colonial rule, one of the leading figures of Indian liberalism, eulogizing feudal manners and unqualified devotion to the state, even as he vacated his exalted position and the country celebrated the birth of the new republic – it was a moment of fitting juxtaposition that laid bare the contradictions inherent in India's transition to democracy.

Rajaji's views seem like a paean for a mythical past where the state held unrivalled power, and perhaps they were. But more than a yearning for the glories of the ancient past, they probably represented the dawning of the realization that the relationship between the rulers and the ruled had now been altered forever. How or indeed why such unqualified reverence for the state was to be restored, or how compatible this view was with the new democratic and republican constitution, was anyone's guess. Rajaji did not elaborate. But his statement graphically revealed the deep ambivalence within the Congress establishment towards the Constitution and individual rights, and the establishment's tendency to prioritize the interests of the state over the personal freedoms of citizens, as well as its distrust of citizens who would choose to exercise the rights that the Constitution was granting them. Just how strong this tendency and this distrust were would soon become apparent.

The Beginning

In any event, it did not take long for the government to start tripping over the new Constitution. Two weeks past the birth of the new republic, the government was already running afoul of constitutional provisions that it had drafted only a short while ago. On 8 February 1950, exactly fourteen days after the new Constitution came into force, the Bombay High Court struck the first judicial blow by releasing suspected communists who had been detained indefinitely under the Bombay Public Safety Measures Act, finding that such open-ended preventive detention ran counter to constitutional provisions.

What had happened was this: in May 1949, twenty-eight alleged communists had been detained in Bombay under orders issued by the commissioner of police using powers conferred by the draconian Bombay Public Safety Measures Act. Detained without charge, the unfortunate detainees languished in prison without a trial for eight long months, even as the country's representatives debated high constitutional principles and drafted independent India's new Constitution. As later events in Salem showed, the threat of a grisly death at the hands of the police was ever present. With nothing but the government's whim as a cause, no access to mechanisms of justice, no possibility of parole and little chance of reprieve or release, the twenty-eight detainees faced the bleak prospect of unending detention as 1950 dawned. Almost two years after independence, with democracy on the anvil, little seemed to have changed for those on the receiving end of government power and police batons.

On 26 January 1950, the situation was turned on its head in ways that no one – government or dissident, police or detainee – had ever anticipated, let alone prepared for. The new Constitution expressly forbade indefinite detention under Article 22, which required an advisory board to approve detentions beyond a period of three months. That heavy-handed state repression could not go hand in hand with the new republican Constitution now became glaringly obvious. Indefinite and open-ended preventive detention was conspicuously and unarguably unconstitutional. The chapter on fundamental rights handed these detainees a powerful new tool to check the dominance of the government, and make a bid for freedom.

As the Yale historian Rohit De has argued, the Constitution, a document of high principles and supposed elite consensus, came alive in the popular imagination as an avenue to renegotiate the relationship between the rulers and the ruled, between ordinary citizens and officers of the state.[27] The detainees were no longer subjects seeking the government's leniency and clemency; they were free, rights-bearing citizens, newly empowered by the Constitution written in their name, with the ability to knock on the doors of the highest court of the land to demand the liberties guaranteed to them. Suddenly, there was a power beyond the government, beyond the state itself: the power of the sovereign promises that the people of India had made to themselves, which the government, watched over by the courts, was duty-bound to uphold. Taking these promises to heart, the twenty-eight detainees took their battle to court.

On 6 February 1950, in one of the first major invocations of fundamental rights, the detainees filed a petition before the Bombay High Court challenging the validity of the Bombay Public Safety Measures Act 'in so far as it relates to the detention of a person for more than three months without the opinion of an Advisory Board as required by the Indian Constitution (under Article 22)'.[28] No such advisory boards existed. Caught unprepared, the state found it impossible to fight back. There was a short hearing on 7 February, at which the Bombay government argued that the Constitution could not be applied retrospectively, despite this principle of its applicability to all existing laws being firmly enshrined in the Constitution itself.[29] Predictably, the court refused to buy the government's flimsy arguments, and on 8 February 1950 a full bench set aside the orders passed by the commissioner of police. The court took the opportunity to warn the police against using such 'public security measures' as a cloak and guise to override ordinary criminal law, making no bones about where judicial inclinations lay.[30]

If this wasn't embarrassing enough for the new democratic government, other setbacks soon followed. The Opposition, led by the Socialist Party and the Peasants and Workers Party, demanded the immediate repeal of public security measures in view of their manifest incompatibility with constitutional ideals and civil liberties.[31] Two days later, the same Bombay High Court held that the government had no power to extern a person from the province under the Bombay Public Safety Measures Act.[32] The Allahabad High Court declared that the wide-ranging detention provisions in the UP Public Safety Act were inconsistent with the Constitution. The Patna High Court, which, on 19 January – exactly a week before the Constitution came into force – had upheld the Bihar Public Safety Ordinance,[33] had a change of heart on 15 February and declared the entire Act ultra vires of the Constitution and hence void.[34] Indefinite preventive detention with no recourse to appeals was effectively consigned to history.

Sardar Patel, the man who had piloted the chapter on fundamental rights and established the principles of their foundation, was caught in a bind. For the tough, no-nonsense home minister responsible for the new republic's security, the choice was stark. Support civil liberties and allow preventive detention to end, as Opposition figures demanded? Or prevent the erosion of the coercive power at the government's disposal, as he and his ministry desired? He plumped for the latter. Facing armed communist rebellion in Telangana (and the prospect of it elsewhere), habituated to heavy-handed and repressive methods, still in the process of coming to terms with the new constitutional order, the Government of India scrambled to undo the damage to its legal arsenal.

A new Preventive Detention Bill was hurriedly drawn up to bring the various security acts in the provinces into one central Act conforming to the preventive detention provisions in the Constitution. Advisory boards were swiftly created. Moving the bill in Parliament, Patel described it as an emergency legislation against communists, who 'constituted a danger to the existence and security of the state', which, as he observed, 'cannot deal with them under the provisions of ordinary law'.[35] The safety and security of the newly created republic apparently could not be defended without such drastic legislation – not even against its own citizens in peacetime.

The new legislation was unanimously passed on 25 February 1950 after Patel threw his weight behind it. But it also became clear that Parliament was not entirely comfortable with such repressive legislation. During the debate, Rohini Kumar Chaudhary[36] gave vent to the frustrations of many when he dramatically rose to say that 'had not the Sardar been the author of the Bill, I would have called it a black bill',[37] demonstrating the lingering apprehension in certain sections about the government's inability to work within the bounds of ordinary legislation. Curiously, however, or perhaps predictably, instead of supporting the courts in doing their job – striking down legislation inconsistent with the Constitution that he himself had drawn up, and upholding the principles he himself had laid before the Constituent Assembly – the home minister took the opportunity to complain that judicial pronouncements were creating major difficulties in the states.[38] For those watching the government's attitude towards constitutional morality, it was not a good omen.[39]

How deeply the Sardar held these views is impossible to determine with precision. But the fact that he chose to forego the chance to support the courts indicates a broader sense of annoyance with being held back by constitutional provisions and judicial procedures, and a prioritization of the needs of the state over the freedoms of the individual. Prime Minister Nehru and Deputy Prime Minister Patel differed over many great questions of policy. The use of sweeping powers under the public safety measures, employed in the fashion of their colonial predecessors, was not one of them (a hesitant Nehru's protestations that they should not function like the British government notwithstanding).[40] Their commitment to civil liberties and individual freedom, or the lack thereof, represented a rare consensus between the two giants of Indian politics.

For the moment, preventive detention survived. Parliamentary intervention created a new legal framework to enable the government to continue jailing citizens without charging them or presenting them in court, or even informing them of the reasons for their arrest. The government breathed a sigh of relief. But even as one debate over public safety legislation was ending, another, altogether more contentious, was only beginning. Its roots also lay in the tumultuous weeks following the inauguration of the Constitution. This time, the flashpoint was the freedom of speech.

Confrontation Over Free Speech

On 11 February 1950, barely three days after the Bombay High Court freed the twenty-eight communist prisoners in Bombay, over 200 communist prisoners in the Madras province went on strike in Salem Central Jail. Demanding that they be treated as political detainees rather than as common criminals, the prisoners refused to comply with the jailors' instructions to work in the workshop or wear the black caps worn by ordinary inmates. A posse of policemen attempted to get the prisoners to revoke their strike and withdraw their demands. The 'rabid' communists, according to the minister for jails, Madhava Menon, then attempted to attack the policemen with the 'timber parts of their looms'.[41] In the ensuing fracas, several policemen, including the deputy jailor, were injured.[42] So the matter might have ended – a minor footnote in a regional newspaper.

But the men in uniform, personifying the might and majesty of the state, refused to take such insubordination lying down. The enraged policemen retaliated by locking the 200-odd offenders in a hall with no means of escape and opening fire on them, killing twenty-two people in cold blood and injuring 107 others in a gruesome demonstration of the new republic's lack of respect for the life and liberty of its citizens.[43]

The Communist Party had repeatedly asserted that transfer of power from the British to the Congress did not mean freedom for the people. The savagery of the killings – and the cavalier attitude of the Madras government, which justified the firing – lent credence to this assertion, and left even those without communist leanings shocked and disturbed. Other prisoners went on a hunger strike to protest against the incident. An uneasy Sardar Patel wrote to the Madras government to express his concern about the number of casualties.[44] A visibly distressed Nehru fretted about the damage to the government's reputation and confided his fears to Patel: 'We are losing the support of the public and a feeling is rising against the police such as existed under the British regime.'[45] 'There can be little doubt', he wrote, 'that people in India as well as abroad are greatly perturbed at these developments.'[46]

Among the many perturbed people, however, few were as outraged as the young Romesh Thapar,[47] editor, printer and publisher of *Cross Roads*, a left-leaning weekly based out of Bombay that was sympathetic to the communist cause and strongly critical of the Congress party, especially its dubious commitment to civil liberties and its eagerness to jail its communist opponents.[48]

In February, *Cross Roads* published a series of articles criticizing the Madras government over its high-handed actions and its appalling handling of the situation. Wary of further disaffection and afraid that public criticism would hasten support for growing communist activity in parts of the state, the Madras government responded on 1 March by banning circulation and distribution of the magazine in the province under the relevant sections of the Madras Maintenance of Public Order Act. In its issue of 17 March, *Cross Roads* replied by launching a broadside against the Congress government in Madras, calling the attack on its circulation 'one more proof that the Congress rulers are afraid of the truth. Their ways are the ways of Hitler and Mussolini. They are out to muzzle the voice of the common people.'[49]

Thapar himself was an unusual figure. Nephew of General P. N. Thapar, distantly related to Nehru, he was an establishment man who developed Marxist leanings over the course of his education in England and remained a lifelong member of the Communist Party of India. He was well connected in journalistic circles, having been trained and introduced to journalism by the legendary Frank Moraes, the man who became the first Indian editor of the *Times of India* in 1949. Born to wealth and privilege, Thapar had started *Cross Roads* out of a sense of ideological conviction, editing and funding the magazine himself. With age, his radicalism would mellow and he would find himself aligned with the Congress establishment in the 1960s and 1970s, receiving several sinecures of power in the process.

But in 1950, as a young, articulate and fiery radical, with the strength of the (officially banned) Communist Party behind him, Thapar was not one to roll over easily. He decided to take the fight back to the government, and the new Constitution became his primary weapon. In its issue of 1 April, *Cross Roads* appealed to its readers to raise funds to legally challenge the ban, and in its issue of 7 April, it proudly announced the filing of the petition in the Supreme Court.[50] The stage was set for a legal showdown.

Interestingly enough, this was not the only province *Cross Roads* was banned in. It had also been banned in Bombay in July 1949 for criticizing police action against trade unionists. As a curious aside, the headline for the offending article in that case had been written by a young college student visiting Bombay for a holiday: Romesh's sister Romila, who would go on to become one of India's most distinguished historians.[51] Though the ban there had been stayed by the Bombay High Court after several rounds of litigation in October 1949, the matter still remained sub judice when the ban in Madras came into force.

* * *

Thapar's fight with the government in Bombay and Madras was mirrored by another confrontation in Delhi during the same period. In this case, the offending publication was from the opposite end of the political spectrum – the *Organiser*, the weekly news magazine of the Rashtriya Swayamsevak Sangh (RSS), the Hindu nationalist organization that had been briefly banned from February 1948 to July 1949 after accusations of involvement in Gandhi's assassination.

In February, in the context of widespread communal rioting in Dhaka and elsewhere in East Pakistan and the migration of thousands of Hindu refugees into West Bengal, the *Organiser* published some items criticizing Nehru and his policies about Muslim evacuee property, the refugees streaming across the border and the volatile situation in East Pakistan. These included cartoons of Nehru and Liaquat Ali Khan, the Pakistani prime minister, and a piece titled 'Villains vs Fools', which argued that 'the villainy of Pakistan is matched only by our own idiocy'.[52] In other articles, it demanded the disbursement of Muslim evacuee property to Hindu refugees, who it claimed were being forced by penury to exchange blood for bread at blood banks.

January and February 1950 had been particularly bloody months for Bengal. As thousands upon thousands of refugees fled pogroms in East Pakistan, the communal situation deteriorated in West Bengal and the police were frequently called out to deal with disorder. Nehru, who had been proposing confidence-building measures and joint commissions to a reluctant Liaquat Ali Khan, came under immense pressure both from within his own party and outside to respond to the situation, even if it meant a forced exchange of populations or military action against Pakistan.[53] So sharp was the disapproval of the government's approach in certain quarters of the Congress that an irate prime minister even threatened to resign, accusing his colleagues of being 'out of touch with the government's policies and activities'.[54]

Leaders from Bengal, such as the minister of industries and supplies, S. P. Mookerji, supported by the right-leaning press, were particularly scathing in their criticism. Others such as Mahant Digvijainath, the general secretary of the Hindu Mahasabha (and a spiritual predecessor of Yogi Adityanath),[55] demanded an annulment of Partition and reunification of India and Pakistan for the benefit of both, pledging their allegiance to the idea of 'Akhand Bharat' – a demand the government considered unwise, undesirable and downright dangerous, describing it as 'the stupidest of proposals' and a 'direct incentive to conflict'.[56]

The prime minister himself was equally desperate to avoid any such precipitous action, especially military action, that could jeopardize the upcoming meeting with his Pakistani counterpart. He was deeply troubled by the open derision of his leadership and the vocal demand for a decisive showdown with Pakistan by the Hindu

Mahasabha – which he accused of trying to push and bully him into war, much against his own wishes.[57] He was even more annoyed with the role of the press, especially the vernacular press, where the Mahasabha demand had found wide echo. 'I feel the Calcutta papers are responsible for a great deal of mischief and this must be brought home to them. They are playing very irresponsibly with fire,' he later complained to Bidhan Roy. 'The Hindu Mahasabha and RSS propaganda both for war and for a Hindu State has a very bad effect in the present tense situation.'[58] When questioned on the issue later, he harangued journalists for running down his reputation with a campaign based on 'malicious misrepresentation of facts' and outright fabrications.[59]

Such trenchant criticism of Pakistan, and the government's policies towards it, by the Mahasabha and the RSS infuriated Nehru, who scorned their idea of nationalism and resented the public pressure they brought to bear. 'I find that progressively we are being driven to adopt what is essentially the Pakistan or Hindu Mahasabha policy in this respect,' he lamented to Patel.[60] 'I am being pressed all round for what is called action. This is a euphemism for war,' he later wrote to Rajagopalachari. 'I do not react to it favourably and, being perverse, hate being bullied.'[61] Just how much he resented this supposed 'bullying' would soon become apparent. Visibly riled, he wrote to his chief ministers on 1 March:

> I am certain that the Hindu Mahasabha policy is fatal for India. Their talk of putting an end to partition is foolish in the extreme. We cannot do so, and we should not try to do so. If by any chance partition was ended, while present passions last on either side, it would mean tremendous new problems for us to face. We would be worse off than ever. Therefore, there must be no thought of putting an end to Partition and having what is called 'Akhand Bharat'.[62]

On 2 March, the Central Press Advisory Committee met to consider the items published in the *Organiser*, and the very same day, the chief commissioner of Delhi issued a 'pre-censorship order' under the East Punjab Public Safety Act, requiring the editor and publisher to submit to the government for approval all communal matters and news and views about Pakistan, including cartoons, other than those derived from official sources.[63] The order was a blatant attempt not only to curtail criticism of the prime minister and the government, but, more specifically, to make public discourse on Pakistan conform to the government's view. It was a clear indication of where the government's inclinations lay, the grand promises of the Constitution notwithstanding.

K. R. Malkani,[64] the dedicated editor of the *Organiser* (who would go on to achieve the dubious honour of becoming the first man to be arrested during the Emergency), however, was not to be cowed. In the very next issue, he defiantly wrote:

> To threaten the liberty of the press for the sole offence of non-conformity to official view in each and every matter, may be a handy tool for tyrants but [is] only a crippling curtailment of civil liberties in a free democracy … A government can always learn more from bona fide criticism of independent thinking citizens than the fulsome flattery of charlatans.[65]

In the issue of 13 March, he again advised the government:

> If the administration earnestly wants ugly facts to not appear in the press, the only right and honest course for it is effectively to exert itself for the non-occurrence of such brutal facts. Suppression of facts is no solution to the Bengal tragedy. Surely the government does not hope to extinguish a volcano by squatting the more tightly on its crater.[66]

On 10 April 1950, within days of the *Cross Roads* petition, Malkani and Brij Bhushan, the *Organiser*'s editor and printer, respectively, followed Thapar to the Supreme Court. Here, too, the Constitution became the primary weapon against the high-handedness of the executive.[67] The RSS and the communists, the two opposite poles of the ideological spectrum, found themselves on the same side as victims of the government's aversion to criticism and its eagerness to control dissenting opinion. Coincidentally (or perhaps not), in the past, both magazines had openly derided the Congress party's lack of commitment to fundamental rights and called for the repeal of the draconian public safety acts.

In court, the *Organiser* was represented by N. C. Chatterjee,[a] former president of the Hindu Mahasabha (and father of future communist stalwart Somnath Chatterjee),[68] who argued that the pre-censorship order was an infringement on freedom of speech, and in fact the East Punjab Public Safety Act itself was void because it did not fall under any of the provisos in the Constitution under which fundamental rights could be abridged.[69] This case in itself was curious, succinct and informative – and an example of a great tradition of liberal thought within the Hindu nationalist movement that now seems to have been lost and forgotten.[70]

* * *

Over the course of April and May 1950, the Supreme Court concurrently heard both cases: *Brij Bhushan v. The State of Delhi*[71] and *Romesh Thappar v. The State of Madras*.[72] Raising, as they did, vital questions about the interpretation of Article 19(1) of the Constitution of India, which guaranteed freedom of speech, both cases attracted widespread attention. While the hearings unfolded, outside the courtrooms concern about the government's disdain for fundamental rights and its reliance on restrictive colonial-era laws was mounting. Questions were raised about the prime minister's own beliefs, and leading political and legal figures denounced him in the most excoriating terms.

The socialist leader Jayaprakash Narayan took the opportunity of his address to the All India Civil Liberties Conference on 16 April to lambast the government. 'The Prime Minister of India talked in the language of dictators when he maintained that when we had to choose between security of the state and freedom of the individual, we must choose the former,' charged Narayan. In the name of 'emergency' (for which he coined the caustic term *sankatvad*) and security, there had been cases of arrests and detention that had no relation to the security of the state, he warned, and 'while lip service was being paid to the ideal of democracy, freedom and civil liberties, those in power did not mean what they said'.[73]

---

[a]Nirmal Chandra Chatterjee (1895–1972) was a lawyer and jurist. He went on to become a judge at the Calcutta High Court, and later served as the vice-president of the Supreme Court Bar Association as well as the president of the All India Civil Liberties Council. Politically associated with Hindu revivalism, he was elected to the Lok Sabha as an independent candidate in 1952.

The chief justice of the Bombay High Court, M. C. Chagla, castigated the government while giving a public lecture in Poona on 1 May. He took the opportunity to emphatically declare that the Constitution was supreme, that any law that violated fundamental rights was ultra vires of the legislature and void, and that judges were the ultimate and final interpreters of the Constitution. In his long speech, he warned against the dangers of emergency legislation and the tendency of the state to seek more and more special and extraordinary powers because 'the executive could always see clouds on the horizon and every cloud was capable of bringing about a storm'.

Chagla then proceeded to deliver a stinging rebuke to the Congress party. To directly quote a news report of his speech:

> Ultimately, since it was the party in power that makes laws, ... it was therefore for that party to place limitations upon its own power and be neither ruthless nor dictatorial in its exercise. But these limitations were objective in their nature and it was for the judiciary to decide whether the limitations conformed to the objective standards laid down. The Constitution had not left it to the party in power in the legislature or the caprice of the executive to limit, control or impair any fundamental rights the right to express opinion, however critical it might be of the government or society as constituted, was one of the most fundamental rights of the individual in a democratic form of government. A facile concurrence with the policy of the rulers was not necessarily a sign of patriotism.[74]

At the Democratic Convention in Lucknow – a joint session of the Democratic Party and the UP Zamindars Conference – the prominent jurist P. R. Das,[75] president of the All India Civil Liberties Conference, brother of Congress stalwart C. R. Das and a former judge of the Patna High Court, bluntly declared:

> We have in India today a one-party state just as Hitler's Germany was a one-party state, Mussolini's Italy was a one-party state and Stalin's Russia is a one-party state The danger which I apprehend is that the government may suppress all political parties which do not believe in the Congress government on the plea that the interests of public order demand that these parties should be suppressed.[76]

In Bengal, no less a person than its highest constitutional functionary, Governor Kailash Nath Katju,[77] himself a noted jurist (and future Union minister), felt compelled to go on record with the warning: 'We must take care that in the name of preservation of State and stopping of subversive activities we may not stifle democracy itself.'[78]

Narayan, Chagla, Katju, Das – this was not criticism by fringe figures. But even such pointed criticism from the highest ranks of the intelligentsia failed to moderate the government's stand. The legal battle continued.

* * *

The Supreme Court finally gave its verdict on both matters on the same day, 26 May 1950. In the case of *Cross Roads*, the court quashed the order banning its circulation in Madras. It further held the relevant sections of the Madras Maintenance of Public Order Act, which authorized the government to prohibit circulation of documents in the state on grounds of public safety, to be ultra vires and hence void. It noted that 'unless a law restricting freedom of speech and expression is directed solely against the undermining of the security of the State or the overthrow of it, such law cannot fall within the reservation under cl. (2) of art. 19 of the Constitution'.[79] In the *Organiser* case, again, the court held that the grounds on which the restriction had been imposed under the East Punjab Public Safety Act did not fall within the reservations provided in the Constitution. As a result, not only was the pre-censorship order quashed, but the relevant section of the Act was also held to be invalid and 'repugnant to the Constitution'.[80]

The judgments expressed a singular precept: that the grounds on which the fundamental right to freedom of speech could be abridged were written in the Constitution itself, and only laws pursuant to those grounds could be held valid. In other words, laws could only impose restrictions based on the criteria in Clause 2 of Article 19 in the Constitution itself: libel, slander, defamation, contempt of court or undermining the security of the state. Any other reason, including public order, was unacceptable. Under no law could freedom of speech be restricted, a publication banned or subjected to censorship because it supposedly constituted a threat to public safety or had the potential to create disorder. In order to justify restrictions on free speech, the magnitude of disorder had to be so great that it seriously imperilled the security of the state.

These were landmark judgments, declaring that the opinions of individual citizens and the views of the press could not be restricted by law on the grounds that they were prejudicial to public order. They ratified the principle, to quote directly from the judgment, that:

[V]ery narrow and stringent limits have been set to permissible legislative abridgement of the right of free speech and expression, and this was doubtless due to the realization that freedom of speech and of the press lay at the foundation of all democratic organizations, for without free political discussion no public education, so essential for the proper functioning of the processes of popular government, is possible.[81]

The Supreme Court's attitude and the principles it delineated were a resounding blow to the government's attempt to regulate free expression, stifle critical voices and circumvent their own constitutional provisions. As a frustrated Patel wrote to Nehru, the bottom had been knocked out from penal laws for control and regulation of the press. Sedition could no longer be a crime.[82]

In this first major confrontation, the Supreme Court came out decisively in favour of individual freedom and civil liberties. It refused to buy the government's argument that public safety could be equated with the security of the state, or that the security of the state could be seriously threatened by such critical opinion. The judgments were widely welcomed as laying the foundation of the freedom of the press and, as one newspaper remarked, 'made it clear that criticism of the government, creating disaffection or bad feelings towards it was not to be regarded as a justifying ground for restricting the freedom of the press unless it was such as to undermine the security of the state'.[83] The dreaded public safety acts were toast.

For the governments, both in the provinces and in Delhi, it was an embarrassing defeat. For dissenters, Opposition figures of all political persuasions, writers, thinkers and intellectuals, this was a major victory that kept the heavy-handed state in check. No longer was it possible for the government to ban publications critical of the Congress party on the subjective assessment of a threat to public order, to stifle dissenting voices by subjecting them to censorship or, indeed, to even contemplate new laws for doing so. Henceforth, nothing short of seriously undermining the security of the state would do.

In the Constituent Assembly, Nehru and Patel had been hailed as 'champions of personal freedom', leading a new government, our own government, which would no longer threaten civil liberties. Four months after the Constitution's inauguration, it was becoming increasingly clear that the champions of personal freedom had feet of clay, that beneath the surface of an ostensibly democratic leadership lurked deeply authoritarian instincts. Evidently, the clear dividing line between the colonial and the post-colonial state that had existed in the minds of many of the Constitution's founders was more blurred than had been thought, and the establishment's ambiguity towards fundamental rights deeper than had been imagined. How much of the new republic represented a rupture from the past, and how much of it represented a continuity, was a ratio still being worked out within the top echelons of power.

Yet, as Jayaprakash Narayan maintained, the central problem wasn't simply the repressive tendencies of the state, but the inability of the masses, or indeed their leaders, to associate the idea of freedom with civil liberties rather than national freedom.[84] This three-way contradiction – between an expansively liberal, enlightened and progressive constitution, a heavy-handed and overbearing state, and a governing party with questionable commitment to fundamental rights – was still to be properly resolved. Further conflict was inevitable. And as one chapter of the confrontation ended in New Delhi, another one, altogether more serious, was already brewing in Uttar Pradesh and Bihar. This chapter would concern the Right to Property and the Congress programme of land reform, and it would shake the government and the establishment to its foundations.

2

Will the People Wait?

The Stage Is Set

In 1949, before it got down to the more arduous task of drafting and debating zamindari abolition and land reform legislation to enable acquisition of zamindari property, the Bihar Legislative Assembly passed the Management of Estates and Tenures Act to allow the government to take over management of zamindari estates, in anticipation of the eventual dispossession of the feudal magnates once the Constitution of India came into force. While it prepared for final acquisition, the state would manage the estate and pay the proprietor 20 per cent of the revenue.

Land reform had been a central part of the Congress agenda since the 1930s, and the major pivot around which its grand plans for social engineering revolved. Zamindari abolition and land redistribution were to be the new republic's biggest social reforms, meant to usher in a social and economic revolution that would remake the social and political fabric of the countryside – breaking feudal power and creating a bourgeois (and more equal) landowning village society more to the Congress's liking. Most states were thus already gearing up for political combat over land redistribution when the metaphoric first bullet was fired in the far-flung district of Hazaribagh[1] in the dying days of 1949 – even before the Constitution was formally adopted – inaugurating, in deceptively innocuous fashion, a legal confrontation that was to shake the republic to its core.

In Hazaribagh, the proud and spirited Raja Kamakhya Narain Singh of Ramgarh – future Swatantra Party stalwart and Cabinet minister who became the first person in India to use a helicopter for an election campaign – received a notice from the deputy commissioner informing him that he was soon to be stripped of his power to manage his estate and his employees.[2] The raja promptly applied for, and received, an order of injunction from the subordinate judge at the Hazaribagh district court, restraining the government from taking over the management of the Ramgarh estate.[3] In a brazen display of bureaucratic power, however, the deputy commissioner calmly brushed off the injunction and had it proclaimed by the beat of a drum across the district that people were no longer required to pay rent to the raja.

Stunned by such open defiance of court orders, the Patna High Court in January 1950 issued a ruling calling upon the state government to show cause why proceedings for contempt of court should not be started against the deputy commissioner and his subordinates for violating the orders of the subordinate judge.[4] Stung and embarrassed, the government scurried to file an appeal against the injunction in the high court. The court in turn, after a few short hearings, dismissed the government's appeal in February 1950 and maintained the injunction against the takeover of further zamindari properties.[5] In the interim, with the Constitution having come into force, the court took the entire Management of Estates and Tenures Act up for examination to judge its constitutional validity in a separate suit instituted by Bihar's pre-eminent zamindar, Maharaja Sir Kameshwar Singh of Darbhanga,[a] one of the new Constitution's authors and a member of Parliament.[6] The Bihar government was left red-faced.

Meanwhile in Delhi, as March rolled into April, communal strife in Bengal continued to occupy much of the distressed prime minister's attention,[7] as it would continue to do over the first half of 1950. He was particularly irritated by Sardar Patel's private insistence on a 'well-considered, firm and determined'[8] approach vis-à-vis Bengal and Pakistan during Cabinet meetings and parleys

---

[a]Maharaja Sir Kameshwar Singh Gautam Bahadur, KCIE (1907–62) was the last ruler of the Darbhanga Raj, the largest landed estate in India. A noted philanthropist, he attended the Round Table Conferences of 1931–3, and was a member of the Council of State (the Upper House of the legislature of British India) from 1933 to 1946, the Constituent Assembly from 1946 to 1950 and the Rajya Sabha from 1952 to 1962.

with MPs, an attitude he believed was providing cover for those who wanted a clash with Pakistan – not least his critics in the RSS and the Hindu Mahasabha. Hectored by his opponents, pilloried by the press[9] and seemingly undermined by his deputy, Nehru felt besieged from all sides. Not content with the censorship orders against the *Organiser* and the other steps the home ministry had taken to control the situation, he berated the home minister:

> I think we have taken up far too lenient an attitude towards those in India who encourage this communal feeling of hatred and violence. The Hindu Mahasabha talks about Akhand Bharat, which is a direct incentive to conflict. The belief that retaliation is a suitable method to deal with Pakistan, or what happens in Pakistan, is growing. That is the surest way to ruin for India and Pakistan.[10]

Patel, who on this matter had self-confessedly submitted to Nehru's approach despite his own misgivings, was taken aback. 'Our action has been circumscribed only by the provisions of the law as interpreted by our legal advisors and the High Courts,' he responded. 'We put thousands in jail and adopted a policy of release only after we were continuously attacked on the score of maintaining civil liberties.'[11] He pointedly and icily reminded the prime minister:

> We are now faced with a Constitution which guarantees fundamental rights – right of association, right of free movement, free expression and personal liberty – which further circumscribe the action we can take. That means that for every executive action there must be legal justification. If within these limits you feel that our policy towards communal organizations has been lenient, steps can certainly be taken in the manner you may suggest.[12]

Coming from Nehru's oldest and closest colleague, a man known to be forthright and unequivocal, the insinuation was stark and damning. Did Patel believe Nehru to be unaware of constitutional limits on executive power? Or did he consider the prime minister to be willing to discard them if they impeded his will? There is no certain answer. Whether he privately suspected him of not respecting constitutional boundaries will have to remain a matter for debate and conjecture. The impression that Patel was chiding his leader for trying to circumvent constitutional constraints and disregard fundamental rights is, however, impossible to escape. Astute politician that he was, Patel clearly had insights into Nehru's thinking, insights which informed the advice he gave the prime minister. He may have been no champion of personal freedom – once even going to the extent of branding the Constitution's fundamental rights provisions a result of 'idealistic exuberance'[13] – but the home minister was plainly wary of trifling with the Constitution.

Just what Nehru had in mind, or was prepared to countenance, we may never completely know. But Patel's sardonic attempt to educate his leader on the essential foundations of the constitutional order could only imply one thing: that the prime minister was irked by constitutional restraints and willing to disregard them in pursuit of his political goals. With its wry tone, its allusions to extra-constitutional action and its derisive presumption of Nehru's ignorance of even the most basic tenets of constitutional legality, Patel's acerbic reply provided the earliest indication that all was not well between the prime minister and the Constitution to which he had recently pledged allegiance.

Nehru himself gave an inkling of his opinions on the subject a few weeks later while replying to Pakistani complaints about the West Bengal press[14] when he tried to reassure the Pakistani government that every effort was being made to rein the fourth estate in. 'I entirely agree with you that some of the newspapers in West Bengal still continue to write in a way which I consider undesirable,' he confessed to Pakistani foreign minister Zafarullah Khan, '[But we] have to face the difficulty that in view of our new Constitution, the courts do not approve of many kinds of action that used to be taken previously against the press.'[15]

It was an ominous confession, demonstrating his impatience with constitutional constraints and seemingly confirming Patel's private suspicions. How Nehru would face this difficulty, only time would tell. In the middle of this sparring over free speech and constitutional limits on executive action, as the government chafed at restrictions on its power and faced action in the Supreme Court, zamindari abolition and land reform legislation was introduced in the Uttar Pradesh (UP) and Bihar legislative assemblies, setting the stage for a titanic clash between the state and landed magnates.

Battle Royale I

'If the amendment moved by the honourable member is accepted, it would only prolong the period of indefiniteness with regard to land reform,' declared Revenue Minister Hukam Singh on the floor of the legislative assembly on 1 April 1950, arguing that it was the government's intention to pass zamindari abolition legislation as soon as possible.[16] From the Opposition benches, Raja Virendra Shahi of the Democratic Party had moved an amendment to the UP Zamindari and Land Reforms Bill requiring that the assessment of compensation should be known to zamindars before their estates were vested in the state. The amendment was defeated. With the first election then proposed for November, the UP government was keen to have the legislation passed and the process of land reform begun before they went to the public – an aim they shared with their counterparts in Bihar, and the Congress party in general.

Yet, the approaches of the UP and Bihar governments could hardly have been more different. In UP, following the report of a Zamindari Abolition Committee, Chief Minister Govind Ballabh Pant and Revenue Minister Hukam Singh had come up with a comprehensive plan to acquire zamindari estates in a relatively balanced manner and provide for reconstruction in its aftermath. Running to a mammoth 344 clauses, the land reform legislation included uniform compensation levels and rehabilitation grants for smaller zamindars, in order to pre-empt legal challenges and achieve a relatively balanced compromise arrangement that would respect the right to property enshrined in the Constitution. They were confident of closing all legal loopholes and peacefully dismantling the old aristocratic order.

On the other hand, in Bihar, the crucible of social reform, where the state had already taken over the management of several large estates, the Land Reform Bill, at just over forty clauses, was not even a quarter of that length. With its staggered scale of compensation where rates decreased arbitrarily with the amount of land a zamindar owned, it was also obviously on slippery constitutional ground. Having stolen a march over UP, however, Bihar's Revenue Minister K. B. Sahay – a committed anti-zamindar activist and a chief ministerial aspirant – was eager to deliver the coup de grâce to the feudal order and cement his place in history.

Debate began in the UP Legislative Assembly in typically rambunctious fashion, with Congress and Socialist Party members castigating zamindar members for employing dilatory tactics by making long speeches and drawing out the already detailed clause-by-clause debate.[17] Progress was slow, as each clause became a matter of contention, not just with the Opposition, which discussed every single line threadbare and often tabled multiple amendments, but also with its socialist supporters, who frequently felt that the terms being offered to the feudal order were too benign. The assembly voted on every single clause and every single amendment, often after prolonged and heated debate. If that wasn't trouble enough, there was even a small group of Congress rebels who sporadically broke ranks with the party when votes were taken.

Within a week, Congress legislators were so fed up of the protracted deliberations that they proposed limiting discussion on Opposition amendments to ten minutes each.[18] Nevertheless, despite all their efforts, the Opposition continued to fight for every inch, every point was assiduously discussed and progress on the bill was excruciatingly slow, so much so that a major newspaper was to later describe it as 'moving like a cumbersome machine, at a pace mocking in its slowness at the urgency of the problem'.[19] As April wore on, frustrated Congress members, worried by the possibility of being unable to complete the task at hand in the current session, began to demand that a time limit be set for the discussion of this bill. After several days of tempestuous arguments over the government proposal to set a time limit of thirty days for the debate – ironically reported as a 'battle royal' by the press[20] – the government, with support from the Speaker,[21] successfully managed to pass a resolution on 25 April limiting the debate to forty days.[22]

Predictably, the manner, quantum and mode of payment of compensation came to be the most important issue under discussion. Over the month of May, Socialist attempts to prevent any compensation from being paid to landlords provoked intense debate but were voted down by conservative Congressmen combining with Opposition legislators to vote against socialist-sponsored amendments.[23] Zamindars' attempts at gaining higher levels of compensation were also decisively voted down, often with Congress ministers repeatedly rebuking their opponents for tabling amendments as a method of delaying the inevitable.[24] With government coffers mostly empty and contributions to the newly created Zamindari Abolition Fund trickling in at levels much below expectation, compensation methods emerged as a major source of anxiety for the government and the Congress leadership.[25]

Outside the assembly, the government set up a Zamindari Abolition Publicity Board under the chairmanship of Chaudhary Charan Singh (the future prime minister who almost single-handedly dismantled Congress supremacy in UP) to rally public support for the measure and encourage farmers to contribute to the Zamindari Abolition Fund and acquire land rights by paying ten times their annual rent to the government. Charan Singh and other senior ministers toured the countryside extensively, rousing people to make the zamindari abolition programme a success.[26] 'Landlordism in every form will soon end in UP and zamindars would be compensated,' he imperiously decreed at one of his earliest meetings, 'but the government was completely free to decide the nature and time of compensation.'[27] 'Money or no money, *bhumidar*[28] or no *bhumidar*, the zamindari system will go lock, stock and barrel,' other state leaders proclaimed at another.[29]

The Congress high command directed all its Provincial Congress Committees to launch extensive public campaigns 'to educate the peasants of the country' about their zamindari abolition and land reform programme.[30] As commanded, the party threw its considerable organizational weight behind its flagship social policy – the pivot for their project of reforming and remaking the Indian social and economic order – and the effort to take it to the people. Congress political figures, often accompanied by bureaucrats and government functionaries, held thousands of public meetings across the northern states. In one such meeting in Meerut, for example, District Congress Committee President Raghubir Singh, accompanied by the deputy land reforms commissioner and the district magistrate, called on the public for support, declaring the 'abolition of zamindari a revolution as big as the attainment of independence'.[31] The pattern was replicated across the length and breadth of the Gangetic plain, and in Uttar Pradesh alone, nearly 35,000 such public meetings were held over the course of the official drive for the Zamindari Abolition Fund in May and June.[32]

In contrast, in neighbouring Bihar, where the government was already facing legal action by zamindars and the new Land Reform Bill ran up to a rather spartan forty-three clauses, the assembly moved at a brisk pace. The bill, which had already gone through a Select Committee by February, was ripe for passing. By the middle of April, over twenty clauses of the bill had been passed, including controversial clauses on the assessment of compensation.[33] Within the next week, another eight clauses had gone through, including the contentious Clause 24 relating to the rate of compensation, which would range 'between three times of the net income exceeding Rs one lakh and 20 times of the net income exceeding Rs 500'.[34] Three more days of debate, and by 23 April the *Hindustan Times* was able to triumphantly report that the Bihar Land Reforms Act had been passed by the assembly and would soon be sent to the president for his assent.[35]

Even as major landed magnates alleged that the scale of compensation was unconstitutional, that payment in non-negotiable bonds was no compensation at all and that major litigation was almost sure to follow,[36] the Bihar government and Congress party figures were convinced that they had won this round and believed that a presidential assent would soon be forthcoming. The jubilant, expectant feeling was contagious. Shamed by the seeming urgency being shown by their counterparts in Bihar, the UP Legislative Assembly, in an attempt to catch up, even passed forty-two clauses of their own land reform bill without discussion one fine day in May, causing Opposition members to stage a walkout in protest.[37]

In this manner, as May wound to a close, the mood within the UP and Bihar governments, and indeed the Congress organization, remained upbeat and optimistic. Landlord members in the state assemblies were too few to offer any significant resistance, even when supported by Congress rebels. There was near-unanimous consensus among front-line politicians, and reluctant but obvious acceptance of the inevitability of zamindari abolition within the ranks of the zamindars. There might have been setbacks in the Supreme Court, unconstitutional attempts to silence criticism might have been shut down and critics might have had a field day in the press, but zamindari abolition and land redistribution, the primary social policy that they were going to take to the people and use to usher in a socio-economic revolution, was about to become reality.

The Congress position in the countryside was to become unassailable and the landed aristocrats and feudal magnates – the most potent sources of future political resistance – were to be largely swept aside. With the Land Reforms Bill in Bihar passed, and the land reform bill in UP making slow but steady progress, there was little to stand in the way of this vision. The scale and method of compensation were supposedly the only bone of contention remaining. Or so the establishment presumed, convinced that the righteousness of its cause justified the use of all legal and extra-legal means. It would not be long until it was proved spectacularly wrong.

The penny dropped on 6 June 1950, when the Patna High Court decided the suit that had been instituted by Maharaja Kameshwar Singh,[38] pricking this bubble of optimism and certainty. In the first judgment of its kind, the court held the Bihar Management of Estates and Tenures Act to be an unconstitutional law, and hence illegal and ultra vires of the state legislature.[39] Observing that the drastic and far-reaching restrictions placed on the power of the proprietors to deal with their property with no corresponding compensation left them practically without any rights over their own property, the court held the law to be void ab initio – both before and after the creation of the Constitution.[40]

The decision came as a bombshell, leaving the Bihar government and its Congress leaders shocked and rattled. The judgment reiterated the judiciary's commitment to fundamental rights, especially the right to property, and pitted the Constitution directly against the government's stated policy. It threw open the entire question of land reform and the modus operandi for achieving it, unlocking an avenue for potential resistance and effectively putting the government's plans of presenting the country with a fait accompli into jeopardy. The atmosphere of expectant certainty dissipated. And as politicians, zamindars and legal experts pondered possible consequences, confusion and apprehension radiated outward through the country.

Confusion Descends

On 2 June, the Allahabad High Court delivered a tongue-lashing to the Uttar Pradesh government, taking inspiration from the Supreme Court verdicts of the preceding two months. 'It is the right of every citizen in a democratic state to spread disaffection against a particular party Government,' the court categorically informed the provincial government as it ordered the release of one Ahmad Ali, who had been detained in Agra jail for campaigning against the government and distributing pamphlets spreading disaffection against the Congress. 'The right is, of course, subject to the condition that disaffection should not be spread as to result in violence and there should be really no incitement to the use of violence or other illegitimate courses,' it clarified.[41] Since there was no incitement to violence or other illegal acts, there was no case, the court reiterated to the prosecution counsels, politely advising them to adhere to the Constitution.[42] It was a harbinger of things to come. The court's admonition was but a thinly veiled warning about the strident position of the judiciary when it came to fundamental rights. The government would have done well to heed its advice.

Further away, in Delhi, June began on a portentous note for the Congress with the resignation of John Matthai,[43] finance minister in the Nehru Cabinet. After S. P. Mookerji (minister of industries and supplies) and K. C. Neogy[b] (minister of relief and rehabilitation), who had resigned in protest against the Nehru–Liaquat Pact in April, this was the third such resignation to rock the government. A distinguished economist and professor, Matthai had repeatedly clashed with Nehru over the creation of a Planning Commission, the tendency of the prime minister to disregard the authority of the Standing Finance Committee and throw government expenditure into disarray, and most importantly, his grave misgivings about the government's 'soft policy' towards Pakistan and the communal situation in Bengal, which he described as a 'policy of appeasement' that threatened to barter away vital national interests.[44] Turning his back on the government, he accused the prime minister of undermining the functioning of Cabinet responsibility with his undue authoritarianism.[45]

---

[b]Kshitish Chandra Neogy (1888–1970) was a Congress politician from Bengal. First elected to the Central Legislative Assembly in 1920, he was a member of the Constituent Assembly from 1946 to 1950 and Minister for Relief and Rehabilitation in the Nehru Cabinet. He resigned in 1950 over the Nehru–Liaquat Pact, and later chaired the First Finance Commission of India from 1952 to 1957.

Matthai,[c] as the newspapers pertinently observed, was neither a Congressman nor a Hindu, and not even a politician.[46] Once described by Viceroy Wavell as 'the most capable and intelligent' minister in the pre-independence interim government,[47] he was an academically gifted, non-political outsider who had been brought in for his professional expertise. His dramatic resignation and his open denunciation of Nehru thus greatly encouraged the claim (and rumoured reports) that the prime minister wished to have in the Cabinet only those ministers who were wholehearted supporters of the Nehru–Liaquat Pact and the government's broader Pakistan policy.[48] The *Times of India* unabashedly reported 'the view that Dr. John Matthai's resignation was demanded by the Prime Minister as a step towards the appeasement of Pakistan' on its front page.[49] Coming close on the heels of legal defeats in the Supreme Court, the failure of ham-handed attempts to curtail criticism of the government's policies and the resignations of Mookerji and Neogy, Matthai's resignation seriously dented the government's reputation.[50]

Mookerji had been a Hindu Mahasabha leader and was ideologically opposed to the Congress vision. Neogy was from Bengal, acutely perceptive of public opinion in his home province and conscious of his own political compulsions. Their criticism could well be ignored by Nehru or dismissed out of hand as borne out of partisan politics or ideological commitments. But the accusations levelled by an ostensibly neutral figure like Matthai – a soft-spoken, academically inclined Syrian Christian from Kerala (whose nephew Verghese Kurien became the architect of India's white revolution) – were much harder to shrug off.[51] From the naval cruiser *INS Delhi*, aboard which he was vacationing, a wounded Nehru complained that his peaceful holiday at sea had been disturbed.[52]

With the press openly speculating on the prime minister's authoritarian impulses and the clampdown on criticism of his Pakistan policy, and even private dissent within the Cabinet, the image of Nehru as an imperious figure averse to criticism and

---

[c]John Matthai CIE (1886–1959) was an economist from Kerala who served as the Minister of Railways and then Minister of Finance in the Nehru Cabinet. He resigned in 1950 after differences with Nehru and later served as the vice-chancellor of the University of Bombay. He was a Syrian Christian by faith.

ideological challenge continued to gain ground. Bengali public opinion, already hostile, saw Matthai's public utterances as further evidence of the prime minister's duplicity.[53] Having dealt with a bruising few months, Nehru himself continued to write about his frustration with the situation.[54] And it was as these allegations and counter-allegations captivated major figures at the highest levels of the Union government that news of the decision of the Patna High Court striking down the Bihar Management of Estates and Tenures Act arrived.

The judgment took the Congress establishment entirely by surprise. Initially, there was bewilderment. This had not been thought possible. The legal foundations had been thoughtfully and intricately laid. After all, even within the Constituent Assembly, the impending task of land reform and the anticipated legal challenges had been discussed extensively by the Subcommittee on Fundamental Rights when drafting the right to property into the chapter on fundamental rights to ensure constitutional support for zamindari abolition. It was for precisely this reason that Article 31, the right to property, had been drafted as a separate article, disassociated from the right to life and liberty.[55] The matter was thought to have been closed. The judgment pulled the rug from under the government's feet, and as it faced the prospect of further judicial challenge to its flagship policy, there was anxiety and consternation within its ranks.

For the Congress party as a whole, which had been committed to the policy since the 1930s, the judgment caused much embarrassment and humiliation. Zamindari abolition and land reform were the lynchpin of its social agenda, a policy on the basis of which it was going to approach the people for votes in the upcoming election. It had invested, and indeed continued to invest, enormous time and effort in its mass contact programme, and staked its prestige and reputation on the outcome. Across the country, its leaders and workers were going from village to village, informing people about their much-touted land reform programme and promising a social revolution. Even the state machinery had been co-opted. From district presidents like Raghubir Singh to senior Cabinet ministers like C. B. Gupta,[56] right up to the all-powerful high command, thousands had put their stature and influence on the line. They had proclaimed the end of the old order and the inevitability of zamindari abolition. The party's hegemonic standing had lent their words an aura of invincibility. The shock judicial defeat, even before the major tasks of their land reform agenda had begun in earnest, thus felt like a metaphoric slap on the party's face. It was a blow to its standing.

The court's decision put Congress workers and leaders, still traversing UP and Bihar rousing the people to their cause, in a peculiar position. The UP bill was yet to be passed. The Bihar bill awaited a presidential nod. Zamindari abolition and acquisition had not even properly started. With all the influence and power that their word represented, they had guaranteed the redistribution of land. And now, the entire programme had become open to question. The air of certainty evaporated. The halo of authority around the words of senior figures began to dissipate. Zamindari acquisition and redistribution could no longer be assumed to be a foregone conclusion. How would this situation be explained to the public? How were they to be told that the words of Congress leaders were not infallible?

The Bihar government, led by Sri Krishna Sinha, reacted with panic and fury. Revenue Minister Krishna Ballabh Sahay,[57] livid at being thwarted by the courts, came up with an audacious new plan – 'a bombshell to the zamindars' – to use the Cess Act to temporarily take over estates that had fallen into cess arrears over Rs 15,000.[58] In large sections of the provincial Congress unit, where the mood was virulently angry, there was a strong backlash against the Constitution. The Bihar government fully agreed with their view – Congress policies and commitments were non-negotiable, Constitution or no Constitution. They looked to their national leaders for action.

'As the Indian Constitution has been found to be the stumbling block in implementing the Congress manifesto to abolish zamindaris in a peaceful manner,' the *Times of India* reported on 10 June, 'the Bihar Government, it is learnt, will approach the Indian Parliament to amend the Constitution.'[59] It was the first public expression of the desire within certain powerful sections of the Congress to amend the Constitution, the first public acknowledgement of the opinion that the Congress manifesto and its social policies trumped the Constitution and constitutional freedoms, the first ever description of the Constitution as a stumbling block on the Congress-directed road to progress.

Barely four months into the new republic, the Bihar government and its leading figures became the first ones to publicly demand that the Constitution be subordinated to the Congress party's social agenda. Suspicions about Congress's commitment to the Constitution, which had so far remained a matter of private conjecture or the subject of an occasional hint by the Opposition, appeared to be vindicated. Perhaps sensing the mood from faraway Kerala, where he was on an official trip, Union Law Minister B. R. Ambedkar cautiously reminded his colleagues that on their observance of constitutional morality depended the success of the new republic's experiment in parliamentary democracy.[60] Few, it seemed, wanted to listen.

For their part, the zamindars in Bihar attempted to extend an olive branch, announcing that they did not want to put obstacles in the way of the government's attempt to improve economic conditions, if it only approached the issue with a generosity of spirit – in the manner that Sardar Patel had settled the issues of the princes. The leader of the zamindars, Maharaja Kameshwar Singh of Darbhanga, stated that 'he was anxious to cooperate with the government in improving the existing land system and implementing the Congress manifesto, if the government discussed the problem in an imaginative manner and gave the zamindars a fair deal'.[61] 'It is for the judiciary alone to examine the laws and determine how far they are consistent with fundamental rights,' an editorial chimed in. 'It may be a cumbrous process, but it is inevitable.'[62]

The Bihar Congress, embarrassed and vengeful, was, however, in no mood for any sort of compromise. The zamindars might have won this round, but the bigger blow of abolition and acquisition was yet to come. Over June and July, as the government was forced to return the estates it had taken over,[63] it strenuously urged the Cabinet and the president to give immediate assent to the Bihar Land Reforms Bill.[64] An alarmed Central government, well aware that it was navigating a constitutional minefield and reluctant to rush into another debacle, parried the thrust by appointing a special committee of the Cabinet to examine the bill and the issue of compensation.[65]

In Lucknow, where the Land Reform Bill was still being debated in the assembly, a circumspect Charan Singh assured landholders that the UP government would pay compensation for the abolition of zamindaris, and in one lump sum if possible.[66] With the Reserve

Bank of India estimating the Zamindari Abolition Bill to come up to Rs 414 crore, the probability of this actually happening ranged from negligible to non-existent.[67] The mood was equally sombre. Nevertheless, when the assembly reconvened in July after a recess, the slow, tiresome process was accelerated in an attempt to pass the legislation as quickly as possible. One particularly productive day, the assembly passed seventy-two clauses of the mammoth bill.[68]

The Congress party's socialist challengers, raging at what they saw as unjustified delay in the destruction of the old order, raised the temperature by publicly describing the Constitution 'as a clumsy document that cannot be an instrument of full and complete democracy'.[69] Jayaprakash Narayan, who till then had been reprimanding the prime minister for disrespecting the Constitution and endangering democracy, now passionately stated, 'Left to myself, I would go to the extent of saying that the Constitution should be scrapped and a new one drafted.'[70]

In Delhi, shockwaves rippled through the corridors of power. 'It seems partly because of the Constitution and partly because of the lawyer's opinions and High Court judgments, we have got into a bad tangle,' Pandit Nehru wrote to the home ministry. 'I am quite certain that unless we find a quick way out to deal with the agrarian problems in Bihar and elsewhere, we shall be in serious trouble.'[71] In his note, he plainly and precisely delineated his problem:

> Having for long proclaimed as a major point in our policy the abolition of the zamindari system and having repeatedly made attempts to do so and raised expectations high, we just cannot, on either moral or practical grounds or even on the basis of legal difficulty, stop this process or delay it ... I feel therefore that it is not quite enough for us to accept with resignation the legal difficulties that are pointed out to us, but to find some way out fairly quickly which enables our state governments to deal adequately with their problem of abolishing the zamindari system. If necessary, the matter might have to be put up before Parliament.[72]

Spooked by the issue's potential to trigger a political earthquake, the prime minister was clearly flustered and blamed the Constitution for his problems. He had provided the ideological force and moral leadership for the government's land reform drive. If the unthinkable happened and public expectations were belied, who would shoulder the blame? The fear of lengthy legal battles over land reform and the possibility of further judicial defeats made the government and the prime minister jittery. There was just one question occupying centre stage, however. How was one to act within the bounds of the Constitution when it was pitted against the party's manifesto? Which of the two was paramount? What was the way out?

The court's answer had been unequivocal. The prime minister was still pondering the question and weighing his options. Several thousand miles away in Tamil Nadu, meanwhile, where a plucky woman named Champakam Dorairajan had taken the provincial government to court, another pivotal case was heading towards conclusion. And in the tussle between the state and the Constitution, another front was about to be opened in Madras.

Battle Ordinaire

Much before backward caste assertion and social justice politics had become a trend in northern India, Madras had been known as the land of social reform and social justice. Social justice politics in Madras had been pioneered by the Justice Party – the forerunner of today's Dravida Munnetra Kazhagam (DMK) – which had ruled the province and dominated politics for significant periods in the 1920s and 1930s. From the Justice Party was born the Self-Respect Movement under the leadership of E. V. Ramasamy Periyar,[d] which challenged the dominance of Brahmins and the prevalence of caste-based discrimination in Tamil society. In the 1940s, the Justice Party transformed itself into the Dravidar Kazhagam (DK) under Periyar's leadership and began a vehement fight for social reform, the rights of backward classes, the promotion of 'rationalism' and the negation of a Hindi or Aryan-influenced identity.[73]

---

[d]Erode Venkatappa Ramasamy 'Periyar' (1879–1973) was a social activist and politician. Taking up an 'anti-Brahmanical' stance, Periyar opposed the imposition of Hindi; promoted rationalism, women's rights and the Tamil language; believed in a historically continuous 'Aryan–Dravidian' conflict; and advocated for an independent 'Dravida Nadu' – a separate state for the Tamil people.

Questions of caste and communal representation had been critical to the political philosophy of the Justice Party, and remained so for Tamil politics as a whole. Experiments with using reservations to challenge the caste order and push back against the marginalization of backward castes had begun as early as 1921, when the first Justice Party ministry had taken charge in the Madras province and instituted the first Communal General Order, creating reservations in government departments and in educational institutions to 'prevent the over representation of students belonging to a particular community' and secure the advancement of non-Brahmins in the face of Brahmin monopoly in education, professions and government service.[74]

The Communal GO, as it came to be called, was a rather intricate device for achieving this objective. Out of every thirteen, it strictly reserved seats for students and applicants from six categories in the following ratio: Non-Brahmin Hindus – 5, Mohammedans – 2, Anglo-Indians – 2, Indian Christians – 2, Brahmins – 1, Other Depressed Classes – 1. Since no one from one group could occupy a seat that belonged to another group, the GO achieved two things at the same time: it reserved a certain number of seats for particular categories and restricted the applicants from those categories to that arbitrarily fixed number. So, for example, out of every thirteen applicants, five positions were reserved for 'Non-Brahmin Hindus' – but this was also the maximum number of positions they could occupy. Brahmins competed with other Brahmins for the lone position in their category. In other words, there was stringently enforced and rigid community-wise distribution of seats in universities and appointments in government departments.

Reservations as an administrative tool and a radical politics based on securing greater representation for backward class and marginalized groups in the state apparatus, as well as a great push for 'de-Brahminization', thus formed an enduring legacy in Tamil politics, a legacy that profoundly shaped the electoral arena and was impossible to ignore even when the Congress replaced the Justice Party in the 1940s. The Communal GO itself went through a number of iterations over the 1920s and 1930s and reached its final iteration in 1948 under the Congress government of O. P. Ramaswamy Reddiyar. In this last iteration, the ratio for every fourteen applicants stood at: Non-Brahmin Hindus – 6; Brahmins – 2; Muslims – 1; Anglo-Indians, Christians and

Europeans – 1; Others – 2, Harijans – 2. It was this iteration that was being followed when the dispute erupted.

Once the Constitution of India had come into force, the legal and constitutional validity of the Communal GO immediately came under a cloud. At a glance, its provisions seemed obviously incompatible with the fundamental right of freedom from discrimination enshrined in Article 15 and the fundamental right of not being denied admission to a state institution on caste grounds enshrined in Article 29 of the Constitution, even with the proviso that this would not prevent the state from making special provisions for backward classes. It was, in constitutional terms, a sitting duck. Few, however, paid much attention until 7 June 1950 when, just as the country woke up to the shock judicial defeat for the government in Bihar, two students, Champakam Dorairajan and C. R. Srinivasan, approached the Madras High Court to file petitions praying for writs of mandamus.

Champakam Dorairajan was a middle-aged woman from Madras who had graduated from the University of Madras in 1934 and had decided to attempt to gain admission to the Government Medical College in Madras. She discovered that she had little chance of actually securing admission to the college Bachelor of Medicine and Bachelor of Surgery programme because admissions were strictly regulated according to the ratio set out in the Communal GO.[75] Since she was a Brahmin, the number of seats available to her to apply for was necessarily limited and the qualifying marks required were necessarily higher. C. R. Srinivasan, a young student who had just cleared his intermediate examinations and applied for admission to the Government Engineering College at Guindy, faced a similar predicament. He found that since admissions were governed by the terms of the Communal GO and granted according to communal proportions, there was little chance of his application being considered on its merits, ignoring considerations of caste, race or religion. Both were scandalized and infuriated by what they perceived as completely unjustified discrimination.

* * *

In their petitions – one filed on 6 June and the other on 13 June[76] – both petitioners contended that the Communal GO was an infringement of their fundamental rights, and inconsistent with the provisions of the Constitution. The order, they asserted, violated both Article 15 (1) of the Constitution of India, which guaranteed that 'the state shall not discriminate against any citizens on grounds only of religion, race, caste, sex, place of birth or any of them', and Article 29 (2), which guaranteed that 'no citizen shall be denied admission into any educational institutions maintained by the state or receiving aid out of state funds on grounds only of religion, race, caste, language or any of them'.[77] All that they wanted, they prayed to the court, was for their applications to be considered on their merits, without taking into consideration their religion, caste or sex.[78]

This small, inoffensive prayer from two aspiring students raised one of the most profound questions for the Indian republic. In it lay the genesis of a political fault line that endures to this day. As the first legal challenge to the idea of reservations and the first one to consider the relationship between the Constitution and social justice, the case – as Justice Basheer Ahmed Sayeed observed while accepting the petition – 'involved issues of supreme importance to the future well-being of the state'.[79] Whether the Communal GO was 'discrimination or not will have to be decided once and for all,' reported the *Times of India*.[80] The future of reservations, indeed the future of the government's vision of affirmative action, was at stake.

In court, the petitioners were energetically represented by Alladi Krishnaswamy Aiyyar,[e] a noted lawyer who had been one of the key architects of the new Constitution and, as a member of nine committees in the erstwhile Constituent Assembly, was intimately aware of the nuances involved. Aiyyar argued that the right granted by Article 29 (2) of the Constitution, which in unequivocal terms prevented any discrimination in the matter of admissions to state or state-aided institutions, was an individual right personally granted to each citizen. It could not be sidestepped by granting restricted community-based opportunities, it was not a right granted to people as members of a particular caste or religion. It did not matter if other Brahmins had been admitted. The petitioners asked for their rights as Indian citizens, not their rights as Brahmins. There was no

---

[e]Sir Alladi Krishnaswamy Aiyyar (1883–1953) was a noted lawyer and jurist; he served as the advocate-general of Madras from 1929 to 1944, was knighted in 1932 and was elected to the Constituent Assembly in 1946. He served on nine committees, including the pivotal Drafting Committee chaired by B. R. Ambedkar and the Advisory Subcommittee on Fundamental Rights.

proviso that allowed for special provisions for backward classes in contravention of this article, as there was in Article 16, which prevented discrimination in the matter of appointments under the state. Marks may not be the one and only criterion to decide on admissions, he stated, but then nor could religion, race or caste be the basis of selection, even if the government wanted to support backward sections of society.

The Madras government did not deny that it was following discriminatory practices. Instead, it sought to justify such discrimination on the grounds of public policy and the need for social justice. It rested its arguments on the view that under Article 46 of the Constitution – a Directive Principle of State Policy that enjoined the state to promote the welfare of the weaker sections of society – the state was bound to promote with special care the educational interests of the weaker sections of the people, and that it had sole discretion to decide who these people were. As a result of applying the ratio prescribed by the Communal GO, seventy-seven Brahmins, 224 non-Brahmins, fifty-one Christians, twenty-six Muslims and twenty-six Harijans had been selected for admission to engineering colleges. If caste and community considerations had been ignored, the numbers would have been 249 Brahmins, 112 non-Brahmins, twenty-two Christians, three Muslims and zero Harijans. To avoid such a situation, the state argued, classification and discrimination on the basis of class and community was imperative.

As the Madras High Court examined the virtues of the arguments presented over June and July, the question generated intense passions among ordinary people, especially among those who felt they had been wronged by the Communal GO.[81] With the issues at stake touching on the lived experiences and aspirations of many young people, several letters made their way to newspaper offices, giving voice to the strong opinions against the government's stand.

'The pursuit of a strictly communal policy ... by the Justice Ministry was violently criticized by the then south Indian Congress giants,' wrote an angry man named S. Krishnaswamy, 'but when the Congress came to power, not only were all these measures given a permanent place in the statute book, but also all intelligent opposition to them was crushed by an iron hand.'[82] The communal policy the Congress was following was suicidal, one letter lamented, and not a word of protest had been uttered by supposedly responsible Congress leaders.[83] 'The poison of communalism which ... has been sedulously developed by Government patronage resulted in the Madras Government restricting admissions of Brahmins in appointments and in colleges,' charged another, arguing that Brahmin preponderance in education was because they had taken to modern education early under British rule.[84]

'The governments of the various states constituting the republic should ... give preference to those who are non-communal and non-provincial in their outlook,' advised a citizen from Bombay.[85] In Ootacamund, the state's finance minister mounted a public defence of the Communal GO, stressing that the advanced communities in the state could afford to make some sacrifices for their less advanced brethren.[86] The effect of the order 'is not some sacrifice, but almost total effacement,' promptly retorted a major newspaper, observing that the 'road of communal rationing may be short, but it is full of pits.'[87] The only way Article 46 could be interpreted, it maintained, was through the provision of free tuition, free books and free lodging and boarding.

On 27 July, a three-judge bench of the Madras High Court pronounced its verdict. It found that grounds of religion, race and caste could not be the basis for admissions, and hence the Communal GO violated Articles 15(1) and 29(2) of the Constitution and constituted a form of discrimination.[88] This was especially true in the case of Article 29, which prohibited discrimination in admissions to state-funded educational institutions, since there was no provision for a contravention of the article to create reservations. The court was vociferous in its condemnation, stating:

The Communal GO denies equal treatment for all citizens under like circumstances and conditions, both in the privileges conferred and disabilities imposed (it) shuts out students having high qualifications solely on the grounds of their caste or religion and lets in others with inferior qualifications on the same ground As the articles of the Constitution stand at present, it is difficult to see how the state can make discrimination between applicant and applicant on the grounds of religion or caste, and restrict the number of seats that could be secured by applicants of any particular religion or caste, or prescribe different qualifications to applicants of different religions or castes to the advantage of some and the disadvantage of others Does social justice or the welfare of the state require a suppression of the integrity and freedom of the individual personality of the citizen by reason of his belonging to a particular caste? Is the lynch spirit having its roots in caste and colour and religious differences to be fostered and recognized as state policy?[89]

The Communal GO, and the broader policy of reservations, was shot down. Shot down also was the government's reference to the Directive Principles of State Policy. Directive principles were clearly and apparently subordinate to fundamental rights, the court categorically declared, and something prohibited by fundamental rights provisions in Part III of the Constitution could not be introduced through the back door using the directive principles in Part IV. In the court's eyes, if the absence of reservations denied opportunities to backward communities and perpetuated social injustice, then the only real satisfactory solution would be to provide adequate facilities to all applicants.[90] In a nutshell, the court had articulated three firm, unambiguous principles. First, that the directive principles were subordinate to the provisions for fundamental rights, and could not be used to suborn the individual freedom that the Constitution granted. Second, that no matter how altruistic the intention and how noble the cause, the government had to function within the bounds of the Constitution – and fundamental rights were inviolable, except in conformity with the Constitution itself. Third, that the Constitution, after much thought and deliberation, had been framed in a particular way, and even if it reversed previous administrative principles or widely prevalent practices, constitutional provisions had to be upheld. As one of the judges pointedly observed, a vague and undefined principle of social justice could not and did not justify a refusal to obey a plain command of the Constitution by which the legislature, the executive and the judiciary alike were bound.[91]

In the end, the judges were scathing in their critique of the government's views, sarcastically noting:

If the person in-charge for the time being of a state, elected no doubt by a majority of voters at the polls, were free to enforce their own notions of social and economic justice unfettered by constitutional restraints, there is a possibility of serious and undeserved hardship and injury to large classes of citizens ... Declaration of a guaranteed right in Article 15(1) of the Constitution would be worthless if the government could disregard or nullify it by executive acts like the Communal GO (it) would become an empty bauble if the Communal GO regulating admission of students were held to be legal and constitutional.[92]

Another pillar of the Congress party's social agenda had fallen, raising as many searching questions as it answered. Unlike the judgment in Bihar, where the major battle was yet to come, the Madras High Court had effectively taken a wrecking ball to what was an article of faith for much of the Congress. In Madras, there were strikes and agitations as backward class students demanded that the Communal GO be retained and the high court ruling reversed.[93] Flustered members of the Congress Legislative Party demanded an emergency meeting of the party to consider the court's ruling and appealed to the Government of India for intervention.[94]

A panic-stricken but nevertheless still combative Madras government immediately declared that they would appeal against the decision in the Supreme Court.[95] And of course, another judicial battle would be fought, and perhaps even won; the government and the Congress were guarded but hopeful. The one question on everyone's lips, however, was: what now? What if the next judicial battle was also lost? Two weeks later, in the Madras Legislative Assembly, state Law Minister K. Madhava Menon provided a tantalizing answer. 'No particular reservations would be made regarding education,' he stated, and 'the question of an amendment to the Constitution would arise after a definite decision had been reached in the matter'.[96]

Resolves Harden

The news from Madras was greeted with dismay and disbelief in Delhi. It was an even bigger blow than what had transpired in Bihar. Land reform and social justice through reservations had been two central pillars of the Congress agenda. One was now under threat; the other had just been effectively demolished. An article of faith had just been violated. Even though the defeat wasn't final and an appeal to the Supreme Court was being contemplated, the very fact that such a key part of Congress policy, an indispensable component of its social agenda, had outright failed the test of constitutionality caused disquiet and outrage among senior figures.

The court had demonstrated in clear-cut terms the primacy of the Constitution over political and bureaucratic power. It had enunciated a crucial dictum – that transgressions of fundamental rights in the pursuit of government policy, however positive, were explicitly forbidden. Article 15 (1) guaranteeing freedom from discrimination was paramount; not only were considerations of caste or religion irrelevant, they were expressly taboo. They could not be factors under consideration, even if – through fortuitous circumstances – doing so advantaged certain people over others. Where qualifications and standards were to be prescribed, they had to be reasonably relevant to their purpose and the same for all citizens. Examination scores or physical fitness, for example, could be a qualification; religion or caste could not.

The judgment was a powerful and expansive articulation of a new republican vision and an equally powerful indictment of government policy. In what it believed to be the underlying egalitarian spirit of the Constitution, the Madras High Court sought to shut out and resolutely combat 'the tendency to think in terms of caste, race or religion in adjusting relations between the citizen and the state'.[97] The verdict embodied a thorough repudiation of the Congress vision and the government's social agenda. Closely following the adverse judgment in Patna, the defeat in Madras put Congress leaders in a quandary. A flabbergasted party searched for a response.

For the Congress, the problem was twofold. The first problem was that both these issues – land reform and reservations – had been discussed extensively in the Constituent Assembly when the Constitution was drafted. The Constitution had been drafted keeping these issues and Congress policies in mind. It had been drafted by Congress leaders. It represented a social contract that enabled and reflected a particular vision of a political society. Now, when pitted against the Constitution, there was little room to manoeuvre. How to square this circle? The conundrum was neatly summed up by the press:

It becomes a matter for serious consideration when high-ranking leaders of the ruling party, which had an overwhelming majority in the Constituent Assembly, fail either to grasp the content of the Constitution or to respect its provisions. Law makers must in no case be themselves law breakers.[98]

The second and bigger problem, as Nehru had stated in his note to the home ministry,[99] was explaining the situation to the people. Having raised their expectations and asked them to believe in the promises of Congress leaders, how were they to now go back to them and explain legal and constitutional niceties? Who was going to tell the people that the word of the government and the prime minister was not the law, that there was now a greater power, the Constitution of India? And what might happen if they did? In the context of land reform and zamindari abolition – essential parts of the Congress policy and programme with which the prime minister was personally identified – these questions assumed added importance.

Already facing the heat in Bihar, uncomfortable with constitutional restraints and impatient with long-drawn legal and judicial procedures, Nehru had been mulling his options for some time. The news from Madras hardened his resolve. On 3 August, he wrote to his chief ministers:

High Courts sometimes intervene and declare state law as ultra vires. It is clear that we have got to go through this programme of abolition of zamindaris and to avoid all delay, for delay is dangerous. Unfortunately, the law and the Constitution sometimes come in the way. I think we could devise methods which are in conformity with the Constitution. It is certain that if the law comes in the way, ultimately the law will have to be changed.[100]

A full six months and six days since the new republic had been inaugurated, the prime minister was seriously contemplating, and making the case for, amending the Constitution because it was getting in his way; the very Constitution that he had once described as the foundation of the country's republican freedom. Between the Constitution and his own political agenda, his faith in the latter clearly trumped his allegiance to the former.

As Congress figures in Madras demanded the intervention of the Government of India and the overturning of the verdict, shrewd observers quickly realized the gravity of the situation. 'Such redress as they [the Congress party in Madras] want,' the *Times of India* prophetically warned, 'can come only through an amendment of the Constitution which in consequence will have to be modified in such other respects as would destroy its present democratic and secular character.' 'In this context,' it added, 'no purpose can be served even if the Supreme Court were to uphold the High Court's verdict. Those who do not respect the High Court will not necessarily show deference to the Supreme Court.'[101]

Meanwhile in Uttar Pradesh, the final schedule of compensation to the Zamindari Abolition Bill had been passed on 28 July, guaranteeing uniform rates plus rehabilitation grants to smaller landholders.[102] On 4 August, to rapturous applause and wide acclaim, the UP Legislative Assembly 'accomplished the herculean task' of passing the Zamindari Abolition Bill. Angry socialists, disappointed that the bill granted compensation to landholders, abstained from voting. Affecting over two million landholders, this was a major success for Chief Minister Govind Ballabh Pant, who described it as a peasant's charter and an antidote to communism.[103] The measure was greeted by jubilant headlines in the press, such as 'Bhumidari Zindabad: UP Zamindari Abolition Bill Passed'[104] and 'UP's Feudal Order Being Changed'.[105]

But, as had been noticed by keen observers as early as 30 June, 'the hilarious optimism which marked the first stages of UP's Zamindari Abolition drive' had faded away.[106] It had been replaced by a potent combination of fear, apprehension and uncertainty. Jubilant headlines aside, both sides realized that another judicial contest loomed – and after the results in Bihar and Madras, no one could be sure about the outcome. The Bihar bill waited for a presidential assent. The UP bill made its way through the Legislative Council. The government and the zamindars, big and small, sharpened their legal swords and prepared for the upcoming battle.

3

The Deepening Crisis

A Gradual Escalation

On 15 August 1950, the *Times of India* surveyed the state of the nation, and found little to cheer about. It observed:

> The third year of independence saw this country sink deeper in the economic morass surrounding her since the end of the war. The National Government's struggle to pull her out of it has proved ineffective and exposed its inability, even incompetence, to tackle an abnormal economic situation. All of its other achievements ... will fail to impress the common people who only know that life is becoming more difficult for them than ever before even under 'independence' ... The same incompetence has marked the administration's handling of other problems during the year.[1]

It had been a year wracked by a turbulent relationship with Pakistan, persistent communal conflict and refugee influx in Bengal, spiralling prices and food shortages, and high-profile ministerial resignations. But even amid this gloom, the writer noted one bright spot, the most important set of events in the political arena: the inauguration of the republic and 'the beginning of an assertion of fundamental rights guaranteed by the Constitution as a result of judgments given by the High Courts and the Supreme Court'.[2] If 'constitutions mark transformations of polity and codify moments of revolutionary change' – in the words of the legal historian Rohit

De[3] – then the first six months of the new republic truly represented a metamorphosis in the nature of public life in India. And yet, even as the press pointed towards these developments – the ability of the Indian people to use the Constitution to hold the state to account for its sovereign guarantees and the role of the courts in ensuring a vigorous defence of constitutionalism – as a singularly important silver lining in a challenging year, others saw in them the origins of frustration and difficulty.

The passage of the Uttar Pradesh (UP) Zamindari Abolition and Land Reform Bill – with its purported intent to liberate 7.5 million farmers and free 34 million acres of land from 'near-feudal ownership' and its torturous reckoning with close to 1,300 amendments and 1,450 speeches[4] – brought questions about the constitutional status of land reform and redistribution squarely to the centre of political discourse. Nehru's letter to his chief ministers making the case for a potential constitutional amendment if the law continued to stand in his way only served to highlight the seminal importance of it to the government. Combined with the question of reservations and the still turbulent situation in Bengal, it meant that apart from the usual 'personal and group predilections', larger issues of policy and ideology became part and parcel of the negotiations within the party regarding the next incumbent of the office of Congress president, who was due to be elected.[5]

In Madras, where the septuagenarian DK leader E. V. Ramasamy Periyar had been pushed into quietude by his controversial marriage to Maniammai, a party worker almost forty years his junior – triggering a split with his chief lieutenant C. N. Annadurai and the formation of the DMK party – the judgment revived the separatist strand of politics. At a DK rally, Periyar declared that if the Supreme Court upheld the high court's judgment, then the only remedy was to change the Constitution – or the creation of a separate Dravidistan[6] in which laws would be more suitable to the 'people of the south'.[7] Congress and Parliament, however, would not change the Constitution, he taunted, because they were dominated by north Indians.[8] 'Crusaders for a separate Dravidistan are once again on the march, using this time as their shield the Communal Order on admissions to colleges, declared unconstitutional recently by the Madras High Court,' reported an alarmed *Times of India*.[9]

On the other side, the long-running consultations between the Bihar government and the special Cabinet Committee constituted to examine the Bihar Land Reforms Bill and the question of compensation came to a conclusion. After almost two months of talks, on 20 August the committee – which included Law Minister B. R. Ambedkar, Finance Minister C. D. Deshmukh and Labour Minister Jagjivan Ram – decided to recommend to Chief Minister Sri Krishna Sinha and Revenue Minister K. B. Sahay that the zamindari system should be abolished and compensation paid to landholders through bonds redeemable over a period of forty years.[10] Curiously, it failed to either notice or address the proverbial elephant in the room as far as the bill was concerned: its staggered scale of compensation where the rate of compensation went down as the size of the landholding went up. It is impossible to determine with any degree of certainty whether the committee simply glossed over this aspect or deliberately chose to ignore it. Notwithstanding, they left the bill in constitutionally dubious territory.

The recommendation was also extraordinary for other reasons. Three of the committee's members – C. Rajagopalachari, K. M. Munshi and B. R. Ambedkar – had also been members of the Subcommittee on Fundamental Rights in the Constituent Assembly. It had discussed and debated squaring land reform with the fundamental right to property, and it was courtesy of those deliberations that the right to property had been written as a separate article, disassociated from the right to life and liberty – with the personal approval of Munshi, Rajagopalachari and Ambedkar. It was precisely for this reason that Article 31 provided that no person could be deprived of his property save by the authority of a validly enacted law, and this law had to be for a public purpose and provide for a mechanism of compensation. Article 31 permitted the law enacted by the legislature to determine levels of compensation rather than prescribe an abstract principle – and it was thought that this would allow the government to meet anticipated legal challenges from landholders by reducing the potential for judicial interference in the process.[11]

Within the Congress, and indeed within the Constituent Assembly, there had been considerable division regarding the right to property and the extent to which judicial interference might be permitted. The Congress leadership was of the view that courts should be entirely prevented from getting into questions about the quantum of compensation. After much debate and dissent, 'it was largely felt that the final version of Article 31 was a compromise suitable to all'.[12] This version empowered the state to acquire private property provided it was for a public purpose and under the provisions of a validly enacted law, and entailed some compensation. It was felt that the quantum of compensation would thus be framed by the state assemblies in their zamindari abolition legislation, and the courts would not be able to judge the justness or fairness of the compensation mechanisms so prescribed. It was hoped all judicial scrutiny of compensation would be avoided in this way.

Given this background, the members of the special committee not only ignored their own previous experience in framing the underlying constitutional framework, but also failed to address the most contentious part of the bill. Still, the Central government's nod with a minor tweak to the method of compensation effectively gave the go-ahead for a presidential assent and brought matters to a head. The issue could not be brushed under the carpet any longer. There was only one distraction remaining: the election of the new Congress president. That got out of the way soon enough. On 2 September, in the teeth of Nehru's opposition and despite his threats of resignation,[13] Purushottam Das Tandon was elected Congress president with Patel's support, defeating Acharya Kripalani in a keenly and bitterly fought contest, and bringing to the fore another man known for his differences with Nehru and his proclivity for what has often been termed 'soft' Hindu nationalism.[14] It was Patel's last effort to make Nehru understand that his will was not law for the Congress.[15] A disgruntled Acharya Kripalani nevertheless described Tandon's election as proof that 'the totalitarian trends inherent in the new regime have not yet completely swallowed up our (Congress's) organization'.[16] From such a senior and long-standing figure in the Congress,[17] the reference to totalitarian tendencies in the new regime was prescient and chilling. Surprisingly, few took the warning seriously at the time. Unsurprisingly, Tandon would fail to stay in his seat beyond the first year of his three-year term.

At one level, internal conflict and manoeuvring within the party intensified. At another, important constitutional questions became a matter of discussion. And political attention again focused on the Land Reforms Bill in Bihar.

High Stakes, Higher Politics

By early September, the bill had found its way to the Union Cabinet for its approval and advice to the president, and on 7 September, the *Times of India* breathlessly and expectantly reported that the assent of the president was expected any day.[18] Even when the government finally came to a decision, it was panned for the delay, which was believed to have led to a decline in Congress prestige, a loss of faith in its pledges and frustration among the peasantry. 'Somewhat rusty and dilatory as the official machinery has become under the Congress regime,' wrote one commentator, 'there was little excuse for such a delay in regard to this particular measure.'[19] 'Perhaps it is wrong to expect such an effort from a party that in spite of its manifestoes and resolutions', he added sarcastically, 'has proved its incapacity to allot proper priorities and tackle those factors first which keep this nation underfed, disease-ridden, illiterate and in the grip of indescribable poverty.'[20]

Subjected to censure by the press and insistent appeals from the Bihar Congress, the Union Cabinet met to consider the bill on 9 September, and there and then advised President Rajendra Prasad to certify the bill, which had originally been sent to him for assent in June.[21] After months of preparation and discussion, the moment of revolution had finally arrived. There was no going back.

The president, who for his part had opposed the idea of class conflict and had spent much of his time as Congress leader in Bihar attempting to bring about an amicable settlement between landlords and tenants,[22] balked at the advice that had been tendered to him. He was no revolutionary, and had only truly wanted either stronger tenancy laws and a change in the behaviour of the zamindars or, failing that, zamindari abolition with full and just compensation to landholders. He had already let the prime minister and the Cabinet know about his views in this regard via a minute sent on 8 September – a minute that had been read out aloud in the Cabinet and then promptly ignored by the prime minister and his colleagues.[23]

The highest constitutional functionary in the country was astonished by the Cabinet's response. Having presided over the Constituent Assembly and thus being well aware that the government was treading on thin constitutional ice as far as the right to property and the question of compensation were concerned,

Rajendra Prasad tarried by asking Attorney-General M. C. Setalvad for his opinions, both on the Bihar bill vis-à-vis Article 31 and, more controversially, on the general powers of the president to accept or reject the advice of his council of ministers.[24] Ideologically opposed to radical socialism and committed to respecting the fundamental rights guaranteed in the Constitution, Prasad played for time – and more legally sound advice.

From Bombay, where he had been recuperating after an illness – and hence had been unable to attend the crucial Cabinet meeting – Sardar Patel wrote to Nehru counselling caution. 'As you know, the President is rather strong in his convictions on this problem,' wrote Patel, 'and I think we should avoid giving any impression that such a well-considered note of his met with a summary reception at the hands of the cabinet.' 'I would suggest', he urged Nehru, 'that the note might be referred to the Home and Law Ministries for joint consultation.'[25] But the prime minister was in no mood to wait. With the election of a right-wing Patel protégé as Congress president,[26] a pivotal and potentially bruising session of the Congress coming up at Nasik, continuing communal problems in Bengal, unrelenting criticism in the press and big defeats in the courts, Nehru was desperate to reassert control and fight back. He was now a man on a mission.

'I find from the Home Ministry that they have not yet received your certificate for the Bihar Land Bill,' he curtly informed President Prasad.

> Yesterday I conveyed to you the request of the Cabinet ... and I also pointed out that there was a certain urgency about the matter which has been delayed long enough. I do not know what difficulty has arisen now to postpone this still further. I would request you, therefore, again to be good enough to certify this Bill. Any other course would render my position as Prime Minister and that of the Government difficult.[27]

A flummoxed Rajendra Prasad responded by informing Nehru that in view of the urgency he attached to the matter, a presidential assent would be given without waiting for the attorney-general's opinion.[28] The bill was duly certified the same evening on 11 September. With the bill now secure in his hand, the prime minister turned his mind to Patel. 'The Cabinet was strongly of the opinion that the advice tendered by them to the President should be acted upon, both from the constitutional and the practical points of view,' he peremptorily informed his deputy. 'I do not think, therefore, that any occasion arises now for a reference of the Bill to the Law or Home Ministry.'[29]

Now firmly in the driving seat, Nehru declared to the press that the Congress had laid down the policy of putting an end to the *jagirdari* and zamindari systems in order to attain a prosperous peasantry. This now had to be given effect to as speedily as possible.[30] The news of the presidential assent evoked mixed feelings in Bihar. Large zamindars, already preparing for a legal showdown, served legal notices on the state government, demanding that their estates not be acquired under the Bihar Land Reforms Act, which inter alia was unconstitutional and ultra vires of the legislature.[31] The secretariat busied itself in adapting the compensation schedule to comply with the Union Cabinet's recommendation and prepared to launch its agrarian revolution.[32] The die was cast.

Meanwhile in UP, the state government had woken up to smell the judicial coffee that had been brewed in Madras and 'directed that the existing orders providing for communal representation in services in cases in which recruitment is not made by competitive tests cannot stand and are accordingly abrogated'.[33] The government's direction brought home to everyone that communal reservations were now a constitutional anathema, and judicial decisions in faraway Madras had profound consequences across the length and breadth of the country. It was in these circumstances, with weighty constitutional questions begging answers, that the Congress party gathered at Nasik for its first general session in the new republic.

Nehru Ascendant

The election of Purushottam Das Tandon, much against his wishes and in spite of his threats of resignation, had so angered Nehru that he had decided to refrain from joining the new Congress Working Committee. He had already communicated his decision to Patel, and continued to hold out his threat of resigning from the government and refusing to work with the new guard. As the Nasik session of the Congress approached, Tandon, who was already facing brickbats from Kripalani and others, was equally anxious to avoid further internecine conflict and bridge the gap that was threatening to grow into a yawning chasm between the two wings of the organization. He was willing to concede ground in order to avert a public clash with the prime minister.

Nehru sensed an opportunity. 'Among many people who supported Tandon, there is now a feeling that they should do their utmost to please me and prevent me from taking any further step. Hence their desire to pass resolutions sponsored by me,' he wrote to his sister Vijaya Lakshmi Pandit, then India's ambassador to the United States.[34] 'But I am quite clear that even if my resolutions are passed,' he informed her, 'I shall not join the Working Committee. How far I cooperate with it in the future will depend upon circumstances.'[35] He was clearly edgy about his own position within the party's framework and unsure of his grip on the party organization.

At Nasik, the prime minister came out all guns blazing. Addressing the Youth Congress, he invoked the Father of the Nation and reminded his audience about 'the emphasis Gandhi had always laid on dignity of labour and not on fighting elections as was the case with Congressmen of today'.[36] 'It is disgusting to see many a so-called leader today merely talk and manoeuvre to get elected to some office or the other,' he roared, 'rather than do constructive work in the interests of the country.'[37] It was a barely concealed reading of the riot act to Tandon and his supporters, whose victory Nehru attributed to the machinations of Patel, the arm-twisting of delegates and the manipulation and misuse of official machinery.[38] Tandon, and the rest of the Congress party, received the message loud and clear. The prime minister needn't have worried.

Addressing the session, he assertively demanded that if party members continued to desire his leadership and place faith in his abilities, they would have to fall in line behind him and his policies. With particular reference to the communal situation in Bengal and his policy towards Pakistan, and what he believed to be almost an existential threat from organizations such as the RSS and the Hindu Mahasabha, there would be no room for dissent. 'Hindu communalism' was to be resolutely fought, and talk of 'firm action' against Pakistan was to be vehemently discouraged – and with this position no compromise was possible as long as Nehru was the prime minister. The radical socialists Algu Rai Shastri and Shibban Lal Saksena accused him of 'coercing the Congress into accepting his standpoint' and charged him with being unwilling to brook any criticism.[39] But with the rapidly ailing Patel mostly confined to his sick bed – he made only one speech over the entire session – and the Congress 'right wing' shying away from a fight, little resistance was on offer. Nehru's approach was eagerly and fervently endorsed by the assembled party members.[40]

Following a nudge from Patel, even Tandon, who had been rumoured to have different views on the subject, hastily submitted and declared his allegiance to Nehruvian secularism while deprecating all talk of a 'Hindu Government'.[41] A similar situation unfolded when it came to the question of economic policy and land reform. The Subjects Committee promptly adopted Nehru's economic plan centred on a controlled economy, and despite objections from certain quarters, the party emphatically endorsed the prime minister's position on land reform and zamindari abolition.[42] Tandon himself obligingly reiterated that the party had been committed to zamindari abolition since 1930, and continued to remain so.[43]

The Nasik Congress turned out to be a remarkable and unabashed personal triumph for Nehru. Some had been expecting a split within the ranks of the party leadership, perhaps even the departure of a senior figure like Kripalani. Others had predicted a moment of truth over Pakistan and communal violence in Bengal.[44] Still others had expected Tandon to 'unfurl the flag of Hindu revivalism and declare a *dharma-yuddha* against secularism'.[45] In the end, none of those eventualities materialized. Instead, Nehru's resolutions were carried through by large majorities, demonstrating the capitulation of more conservative elements within the organization – derisively called the 'Patel group' – and the preponderant influence of Nehru's personality. 'There is a tendency to please me within limits, and therefore the resolutions have gone through,' he observed to Vijaya Lakshmi Pandit.[46] It was unmistakable: the party now lay prostrate before him, the unchallengeable wielder of executive power.[47]

As C. Rajagopalachari commented, 'there could not have been a more thumping vote of confidence in the Prime Minister than what was by implication given at Nasik'.[48] The prime minister who emerged from the Nasik session was vastly more powerful than the one who had entered it. He had fended off challenges from the left, the right and even the remnants of the Gandhians. He had tamed a potentially rebellious Tandon; he had convinced his party colleagues to endorse his policies and ideological suppositions; and he had forced the party to fall in line behind him. Having secured the party's backing, demonstrating his popularity, pushing his detractors onto the back foot and making his policies into Congress doctrine, Nehru was now very firmly in charge.

Nehru's critics quickly realized that they had little chance of dividing the party ranks against him. The picture was clear: they would either have to sit tight or seek avenues outside the party. His stature and reputation considerably enhanced and his hold over the party cemented, all thoughts of resignation were promptly forgotten as Nehru turned to cutting Tandon and the new Working Committee down to size. But he was right in that there were limits to the tendency to please him. Indeed there were, and Tandon delineated them in his presidential address when he gave 'his unqualified support' to the Constitution, calling for it to be worshipped as a symbol of the country's collective will and aspiration, and describing defiance of the Constitution as a criminal act.[49] It was a remark directed as much at Nehru as it was towards his friends in the Hindu Mahasabha.

Nevertheless, the prime minister returned from Nasik with a spring in his step. With his popularity unquestionable and his authority unchallengeable, with his policies on everything from Pakistan to zamindari abolition definitively endorsed, he now strode like a colossus over the political arena, in a position to dictate terms to his party. Directions were issued to ministers and chief ministers to make their administrative activities conform to not only the words, but also the spirit of the Nasik Congress.[50] 'So far as Congressmen are concerned,' he informed his chief ministers, 'they are bound by the directions issued by the Nasik Congress … which must be understood and acted upon.'[51]

As he now turned his attention back towards the Land Reforms Bill in Bihar and his plans to rapidly rearrange the socio-economic fabric of the nation, the Constitution really was the only potential obstacle left in his path. His ascendancy was complete.

Events Crowd In

While attention was riveted on Nasik and the internal politics within the Congress, another vital legal battle had drawn to a close in Madras. In a ham-handed attempt to suppress organizations that the government disapproved of – chiefly Hindu groups, trade unions and propaganda associations functioning as fronts for the Communist Party of India – the Madras government had passed the Indian Criminal Law Amendment (Madras) Act that empowered the state to declare an association unlawful based on its own subjective assessment of the situation. The People's Education Society, a society supposedly promoting social and political education among the public (in short, indulging in communist propaganda), which had found itself banned under the abovementioned law in March 1950, had challenged its ban and the constitutional validity of the law in the Madras High Court.[52]

On 13 September, the court held the Criminal Law Amendment (Madras) Act unconstitutional and hence void. The government had boldly asserted before the court that it had 'the prerogative to declare associations unlawful and imprison their members in the interests of public order'.[53] 'Such an argument was never heard in England after the Magna Carta and assertions of such prerogatives cost an English king his head,' the bench sternly admonished the Madras advocate-general, 'and such a contention is unthinkable under our Constitution.'[54] In a strongly worded response, the court described the Act as an 'illustration of the exercise of naked arbitrary powers' and affirmed the primal importance of Article 19 of the Constitution, which guaranteed the right to form associations or unions. Such rights, as the bench observed, could not be tamed by ordinary legislation.[55]

Through this judgment, the judiciary struck another blow for civil liberties. Another repressive law bit the dust. Another ungainly attempt to trample on constitutional rights and assert executive power came to nought. The government received another reprimand from the judges, and was forced to surrender another tool in its arsenal. Having repeatedly been raked over the coals over its lack of commitment to fundamental rights and constitutional provisions, the verdict represented another major embarrassment for the Congress party – especially in the run-up to Nasik. Whether anyone within the organization was paying much attention was anyone's guess. But to those who were, it was now apparent that when it came to defending civil liberties in the face of executive power, there was going to be no vacillation or prevarication from the third pillar of the state. Government attempts to stymie and evade the Constitution were going to be vigorously contained.

For the Congress party, with its commitment to zamindari abolition and nationalization newly reaffirmed at Nasik, the resolute position of the judiciary now represented a major concern. In Bihar, where the new Land Reforms Act had just become operational, and in Delhi, where Congress grandees believed their prestige was at stake, it was a cause of existential anxiety. With the first ever general election planned for May 1951 and Congress pledges of social revolution remaining unfulfilled, state governments grew restless and uneasy. In certain provinces – Bihar, Madras and Punjab, for example – anxiety levels were high enough for the administration to attempt to delay the election by studiously obstructing all preparations.

An annoyed Nehru chided his chief ministers:

> I have written to you frequently about the necessity of having our general elections the latest by May next year. This was easily possible and yet is possible if we work hard. I am sorry to say, however, that some State Governments do not appear to appreciate this urgency and perhaps imagine that they can prolong the preliminaries for as long as they like ... All kinds of obstructions have been placed in the way of preparation. It would almost appear that there is a deliberate desire not to have these elections fairly early next year.[56]

It wasn't an appearance. There was indeed a deliberate desire to avoid early elections on the part of Congress governments afraid of going to the people. With zamindari abolition, reservations and nationalization still under a constitutional cloud, they were unwilling to face accusations of broken promises. Food shortages were rife, inflation was rampant and the economic outlook remained dire. In this setting, unnerved state governments were keen to put off the prospect of facing a restive population for as long as possible. Earnest as he was in his desire for early elections, there was precious little Nehru could do to either force the hands of his obstructionist chief ministers or assuage their fears. But as he returned from his resounding triumph in Nasik, events took on a momentum of their own.

The Bihar government issued a notification under the Land Reforms Act on 24 September declaring that from the following day, the three largest estates in the province – belonging to Maharaja

Sir Kameshwar Singh of Darbhanga, Raja Bahadur Vishweshwar Singh of Darbhanga and Raja Bahadur Kamakhya Narain Singh of Ramgarh – would pass to and become vested in the state. Already prepared for battle, the three zamindars immediately applied to the Patna High Court for an interim injunction restraining the Bihar government from taking possession of their property. An interim injunction was quickly granted two days later, and a suit was instituted to challenge the constitutional validity of the Land Reforms Act.[57]

The injunction effectively restrained the state from taking possession of any landed property until the suit was decided, dashing any hopes the Bihar government had entertained about a swift resolution of the property conundrum. Dreams of expeditious takeover of property, brisk disbursement of land and rapid transformation of the countryside receded into the distance. Zamindari abolition was temporarily halted as the Bihar government was directed to prepare a rejoinder. The threat to the Congress's social agenda was no longer an academic question; it could no longer be ignored. The possibility of zamindari abolition, the most important element of the government's socio-economic agenda, being declared unconstitutional was now very real. From the heady days of May and June, the fall in morale was steep and agonizing. The single most important legal battle in the history of the republic had begun.

Fear gripped the Bihar government. Sri Krishna Sinha, Bihar's beleaguered chief minister, was now well and truly in a legal and constitutional soup. Legal and constitutional complications, however, were only one problem. The bigger problem was political – and it was a problem for the entirety of the Congress party. A vivid, eloquent vision of a Congress-directed highway to 'progress' – on which zamindari abolition and land redistribution were crucial milestones – had been conjured up and steadily sold to the public over the years. Animated by this vision, thousands of Congress leaders and workers had gone forth promising social revolution. Along with the devout pledges of Congress leaders, this entire vision was now under serious threat. The party's agenda or the nation's Constitution – which was to have the government's primary loyalty? The question needed an answer.

A flustered Sinha wrote to Nehru on 15 October expressing his helplessness at the situation and pleaded for Central government intervention. The prime minister, equally agitated by the situation, was sympathetic towards Sinha's predicament. 'I am as concerned as you are with these quibblings of lawyers coming in the way of our social progress,' he replied on 19 October. 'I entirely agree with you that we shall have to consider seriously an amendment of the Constitution. I am consulting the law ministry in regard to it.'[58]

Tipping Point

Evidently unmindful of the great legal and constitutional conflicts that had been flowering around them, and seemingly oblivious to the clear and uncompromising stance taken by the judiciary with reference to the Constitution, the Punjab Legislative Assembly waded into the debate over reservations and constitutional provisions in the opening week of October by passing a resolution demanding reservation of posts and employment opportunities in favour of 'statutory agriculturists'[59] and backward classes.[60] The passage of the resolution confirmed that caste divisions and urban–rural conflict in Punjab were as sharp as ever.

Punjab Cabinet ministers excitedly went on record with assurances that the resolution, which they labelled 'a triumph for rural interests', would definitely be implemented in the near future. 'How little Ministers and legislators understood the Constitution, or having understood it, honour its provisions is illustrated by the passage of this resolution,' a prescient commentator observed.[61] This 'triumph for rural interests', as the incisive commentator noted, was in fact a defeat for the Constitution, which it was 'the duty of Congressmen more than others to respect'.[62] Whether Punjab's legislators and ministers were wilfully ignorant about what had transpired in Madras or whether they were simply wet behind the ears when it came to constitutional matters is anybody's guess, but the impression that Congress leaders were amenable to playing fast and loose with the Constitution was now becoming unmistakable.

A few days later in Bihar, where the state administration was already panicking about land reform, the Patna High Court passed another judgment further embarrassing the government. The case had started in the remote district of Purulia, where Shaila Bala Devi, the proprietor and keeper of the Bharati Press, had published a Bengali pamphlet titled *Sangram*, calling for a revolution in India – 'a good deal of demagogic claptrap with some pretence to poetic flourish', in the words of the judges.[63] The government had retaliated by using the Indian Press (Emergency Powers) Act, a colonial-era law once used with merry abandon by the government's British predecessors to muzzle critical opinion, to order her to deposit a security amount of Rs 2000 that would be forfeited if they believed the press was publishing material inciting violence.[64] An aggrieved Devi had taken her case to the Patna High Court arguing that Section 4(1) of the Press Act, under which the government could demand and seize security amounts, was inconsistent with the right to freedom of speech.

On 13 October, the court upheld Devi's contention and declared the aforementioned part of the Press Act unconstitutional and void. Legally and constitutionally, the powers conferred by the Press Act had already been curtailed by the principles enumerated by the Supreme Court in the *Cross Roads* and *Organiser* cases. Through these principles, the Supreme Court had essentially erected a legal dyke around fundamental rights which could only be breached if the security of the state was undermined. Following this lead, there was little else the high court could have said. The government should have read the writing on the wall. In legal terms, therefore, it was a good but unexceptional judgment, a rap on the executive's knuckles to remind them that the days of repressive laws and curtailment of 'undesirable' speech were now over.

But in the concluding paragraphs of his judgment, Justice Sarjoo Prasad speculated that people were now free to preach murder and violence with impunity. Since such speech would fall neither under the categories of libel, slander or defamation, nor under the categories of contempt of court or offending against morality and decency, and definitely not under the proviso for undermining the security of or tending to overthrow the state, any legislation seeking to curb this right would have to be declared unconstitutional. 'I cannot with equanimity contemplate such a situation,' the honourable judge mused, 'but the conclusion appears to be unavoidable on the authority of the Supreme Court judgments with which we are bound'.[65]

Justice Prasad's musing was not meant to be a declaration of law, only a statement of what he believed to be an anomalous position that he hoped the Supreme Court would soon re-examine and clarify. It merely pointed towards a potential loophole that he hoped would be closed. It did not reconstitute Article 19, it did not even seek to expansively reinterpret it beyond any reasonable assumption. But for a state accustomed to quasi-arbitrary power and resentful at being deprived of it, and for a political leadership given to authoritarian impulses and acclimated to utilizing coercive methods to tackle criticism, the judge's views provided a perfect alibi for claiming that the Constitution was deficient. They latched on to it with gusto.

Against this backdrop, the Bombay High Court caused another political earthquake on 16 October by declaring the Bombay State Road Transport Corporation (BSRTC) – through which the Bombay government was attempting to nationalize bus routes across the state – an illegal body and terminating its existence.[66] The decision knocking down the much-touted programme came as a huge setback to the Bombay government. For the Congress, which had only recently reaffirmed its commitment to nationalization and controls in nearby Nasik, it was a double whammy.

The story was this: nationalization of road transport had faced persistent legal hurdles right from the word go. In UP, where the government had attempted to nationalize bus routes by executive fiat (denying permits to private operators) in March and April 1950, private bus owners had petitioned the high court, arguing that the exclusion of private enterprise was unconstitutional because it deprived them of the right to carry on any trade or profession.[67] In that case,[68] while the court upheld the validity of nationalization through duly enacted legislation, it had shot down the UP government's attempt to create a state monopoly by preferentially giving permits to its own Regional Transport Authorities while denying them to private operators.[69] An overworked UP government had then had to go back to the drawing board and draft a new Nationalization of Transport Bill, which had pushed their nationalization plans back by several months, besides laying the whole exercise open to potential litigation in the future.[70]

In Bombay, even though the legislative assembly had passed a bill conferring wide powers on the State Road Transport Corporation,[71] the corporation itself had been set up by a government notification even before the Constitution had come into force, using the authority granted by the Road Transport Corporation Act, a Central law that allowed state governments to set up their own corporations by executive fiat. Bombay had been slightly more circumspect than UP, but it still attempted to use the same method of preferentially granting permits to the state corporation while denying them to private operators. Unsurprisingly, the matter landed in the Bombay High Court, where celebrated lawyer Nani Palkhivala, appearing for private bus operators, argued that the state was unconstitutionally attempting to prohibit private enterprise through the back door.[72]

The Bombay High Court partially agreed with Palkhivala, and declared the corporation illegal. It also held the enabling Central act allowing the setting up of state corporations by mere notification, without defining their rights and privileges, to be void, since it amounted to an unconstitutional abdication of legislative functions by Parliament in favour of provincial governments.[73] Again, while the constitutionality of nationalization was not strictly questioned, the court's decision threw the ball back into Parliament's court. Even if it didn't disrupt the government's nationalization plans, the need for duly enacted enabling legislation, albeit a perfectly reasonable demand from the judiciary, meant an inevitable delay in the entire process.

K. Santhanam, Union minister of transport, scurried to draft the requisite enabling legislation, which Parliament would eventually pass on 30 November.[74] A desperately skittish Union government breathed a sigh of relief. Nationalization, another major pillar of the Congress party's social agenda, had survived by a whisker. But it had been a mightily close-run affair. And the very fact that the courts had been presumptuous enough to test the legality of nationalization, the very fact that the possibility of it being struck down had been entertained by the judiciary, put Congress politicians on edge. It was as if the party was under judicial siege. It was in this context that Nehru wrote to the Bihar chief minister on 19 October assuring him that he was going to consult the law ministry about the possibility of an amendment to the Constitution. Land reform, nationalization and the regulation of free expression coalesced into one big problem. Matters were rapidly reaching a tipping point. Constitution or no Constitution, preparations to break the judicial siege would have to begin. The prime minister made up his mind.

The very same day, soon after he had written to Sri Krishna Sinha, Nehru wrote to Law Minister B. R. Ambedkar 'expressing the view that the Constitution's provisions pertaining to law and order and subversive activities needed to be amended. Reflecting on the difficulties the government was having with the courts over other fundamental rights, Nehru added that the provisions affecting zamindari abolition and nationalization of road transport also needed amending.'[75] The prime minister and the Constitution were now on opposite sides. The game, to borrow a term from Sherlock Holmes, was now afoot.

Decisions, Decisions

Two days after the prime minister wrote to Ambedkar conveying his desire for a constitutional amendment, the Union Cabinet met in Delhi. An enfeebled Sardar Patel, now mostly confined to his sick bed, was unable to attend. Nehru was now supremely in command. The Cabinet officially directed the law ministry to examine the issues of land reform, nationalization, regulation of the press, incendiary speech and sedition, and accordingly prepare draft amendments to the Constitution.[76] Others present in the meeting, including Maulana Azad[a], C. Rajagopalachari, B. R. Ambedkar and Jagjivan Ram, concurred with the idea. With Patel's health rapidly failing and Nehru's authority unchallenged, there were none left within the government to question the desirability of a constitutional amendment. Even as the Supreme Court was seized of the matters, much before any judgments had been delivered, the Union government had already decided, at least in principle, to amend the Constitution.

That very day, as the Cabinet deliberated, another petition concerning the infamous Madras Communal General Order (GO) was filed in the Supreme Court. In this case, the petitioner was B. Venkataramana, a Brahmin advocate from Nellore who had applied for the post of district *munsif*[77] in the Madras Subordinate Civil Judicial Service. Venkataramana had degrees in law and

---

[a]Maulana Abul Kalam Azad (1888–1958) was an Islamic theologian, journalist and Congress politician. He became closely associated with Gandhi during the Non-Cooperation Movement and was elected Congress president in 1923 – at 35, the youngest person to ever hold that post – and again in 1940. Later, he served as a member of the Constituent Assembly and as education minister in the Nehru Cabinet.

mathematics, and had done well in the examination and the viva voce conducted by the Madras Public Service Commission. Since the selection was done in June 1950 in pursuance of the strict caste and communal ratios prescribed in the Communal GO, the petitioner had found himself without a spot in the list of selected candidates. On 21 October, he approached the court with a prayer to direct the authorities to consider his application on its merits, without taking into account questions of caste and community.[78] Much to the chagrin of the Madras government, already dealing with the political fallout of the decision pronounced by the Madras High Court on the matter of reservations in educational institutions, the Supreme Court accepted the petition and directed the government to file a reply.

Still hopeful of having a general election by the next summer, Nehru spoke directly to the chief electoral officers of all the states on 31 October and directed them to ensure that an election was held before May 1951. 'The present government,' he informed them, 'could not continue to act as a caretaker government for an indefinite period.'[79] The prime minister's awareness that he was heading a caretaker government that lacked the legitimacy of a democratic mandate was admirable, and combined with his desire for an early election, served to burnish his democratic credentials. But it made his clash with the Constitution, his attempts to undermine fundamental rights and his decision to seek a constitutional amendment in order to have his own way all the more jarring. Holding the ideals of a democrat, he wanted democratic validation, he wanted the boost it provided to his global image – he was just not entirely willing to pay the price that leading a republican government entailed. In any case, with their grand social revolution yet to get off the ground, most Congress chief ministers were reluctant to go to the electorate. They certainly had no intention of complying with Nehru's requests.

In Madras, the government led by P. S. Kumaraswamy Raja had just filed an appeal in the Supreme Court against the high court's decision on the Communal GO. Backward caste groups were clamouring for a constitutional amendment and accusing Congress leaders of betrayal, Dravidian ultras were demanding secession and the Communist Party of India in the Telegu-speaking parts of the state had decided to abandon armed rebellion in favour of electoral politics. In such a situation, given its inability to defend its own social agenda, the party's provincial unit was terrified of going back to the people. What would it tell them? That reservations were unconstitutional and they should simply accept the new status quo and move on? The prospect was too frightening. The party's subsequent failure to win a majority in the next election – with the chief minister and almost half the Cabinet failing to win their own seats – testified to the fact that Raja's fears were not without merit.

A similar state of affairs prevailed in Bihar. With the fate of zamindari abolition still hanging in the balance, land redistribution still a chimera and its ability to stifle unfriendly political voices severely eroded, Sri Krishna Sinha's government dreaded the prospect of facing the electorate. Faith in Congress pledges was running low, and neither Sinha nor his colleagues were in any rush to test their popularity. Likewise, in Punjab, where an intense battle was being waged between the Congress and the Shiromani Akali Dal, the Sikh party, there were growing cleavages between Hindus and Sikhs. Demands for a separate Sikh-majority state were being voiced, and Akali leader Master Tara Singh – a fearsome Congress critic – had been thrown into jail for sedition along with hundreds of his supporters in a blatant misuse of police power.[80] Like their counterparts in Bihar, Congress leaders in Punjab were also loath to face the voter in this situation.

By dragging their feet when it came to ensuring administrative preparedness for an election, the obstructionist chief ministers were effectively scuttling the prospect of it taking place in the first half of 1951. Punjab, Bihar and Madras plainly confessed that they could not hold elections in April and May 1951 and suggested postponing them till October.[81] But they were not the only ones. As the *Times of India* reported on 12 November,

An informal decision to postpone the first general election under the new Constitution until October next year has been made by the government … despite the Election Commission's preparedness to have the preliminary arrangements completed in time, pressure from a good number of states, for one reason or another, has impelled the Central Government to postpone the elections by six months.[82]

Ultimately however, the prime minister himself was in sympathy with this position. In private, he himself had voiced similar opinions, accepting that having raised the public's expectations, he couldn't go back on his word, complaining about the Constitution getting in the way or assuring his party colleagues that the Constitution would be amended to fulfil the pledges in the Congress manifesto. Nehru was personally identified with the policies in question, especially land reform. In spite of his public stance, he was thus equally hesitant when it came to facing the voter while zamindari abolition, nationalization and reservations remained constitutionally suspect – a feeling to which he would freely admit some time later. More importantly, having already declared his resolve to avoid all delay in the fulfilment of the party's social agenda (for delay was dangerous) and having recently instructed Ambedkar to prepare the draft amendment to the Constitution, he was hardly likely to have wanted to get drawn into a lengthy election campaign that would further delay any attempt to settle these questions.

Consequently, the Union government decided to postpone the general election to November 1951.[83] That would give it enough time to win its judicial battles with the Constitution. The volte-face by the prime minister, who had been publicly insisting on early elections till a few weeks ago, caused considerable disquiet in the ranks of the Opposition, which foresaw grave danger to the democratic future of the country.[84] Socialist leaders Jayaprakash Narayan and Acharya Narendra Deva, for example, expressed 'grave concern at the sudden postponement of general elections' and 'called upon the government to lay down a definite programme for holding the election all over the country and give a solemn promise that they will adhere to that programme'.[85]

With his dominance over the party now secured and plans for constitutional change already being drawn up, democratic propriety was, however, far from Nehru's mind. For example, in an apparent concession to constitutional rectitude, the prime minister directed all ministries to refer to him as 'Shri Jawaharlal Nehru' rather than 'Pandit Jawaharlal Nehru', since titles denoting castes and communities – obvious markers of community identity – were now against the Constitution.[86] Yet, behind the scenes, blueprints were already being prepared to maraud the very same aspects of the Constitution in the headlong pursuit of the Congress's social revolution. In the obdurate, unvarnished attempt at building a Nehruvian state, propriety was an early casualty. And in the corridors of power, constitutional amendments could not be expected to remain secret.

Out and About

With whispers of a government attempt to change the Constitution growing louder, the latter part of November 1950 brought little cheer to its leaders. On 16 November, Justice S. R. Tendolkar of the Bombay High Court, speaking under the auspices of the Bombay Progressive Group, publicly warned that 'power was an incomparable intoxicant and the tendency existed in governments the world over to encroach upon citizens' rights'. 'Eternal vigilance being the price of liberty,' he exhorted his listeners, 'it was the duty of every citizen to ensure his fundamental rights were not violated.'[87]

As if on cue, on 21 November, the Allahabad District Zamindars' Association announced its intention to fight the Zamindari Abolition Act in the courts when it was enforced, on the grounds that it would violate fundamental rights that had been guaranteed under the Constitution.[88] Addressing the association's annual conference, Democratic Party MLA Guru Narain

> called upon the zamindars to fight the elections in which the Congress would be just another party with its manifesto before the country ... the Zamindari Abolition Act, the provisions of which were unjust, would be as much an unsettled fact after the elections, with the Congress beaten at the polls, as it was a settled fact today.[89]

On 28 November, the Punjab High Court ordered the release of Akali leader and Nehru baiter Master Tara Singh (arrested for sedition and spreading disaffection against the government), who had been cooling his heels in Karnal jail.[90] Tara Singh had been charged under Sections 124A and 153A of the Indian Penal Code. Section 124A referred to sedition, and Section 153A referred to spreading enmity between groups or classes of people. Both had become constitutionally untenable after the Supreme Court's judgments in the *Organiser* and *Cross Roads* cases. In its judgment, the court restated the position that there could be no dispute that

Section 124A contravened the right to freedom of speech and expression guaranteed by the Constitution and had thus become void. The same could be said for Section 153A.

'India is now a sovereign democratic State,' the court observed.

Governments may go and be caused to go without the foundations of the State being impaired. A law of sedition thought necessary during a period of foreign rule has become inappropriate by the very nature of the change which has come about ... The limitation placed by Clause 2 of Article 19 upon interference with the freedom of speech is real and substantial ... So long as the possibility of its [Section 124A] being applied for purposes not sanctioned by the constitution cannot be ruled out, it must be held to be wholly unconstitutional and void.[91]

The observations were as categorical as the court could possibly get in describing to the executive what the legal and constitutional state of affairs actually was in the new republic. Why governments throughout the country could not understand the obvious was now an open question. Were they simply obstinate? Or were they fundamentally authoritarian and unable to come to terms with constitutional bounds?

The court's decision, as observers and commentators noted, could hardly have been otherwise, given the principles the Supreme Court had already delineated. It conferred no new civil liberty, only confirmed a right already guaranteed by the Constitution. Freedom of speech and expression could only be restricted in respect of subjects that undermined the security of the state or tended to overthrow it. Attempts to promote discontent against the government may tend to overthrow the state – or they may not. But as long as the possibility existed that someone promoting discontent against the government but falling short of endangering the very foundations of the state could be charged with sedition, Sections 124A and 153A of the penal code had to be considered invalid. In plain English, the Congress government was not the state. And being critical of it did not amount to undermining the state.

'The law of sedition is conspicuous by its absence in this saving clause [the grounds for restricting the freedom of speech]; and its omission is inevitable,' noted one commentator. 'The government is not the State, and it is not open to any government, however broad-based on the will of the majority, to assert imperially after the manner of the Grand Monarque: The State? I am the State.'[92] In the words of another, 'A clear distinction thus exists between the Government and the State. To equate the two, as the Attorney-General sought to do, is to negate democratic freedom.'[93] Negating democratic freedom, however, was precisely the plan that the government had – and by this point it was barely bothering to conceal its true intentions.

'Freedom of Speech and Expression and of Association and Assembly,' as newspapers reported, was causing immense disquiet to the authorities.[94] With rumours swirling about Nehru's decision to press for a constitutional amendment, the suspicion that the Congress was out to breach the legal dyke the judiciary had built around fundamental rights appeared to be confirmed. The impression that the government's commitment to the Constitution was just a veneer, an expedient to be junked when the power and authority of the Congress party was questioned, now began to catch on in public discourse. For most discerning observers, it was now becoming glaringly evident that constitutional freedoms were under threat and an assault on Part III was imminent. And resistance started to grow.

The first thing Tara Singh did on release from jail was to state that 'chaos was certain in the country unless it was freed from the Congress' and announce his intention to agitate against the proposed curtailment of fundamental rights guaranteed by the Constitution.[95] He invited both the Communist Party of India and the Hindu Mahasabha to join him on this common platform. 'Reports that the Law Ministry has been asked to draft amendments to the Constitution underline the urgency of speedy disposal of appeals,' urged a major newspaper, and 'attempts to destroy the democratic content of the Constitution at this stage are to be deplored and should be resisted'.[96] Bombay labour leader N. M. Joshi, one of the founders of the All India Trade Union Congress, denounced the free and casual use of repressive powers by the government and warned that giving higher priority to the interests of the state in fundamental freedoms would lead to totalitarianism.[97]

Socialist stalwart Jayaprakash Narayan alleged that the Congress was heading inexorably towards dictatorship and cautioned 'the

people against the contemplated attempt by the Government
to restrict their civil liberties by introducing amendments in
the Constitution'.[98] Speakers at the Punjab State Civil Liberties
Conference challenged the representative character of an indirectly
elected provisional parliament, and its authority to change the
Constitution.[99] The most savage criticism came in an editorial in
the *Times of India* newspaper:

> It is a tragic irony that our popular governments should at every
> stage feel the need of repressive laws against which leaders of
> our struggle for freedom cried themselves hoarse for generations.
> The whirling of time brings some strange revenges. The decriers
> of a Government, once termed Satanic, flatter our previous rulers
> by imitation. They resort to preventive detention even without
> declaring a state of emergency.[100]

Nehru decried Tara Singh's efforts to 'bring about strange
alliances' where the only common factor was a dislike of the
present government and its policies and argued that it only
demonstrated the extreme poverty of Sikh leadership in thought
and action.[101] '[The Sikhs] are excellent soldiers, good farmers and
fine mechanics,' he informed his chief ministers. 'In spite of this they
have repeatedly allowed themselves to be misled and unfortunately,
even past experience does not teach wisdom.'[102] In Parliament,
his Cabinet colleague N. V. Gadgil reprimanded the judiciary for
'going far beyond its legitimate jurisdiction' by pronouncing on the
reasonableness of legislation.[103] In correspondence, Nehru himself
complained about the 'tendency on the part of some High Court
judges to indulge in strong criticism of the government not only
from the bench but also from other platforms'.[104]

The cat, so to speak, was now out of the bag. The confrontation
between the government and the Constitution was now public
knowledge. In the midst of this turmoil, on 15 December, Sardar
Patel, Nehru's deputy and India's iron-willed home minister, a
true political giant of his time, breathed his last. Over the years,
he had exuded an air of calm, collected pragmatism, and exerted
a tremendous moderating influence on some of Nehru's more
radical and authoritarian impulses.[105] He had, for example, firmly
counselled him against trying to use a charge of sedition against
Shyama Prasad Mookerji,[106] advised him to tread carefully on land

reform and cautioned him against straying beyond constitutional bounds. On the other hand, despite his consistent support for constitutional propriety, Patel had been no great friend of personal freedom – and on occasion, had admitted to considering the prospect of a constitutional amendment in the future.[107]

Whether Patel would have resisted the idea of a constitutional amendment, or reduced the size and scope of the one Nehru was contemplating, will remain a matter of conjecture. He had submitted to Nehru's impulses as often as he had contained them. But given his views on the associated issues, it seems quite likely that he would have queered the pitch, especially when it came to provisions concerning the right to property and the right to freedom against discrimination. In India's political landscape, Patel had been the prime minister's only rival – in stature, in popularity and in authority. His death removed from the scene the one man who (should he have desired) had both the political capital and the organizational capacity to either thwart Nehru's plan or check his petulant confrontation with the judiciary. The path to an amendment was now relatively clear.

4

The Gathering Storm

The Year Ends

Amid chatter of a constitutional amendment and an impending attack on the freedom of the press, Prime Minister Nehru addressed the annual session of the All India Newspaper Editors Conference (AINEC) on 3 December 1950. Rights did not exist without obligations, he warned them, and freedom came with responsibility:

> I think I can say that whatever our other failings may be at the present moment, the amount of freedom of expression that is allowed or indulged in by the press can hardly be exceeded in any country in the world. I shall be quite frank with you. Much that appears because of that freedom seems to me exceedingly dangerous from many points of view. Nevertheless, I have no doubt in my mind that the freedom of the press from the larger point of view, is an essential attribute of the democratic process.[1]

The assembled newspapermen, who had been worried by the prospect of being leashed by the government, took Nehru's caveat about the democratic process and his view that 'it was bad to interfere with freedom' to mean that there was no longer any fear of the Constitution being changed to restrict the freedom of the press.[2] Deshbandhu Gupta, AINEC president and a member of Parliament, thanked him voluminously for this assurance. 'Many of us feared', he said, 'that, in view of certain judgments given by the Supreme Court and the High Courts, there might be some attempt to modify the Constitution with a view to curbing the press. I particularly value the assurance you have given in this respect.'[3]

Nehru, who had already directed the law ministry to prepare a draft of the amendment, did not care to correct him. Unbeknownst to the doyens of the press, while they were thanking the prime minister for his graciousness in abandoning the idea of a constitutional amendment, their shackles were already being prepared. Even as his assurances pacified the agitated pressmen, Nehru complained to Bidhan Roy: 'We have been putting up with the most virulent writings in the press, because we were told we could do nothing about it since our judges have interpreted the Constitution.'[4]

In the Supreme Court, where the Patna High Court's decision to strike down the Bihar Management of Estates and Tenures Act had been challenged by the Bihar government, the judges declined to hear the appeal and directed that the matter should be taken up only after the high court had disposed of the application challenging the validity of the Bihar Land Reforms Act.[5] It was another red flag in the government's eyes. In the meantime, G. V. Mavalankar, the Speaker of Parliament, wrote to the prime minister to express his concern about the government's reckless use of ordinances to bypass regular parliamentary procedure and debate, endangering the conventions of democracy even before they had taken root.

'Parliamentary procedure is meant to give the fullest opportunities for consideration and debate and to check errors and mistakes creeping in,' came Nehru's perfunctory reply. 'That is obviously desirable. But all this involved considerable delay. The result is that important legislation is hung up.'[6] Irked at being called out on his errant ways, he offered a simple explanation to the Speaker that discussion and debate were holding up important legislation and taking up too much time. 'We are living in rather extraordinary times both from the national and international points of view,' he added by way of justification, 'and the situation changes from day to day.'[7]

By this point, with the government still feeling like it was under judicial siege and the prime minister feeling like he was being pushed further and further into a corner, notions of democratic process, traditions and conventions were quickly being thrown by the wayside. In the wake of Patel's death, the balance of power in the government had tilted overwhelmingly in Nehru's favour[8] – and with the brakes on his power rapidly dissolving, residual commitments to constitutionalism were also fast being dispensed with. On 18 December, within days of Patel's funeral, he wrote to his chief ministers:

> Recent judgments of some High Courts have made us think about our Constitution. Is it adequate in its present form to meet the situation we have to face? We must accept fully the judgments of our superior courts, but if they find that there is a lacuna in the Constitution, then we have to remedy that. The matter is under consideration.[9]

When the Constitution had been inaugurated, it had been taken to signify a clean dividing line between the colonial past and the republican present; a representation of the nationalist resolve to shake off the state's colonial antecedents; evidence of the new government's commitment to freedom and republican democracy. By December 1950, it was clear that not only was this line more blurred than imagined, but in many cases it did not exist at all. The new republican government, much like its colonial predecessor, was finding it excruciatingly difficult to function within constitutional bounds. Congress figures, the inheritors of the Raj, were proving to be almost as irascible, as intolerant of criticism and challenge, and as eager to jail dissidents as their former British overlords. Judicial pronouncements restricting executive action became identification marks for deficiencies in the Constitution. Fundamental rights, the heart and soul of the Constitution barely a year ago, were now lacunae that needed fixing. Indeed, the Constitution itself was now a problem that needed a remedy.

Over the years, Nehru had been variously described as proud, rash, impatient, stubborn, impetuous, petulant and intemperate. Sardar Patel had interpreted Nehru's conception of his own role as prime minister to be 'wholly opposed to a democratic and cabinet system of government'.[10] The writer Nirad C. Chaudhuri was to call him 'virtually a dictator but not a scoundrel', a dictator without a dictator's will,[11] while his biographer, the Australian diplomat Walter Crocker, would describe him as 'authoritarian in temperament' and 'by nature, intolerant of opposition'.[12] Over a decade before his first taste of executive power, in a fascinating self-portrait, Nehru himself had claimed to have all the makings of a dictator.[13] As the year ended and the first anniversary of the republic approached, the epithet 'authoritarian' began to gain public currency. On the final day of 1950, Nehru affirmed his desire to his chief ministers: '... we have to make clear that no individual in India, whoever he may be, can challenge the authority of the State or of Parliament ... So far as we are concerned, we are not going to tolerate any defiance of the State's authority.'[14]

The Anniversary of the Republic

The UP Legislative Council, which had been making its way through the gigantic Zamindari Abolition and Land Reform Bill, suggested a number of amendments and sent the bill back to the legislative assembly for consideration on 22 December. 'The Government's No. 1 election winning measure – otherwise known as the Zamindari Abolition Bill – has been returned to the Assembly by the Upper House with minor changes,' reported the *Times of India*. 'But the bill is as good as on the Statute Book, for the only freedom now left for Congress MLAs is to vote as they are told.'[15] Zamindar elements within the legislature, emboldened by the stiff fight being put up by their compatriots in Bihar, warned the government that it was counting its chickens 'without bothering to check whether they will be hatched'.[16]

The UP Legislative Assembly, which had been in recess, was summoned back for a special session on the first day of the new year to accommodate the government programme of announcing the end of landlordism on 26 January 1951, the first anniversary of the new republic.[17] In the zamindar camp, preparations to challenge the bill in court were at full speed under the watchful eye of P. R. Das, the acclaimed lawyer and civil liberties activist who had been chosen to pilot the case.[18] After the unpredictable twists and turns that the land requisition battle had taken – and was still taking – in Bihar, political observers watched, enthralled, as another critically decisive clash took shape. Events now moved at lightning speed.

At 5.00 pm on 10 January 1951, the UP Legislative Assembly accepted the amendments recommended by the Legislative Council and passed the final version of the Zamindari Abolition Bill, a full four years and six months after it had first been drafted. As

Democratic Party legislators, led by Nawab Jamshed Ali Khan of Baghpat, staged a walkout in protest, they were heckled from the Congress benches, which rang out with loud slogans of 'Bharat Mata ki Jai'[19] and 'Kisan Mazdoor Raj Zindabad'.[20] Six days later, the final version of the bill went to the Legislative Council, where it was quickly passed and sent to the governor. The governor, in turn, promptly sent it on to the president for his assent.[21] UP Chief Minister Govind Ballabh Pant was determined to bring the curtains down on the old order on Republic Day. The representatives of the old order, inspired by the victories in Bihar, were equally determined to make a stand. Both the government and the zamindars girded their loins for the battle they knew was now unavoidable.

Neighbouring Bihar had its own concerns. It had been asked to file its reply to the suit initiated by the maharaja of Darbhanga.[22] Forty-eight hours after UP had passed its bill, the state of Bihar filed its reply with a prayer to dismiss the maharaja's suit. The affidavit argued that 'the abolition of the zamindari system and the introduction of certain land reforms in the state as envisaged by the Bihar Land Reforms Act are essential to achieve the economic progress of or promote adequately the welfare of the people of the state'.[23] Clause 4 of Article 31, which governed and restricted the right to property, basically stated that if a law for acquisition of property received the president's assent, then notwithstanding anything else said in the Constitution, that law could not be challenged in a court on the grounds that it did not fix the amount, principle or manner of compensation. The state therefore contended that since the Act had received the assent of the president, no question of compensation could be raised in the court – indeed, the court itself was unqualified to adjudicate on the matter.[24]

Meanwhile, in Delhi, true to Nehru's instructions, the law ministry had already got to work to prepare draft amendments to the Constitution. On 6 January, Joint Secretary S. N. Mukherjee – who, as chief draftsman in the Constituent Assembly Secretariat, had played a pivotal role in the drafting of the Constitution – prepared a note detailing his mechanism to safeguard legislation restricting the freedom of speech from the judiciary.[25] The Constitution permitted the imposition of 'reasonable restrictions' on most fundamental rights in Article 19, such as the right to assemble peaceably or the right to form associations. No such qualifications were available as far as the freedom of speech and expression was concerned.

Mukherjee recommended the removal of the word 'reasonable' from all parts of Article 19 to achieve consistency throughout the article, and the addition of a provision to enable the government to make 'restrictions' to the freedom of speech for whatever purposes it desired. In this way, Mukherjee concluded, the government would be able to both draw up legislation imposing restrictions on fundamental rights, and preclude the need to justify the reasonableness of such legislation before the courts.[26]

Mukherjee's superior, Principal Secretary K. V. K. Sundaram, agreed, and proposed a rewording of Article 19(2) to enable the government to impose 'restrictions' (without the qualifier 'reasonable') on the freedom of speech. He suggested that grounds for such restrictions be expanded to include the interests of the security of the state (rather than undermining the security of the state), public order, decency, morality and relations with foreign states.[27] Sundaram, apparently encouraged by Bihar chief minister Sri Krishna Sinha, also came up with the idea of wording the amendment to completely exclude judicial review of zamindari abolition legislation – the genesis of what would become the infamous Ninth Schedule.[28] Both Mukherjee and Sundaram concurred with the government's view that politicians and legislatures were, and should be, the final authority deciding the nature of restrictions on fundamental rights, not the judges and the courts.[29] The notes were sent to Law Minister B. R. Ambedkar and Prime Minister Nehru for their perusal.

Zamindars from across UP gathered in Allahabad and Lucknow in anticipation of a presidential nod for the UP Zamindari Abolition Bill, which was expected at any point before 26 January. They were armed for battle. 'Over 1000 applications for writs of mandamus and prohibition under Article 226[30] of the Constitution against the enactment of the Uttar Pradesh Zamindari Abolition and Land Reforms Bill are proposed to be moved by the zamindars of the State in the Allahabad High Court within the next few days,' reported the *Times of India* on 18 January.[31] The government, the Opposition and political observers of all hues watched with bated breath.

On 24 January 1951, President Rajendra Prasad gave his assent to the bill, described by the *Hindustan Times* as 'the biggest socio-economic Central or State legislation yet'.[32] Chief Minister G. B. Pant, who received news of the presidential assent around 3.00 pm, called it the 'consummation of many years of labour and fulfilment of the Congress pledge to the peasantry' and declared that 'the fabric of the new order' was now complete.[33] Within the hour, hundreds of petitions challenging the validity of the Act were making their way to the high court benches in both Allahabad and Lucknow, pre-empting the publication of the new law in *The Gazette of India*. By the time the day was over, the applications of more than 4,000 zamindars had been filed, sending the authorities into a tizzy. Carrying the briefs of the maharajas of Balrampur and Kapurthala, P. R. Das rolled up his sleeves.

Like their Bihari cousins, UP's aristocrats – the big, the small, the affable, the astute, the benevolent and the degenerate – suddenly and collectively found themselves recast as guardians of fundamental rights. The transformation of India's feudal lords, scorned in Nehru's India as a class of vicious parasites and ruthless exploiters out of step with the republican mood, into defenders and promoters of constitutional freedoms was one of the many moments of supreme irony that the first years of Nehruvian politics was to generate.

The petitions were heard by benches in both Allahabad and Lucknow the next day. Arguing in Allahabad, Das contended that the bill served no public purpose beyond giving effect to Congress policy, and 'public purpose was not public policy. The policy of the party in power was not public purpose'.[34] In his view, even the presidential assent didn't protect the law from challenge because 'an unconstitutional Act was no law, and it did not confer any right and it did not impose any duty'. 'This piece of legislation', he asserted before the court, 'is a fraud on the Constitution. It defies the terms of Article 31. It offends Article 19. It infringes Article 13.'[35] Das prayed to the court to issue an injunction to the state preventing the takeover of any property until the zamindars' petitions were disposed of.

Both benches of the Allahabad High Court granted the zamindars' prayers and 'issued interim injunctions restraining the UP Government from taking possession of the zamindars' properties in UP and from issuing any notification under Section 4 of the Act specifying the date of vesting of the estates in the state ... pending the disposal of the applications'.[36] To forestall any precipitous action by the government while the courts were closed over the weekend, the Lucknow bench even said 'that the order would be drawn up immediately and communicated to the parties'.[37] The socio-economic fabric of Pant's new order was not complete just yet.

The UP government and the Congress leadership were shocked and dismayed. The grand plan for a triumphant announcement of the end of the old order on Republic Day had been blown out of the water. Instead, on 26 January 1951, India awoke to the headline 'Zamindari Abolition in UP Stayed: Allahabad High Court Issues Injunctions'.[38] The old order was not going to give in without a fight. What was to become of zamindari abolition in UP? No one could quite say. Even though the Act itself remained to be examined, the psychological blow was tremendous. Unlike the fumbling in Bihar, in UP, the land reform programme had been painstakingly and fastidiously drawn up under Pant's leadership to reflect his maxim 'justice to all and injustice to none'. If such a meticulous scheme could be stalled, who could predict the future course of events? The very future of zamindari abolition now in the balance, there was confusion and hysteria within the ranks of the Congress party.

Work Begins in Earnest

On the morning of 25 January 1951, the Congress Working Committee (CWC) met at the All India Congress Committee headquarters at 7, Jantar Mantar Marg in New Delhi for over three hours to discuss 'the question of how to galvanize the Indian National Congress so as to maintain its moral and political hold over the people'.[39] Over much of the final quarter of 1950, with the death of Sardar Patel, splits in provincial units in UP and Bengal and the formation of a dissident 'Democratic Front' led by Acharya Kripalani and Rafi Ahmed Kidwai, newspapers had often asked if the party was going to crack or whether the departure of such senior figures would make a dent in its popularity.[40] At the CWC meeting, many in the party, including the prime minister, now 'stressed the necessity of doing something to pull up the Congress organization so that its policy and programme may attract the people much more'.[41] Other more passionate members 'pointed out that the Congress organization had already laid down its economic and social programmes and it was now for the government to give shape to those programmes'.[42]

It was against this backdrop, hours after the CWC meeting, that news of the injunctions issued in Allahabad was received in Delhi. In the meeting, Nehru had been told by several members in no uncertain terms that to attract more people to the Congress, it was imperative that the government implemented the party's social and economic programmes. Zamindari abolition and land reform were a critical part of this programme, the central pillar of its social and economic agenda. The news from UP, coming hours after this meeting and months after a similar set of events in Bihar, must have seemed to him a body blow. With both high courts having stayed the operation of zamindari abolition laws while they decided on their constitutional validity, the entire land reform agenda effectively ground to a temporary halt. It might pass the hurdle, or it might not – but the very fact that the party's social agenda, which he himself had mostly dictated, was having to face up to the Constitution and the judiciary was to him a step too far. The prime minister was livid.

The Allahabad High Court's decision to grant injunctions to 'stop any implementation of this legislation', in Nehru's opinion, raised several starkly important questions. In his letter to his chief ministers on 1 February, he amply and abundantly set out his views:

Parliament, representing the will of the people, decides on certain essential social reforms. These are then, by a process of interpretation of the Constitution, held up by the judiciary. The result may well be trouble in the rural areas of the States concerned. It is the right of the judiciary to interpret the Constitution and to apply it and none of us can or should challenge that. But if the Constitution itself comes in our way, then surely it is time to change the Constitution to that extent. It is impossible to hang up urgent social changes because the Constitution comes in the way, according to the interpretation of the courts. This has happened in Bihar also. We shall have to find a remedy, even though this might involve a change in the Constitution.[43]

It was apparent that the prime minister was more or less set on a particular course of action in pursuit of his social agenda. In the background, the law ministry was hard at work preparing for his assault on the Constitution. But even then, Nehru's views were troubling for several different reasons. First, the injunctions did not 'stop any implementation of this legislation', as he asserted – they only prevented the state from making any move to acquire property while the constitutional validity of the law, which on the face of it shared several similarities with the law struck down in Bihar, remained under doubt. Second, neither in Bihar nor in UP had the courts actually pronounced any judgment on the constitutional validity of their respective zamindari abolition legislations. To all intents and purposes, while both were under a constitutional cloud, their legal validity was still an open question awaiting a judicial decision. Even if the high court was to eventually give an adverse judgment, the possibility of an appeal to the Supreme Court remained. In essence, at this point, land reform was delayed but not denied.

That the prime minister had already decided, even at this early stage, that it was time to change the Constitution because it was getting in his way was firm testament to the undeniable certitude that in the mind of the establishment, the end result of the unfolding legal battle had already been determined. It was proof of the prime minister's belief that victory ultimately belonged to him and the Congress party's social agenda, rather than to the Constitution and fundamental rights. 'Impatient'[44] was an adjective often used in conjunction with Nehru – after all, here was a leader who self-admittedly took recourse to ordinances because regular parliamentary procedure took too long. In this case, however, impatience would be an understatement; and even his peers found themselves hard-pressed to understand, much less justify, the prime minister's almost frenzied rush towards a constitutional amendment.

What Nehru was saying was this: the people's representatives – an overwhelming majority of whom belonged to the Congress party, and all of whom had been elected on a limited franchise under British rule – had determined a social agenda and passed laws to give effect to it. The judiciary was doing its job by examining the laws when their constitutional validity was challenged. No judgment had yet arrived, and when it did, the law might be found constitutional or it might not. But the legal process of testing legislation against the Constitution was taking up time and delaying the implementation of these laws, thus holding up the party's social agenda and hindering the social revolution it had promised. They did not want their social agenda to be held up by such mundane questions of legality and constitutionality. Therefore, to nip such questions in the bud and safeguard against them arising in the future, it was now time to change the Constitution. The logical sequence was breathtakingly audacious.

Barely two months after newspaper editors had cheered Nehru in the mistaken belief that his assurances meant that plans to amend the Constitution and curb fundamental rights had been dropped, formal preparation for a constitutional amendment began in earnest. As the week progressed, a Cabinet Committee was constituted for the specific purpose of examining matters related to criticism in the press and piloting the proposed amendment through Parliament. Apart from Nehru, such luminaries as C. Rajagopalachari, Maulana Azad, K. M. Munshi, Jagjivan Ram and B. R. Ambedkar were made members. A similar committee was appointed by the Congress Parliamentary Party to invite opinions and suggestions from MPs and to make recommendations to the government on the party's behalf.[45] It was reported that Thakurdas Bhargava, Mohan Lal Gautam[46] (whose daughter Sheela would later become a prominent BJP leader), Renuka Ray and Punjabrao Deshmukh were members.[47]

The government's intent to amend the Constitution was now guardedly made public. A newspaper reported on 14 February:

Informed circles suggest, however, that any changes in the Constitution … based on the experience gained in its working during the last year, as well as in light of various judicial pronouncements can only be brought forward at the next session of Parliament in August or September. The present phase of discussions … on the proposed changes in the Constitution is therefore stated to be exploratory in character.[48]

'It is realized in Congress circles', the correspondent continued, 'that they should not hustle through and suggest changes in haste.'[49] Little did the correspondents realize that while they reported on the 'exploratory' discussions within the Congress party, the government's preparations were already moving full steam ahead.

In Parliament, Prime Minister Nehru lambasted the press for its supposedly nefarious role in public affairs. 'May I also say that some periodicals in various parts of India fall very greatly below any standard of decency and legitimate criticism,' he thundered.

Indeed, it has amazed me to find to what depths these periodicals can fall and how they go on giving publicity to an amalgam of falsehood and indecency ... I should say something about this false and malicious campaign ... What I am especially concerned about is the degradation of some parts of our press.[50]

'While appreciating the role of newspapers generally,' he informed his chief ministers, 'I pointed out [in Parliament] that some weekly periodicals specially had passed all limits of decency and were carrying on persistently a propaganda full of falsehood and malice ... to remain silent may also have consequences.'[51] 'I have appealed to the newspaper editors to take it in hand,' he added, '[but] if they fail, then something else will have to be thought of.'[52] It was not an idle threat.

To take his colleagues and other major figures in the party into confidence, the prime minister requested senior leaders for their opinions on the right to freedom of speech and expression and the right to property. Freedom of expression had been wantonly abused, replied Chief Minister Govind Ballabh Pant of UP. 'Venomous and filthy attacks are being made ... against the central and state governments ... maliciously and in an extremely vulgar and indecent manner.'[53] Like the mandarins of the law ministry, Pant also recommended to Nehru that zamindari abolition should be made invulnerable to judicial challenge. He also advised Nehru to think about constitutional support for nationalization.[54] Hare Krishna Mahtab, minister of commerce and industry, stated that 'reasonable restrictions' would lead to an uncertain legal framework and it would be much better to not have any such qualifiers at all. The real culprits in his opinion – 'serious blunders, impediments in the way of economic democracy' – were actually Article 13, which mandated that all laws inconsistent with fundamental rights provisions would be void, and Article 14, which guaranteed equality before the law.[55] Much of the Congress party, Nehru learnt, had now turned against the Constitution and echoed his own views that the people's constitutional freedoms were in need of pruning. As they waited on tenterhooks for the Patna High Court to announce its decision on the Bihar Land Reforms Act, such extreme opinions became the norm within the ruling establishment.

Pandemonium

The Patna High Court ended the suspense on 12 March 1951 when it held the Bihar Land Reforms Act to be unconstitutional and ultra vires because it violated Article 14 of the Constitution by providing for differential rates of compensation for different categories of landholders. It also held that a presidential assent under Clause 4 of Article 31 (that prevented courts from ruling on appropriateness of compensation) did not debar 'the Court from entering into the question of compensation in order to decide whether or not the impugned act offended against Article 14'.[56]

In a searing indictment of the Congress party and the Bihar government's manifest authoritarianism, the judges denounced the Act as an 'unconstitutional law enacted in the belief that the right of the plaintiffs to challenge it and ask for relief from its operation has been taken away'.[57] The court's decision shook the government and the Congress party to its core. It shattered the illusion of the current regime having inherited the absolute power of the Raj. The Bihar Land Reforms Act bit the dust. An entire pillar of the Congress party's social agenda stood virtually crippled. The establishment's worst dreams seemed to be coming true.

For the powers that be in New Delhi, this defeat was an especially 'bitter pill to swallow'.[58] The government had wrangled over the Act for months; it had clashed with President Rajendra Prasad and overruled his objections, and it had threatened him to receive his assent. For the Congress party itself, this had been an article of faith. Party workers and leaders had toured the country to pledge their word, and staked their reputations on the altar of zamindari abolition and land redistribution. As both the government and the party faced the daunting prospect of their entire social programme potentially falling to pieces, there was panic and pandemonium in the corridors of power.

For the prime minister, to whom hysterical Congress leaders from Bihar now turned for deliverance, this was the proverbial last straw. His patience exhausted, a furious Nehru addressed the press and blew the bugle for battle:

> If the Constitution is interpreted by the Courts in a way which comes in the way of the wishes of the legislature in regard to

basic social matters, then it is for the legislatures to consider
how to amend the Constitution so that the will of the people as
represented in the legislature should prevail.[59]

It was an extraordinary proposition: that the ephemeral will of
the people was enough to overturn the very basis of constitutional
democracy. The moment of truth in his confrontation with the
Constitution had arrived.

On 14 March, responding to the prime minister's frenzy over
criticism and freedom of speech and expression, and questions about
the right to property and zamindari abolition in the aftermath of the
Bihar judgment, Ambedkar prepared a long memorandum for the
Cabinet Committee. The rulings of the courts had not recognized any
limitation on the freedom of expression unless it had been specified
by the Constitution, he informed the committee, but he opposed the
deletion of existing limitations and their replacement with others in
order to prevent the Supreme Court from reinterpreting them into
Article 19 through the concept of 'due process of law'.[60] Provisions
for restricting the freedom of speech were already detailed in Article
19 – libel, slander, undermining the security of the state, etc. – and,
in his opinion, rather than adding to them or replacing them, they
should just be amended to the extent of allowing laws placing
such restrictions to be exempted from judicial intrusion.[61]

As far as the right to property went, Ambedkar recommended
that Article 31 be amended so that nothing should prevent the
government from prescribing different principles of compensation
for different classes of people, or affect the validity of any law the
government should create for divesting property owners of their
property. He also added his opinion that 'the Supreme Court
ought not to be invested with absolute power to determine which
limitations on fundamental rights were proper', for if that were
to be the case, then Parliament would be placed in the position
of having to constantly amend the Constitution to proclaim and
uphold its sovereign position.[62] Ambedkar's views were a near
overturning of the constitutional order, an order he himself had
helped draft and institutionalize.[63] They represented a growing
consensus within the government that there had to be a clipping of
the judiciary's wings and a reassertion of what the constitutional
historian Harshan Kumarasingham termed 'the ultimate power of
the central executive'.[64]

On the matter of freedom of speech and expression, the home ministry, now led by Chakravarti Rajagopalachari, the keeper of Gandhi's conscience and future guiding light of Indian liberalism, was one step ahead of the authoritarian curve. It recommended to the Cabinet Committee that the list of grounds to curb the right to free speech be expanded to include 'public order' and 'incitement to a crime', and the expression 'undermine the security of or tend to overthrow the State' be broadened to 'in the interests of the security of the State'.[65] To prevent the courts from adjudicating on what was or was not 'reasonable', Rajaji's ministry recommended that the word 'reasonable' be dropped altogether. The home ministry's note concluded by suggesting that not only freedom of speech, but all other freedoms in Article 19 – freedom of movement, the right to reside in any part of the republic, the right to own property, etc. – also be made subject to martial law, in addition to all the other grounds for restrictions already written in the Constitution.[66]

Accustomed to reigning over a subservient population, given to treating their constitutional freedoms with disdain, uncomfortable with the idea of civil liberties and resentful at its legal armoury being wrecked by the courts, the home ministry wanted little more than to be granted its draconian powers back. Its recommendations represented nothing short of a brazen desire among India's ruling elite to wind the clock back to the glory days of colonial rule, substituting their own selves for their former colonial overlords. Fourteen months into the new republic, they wanted their old punitive measures back. Fourteen months after granting their fellow citizens a comprehensive set of constitutional freedoms, India's rulers were already ruing their over-generosity. They now craved a new legal order that was, in the words of the economist Meghnad Desai, 'firmly founded on old British laws, warmed up for independent India'.[67]

From Nehru to Rajagopalachari and from Ambedkar to Munshi, there was nigh a hint of opposition within the government. Patel was dead. Mookerji, Neogy and Matthai had resigned. There were none left to resist. Within the party, members and leaders hungry for a party ticket in the upcoming general election were unwilling to jeopardize their chances by protesting. As those seated at the high table debated their plans for an assault on constitutional freedoms, there was hardly a whimper of protest from the bottom. Agitated and incensed, the prime minister replied to Ambedkar the same evening, instructing him to 'proceed with the utmost expedition' to ensure that the necessary amendments could be brought before Parliament within the current session.[68] From top to bottom, an establishment enraged at being thwarted by the Constitution now resolved to fight back.

'A recent decision of the Patna High Court about zamindari abolition has raised rather vital issues for all of us,' Nehru wrote to his chief ministers.

> It is well known that the abolition of the zamindari system has been a principal plank in the Congress programme for many years ... If this is to be prevented, then our entire social and economic policy fails and the hundreds of millions of peasants and agriculturalists can well charge us with a breach of promise. An intolerable situation would be created. While our courts have the right to interpret the Constitution and we must respect and honour their decisions, the fact remains that the wider social policy of the country must be determined by Parliament or the State Legislature. Any other course would be a denial of democracy ... The Government is no longer an agency for the mere carrying on of routine functions. It has to lay down social policies and give effect to them. Therefore it has become necessary for us to consider an amendment to the Constitution, so as to remove the lacunae which have apparently crept into it.[69]

The prime minister was essentially making three claims. First, that the failure of the Congress social agenda when confronted with the Constitution should be regarded as an intolerable situation. Since he did not want to face the populace and be accused of breaching his promise, the Constitution would have to give way to the primacy of the Congress programme. Second, that the social policies devised by elected legislatures – sites of popular sovereignty – being held unconstitutional by the courts was a denial of democracy, even if the legislatures had been elected on a distinctly limited and narrow franchise. In true democratic spirit, the Constitution would have to bend to accommodate the 'will of the people' as represented by a legislature elected indirectly and on a limited franchise. Third, the three pillars of the state – the judiciary, the executive and the legislature – were not equal. The executive was to create and give effect to social policy, and it was to have primacy over the other wings of the state, especially the judiciary. It was a slippery slope.

Nehru's views represented a radical departure not only from conventional constitutional thought, but also from what had come to be accepted by the Constituent Assembly. They were a veritable denial of the elemental importance of the Constitution in setting the terms of reference for a political community. They embodied his – and indeed the Congress party's and the post-colonial elite's – vision of expansive, untrammelled executive power, intolerant of dissent, unhindered by constitutional obligations and ideas of democratic propriety, and unencumbered by the restraining powers of the judiciary. From being the charter of republican freedom, the Constitution was now a barrier in the path of progress, an impediment to be overcome. Faced with an obstacle to its will, the government saw only one solution: a blatant reassertion of executive power over the judiciary and a full-scale assault on the offending constitutional provisions.

The same evening, 14 March, the advocate-general of Madras, V. K. T. Chari, wrote to Law Secretary K. V. K. Sundaram 'suggesting that Sundaram's idea to name in Article 31 the tenure laws to be exempted from its reach be expanded to create a separate schedule to the Constitution that would contain acts certified by the President and deemed valid retrospectively and prospectively notwithstanding anything in the Constitution'.[70] The apparatchiks in the law ministry loved the idea of the inclusion in the Constitution of a schedule of unconstitutional laws beyond the purview of the courts. India's democratic politicians, unwilling to submit to constitutional confines, salivated at the prospect of such a power grab. Thus was born the controversial Ninth Schedule, an extraordinary legal device designed to allow laws (and by extension, Parliament and the government) to evade the Constitution, a device that would one day cause Chief Justice Hidayatullah to quip that India's was the only Constitution in the world that needed protection against itself.[71]

The True Position

Contrary to the panic-stricken, apocalyptic interpretations being given to the Patna High Court's judgment, however, the judiciary had neither struck down land reform per se, nor intruded into the legislature's domain to deny democracy. If anything, the court had been broadly supportive of the government's aims and dispassionate in discharging its constitutional duty of adjudicating on the constitutional validity of legislation, a duty and a power provided to it under Articles 13, 32 and 226 of the Constitution.

To the charge, levelled by the zamindars' lawyers P. R. Das and N. C. Chatterjee, that the Bihar Land Reforms Act was not designed to serve any public purpose but only to augment public revenue, the court replied:

> Under our Constitution land, or certain kinds of landed property, are not sacrosanct. On the contrary the Constituent Assembly, by enacting clauses (4) and (6) of Article 31, gave their express approval to legislation abolishing the Permanent Settlement and extinguishing certain rights in land. Whatever our own views may be, we must in my opinion, regard the scheme embodied in the impugned act as a scheme intended to benefit the public. We cannot shut our eyes to the patent fact that the makers of the Constitution regarded it as likely to do so. Whatever construction might have to be put on the expression 'public purpose' in Article 31(2), we are, in my opinion, estopped from saying that the acquisition of tenures and estates is not an acquisition for such a purpose. That it is, has been decided by the Constituent Assembly itself.[72]

In effect, the court declared that since both the Constituent Assembly and the state legislature had decided this was a measure that served a public purpose, the bench should defer to their decision and refrain from deciding what was or was not a governmental function unless 'public purpose' was shown to be a complete impossibility.[73]

Even when the court examined the compensation mechanisms of the Act and struck them down as void because they prescribed a sliding scale of compensation where landholders got different rates of compensation depending on the size of their landholding, it did so not on account of the size, scope, amount or method of compensation, but on account of the fact that such an arbitrary scale was a clear violation of Article 14, the fundamental right to equality before the law. The bench observed:

Legislation which affects only one particular class is permissible so long as it does not discriminate against individuals within the class, so long as it can be said that such a class does, in fact, exist; that there is something to distinguish the citizens composing it from all other citizens. It is, I think, clear that proprietors of estates and tenure-holders may be said to form a distinct class, in that they all enjoy an income which is an unearned income from land ... The impugned Act, however, discriminates between individuals falling within the class which it affects. In fact, it divides the class into a large number of sub-classes, and to these sub-classes differential treatment is meted out. It is quite impossible to say that this sub-division is based on any rational grounds. On what principle for instance, ought a proprietor whose net income is Rs. 20,000 to be given eight years purchase while a proprietor whose net income is Rs. 20,001 is given only six years purchase? At one end of the scale are a vast number of proprietors and tenure-holders who are to be allowed twenty years purchase ... At the other end of the scale are the great zamindars who are to be allowed only three years purchase ....[74]

In other words, what the court was objecting to was simply the unequal situation where some zamindars were to be compensated at the rate of twenty times their net income, while others were to be compensated at the rate of three times their net income – with many others falling somewhere in the middle of this scale. Neither the quantum nor the method of compensation had been the deciding factor in the judgment. It was the discriminatory nature rather than the inadequacy of compensation that had been the problem. The bigger zamindars, as the court observed, were to be given little or no compensation so that the smaller zamindars could be compensated adequately. If there had been uniform rates of compensation, the large landholders would get a lot more and the smaller landholders would get a lot less. This was the crux of the problem.

The judgment, then, did not bolt the door on land reform at all, and in fact the court had conspicuously accepted the inevitability and the intrinsic justice of zamindari abolition as an idea. Indeed, the bench spelled this out openly and precisely: 'If, the State is prevented from invading the plaintiff's right to equality, it is material that the State is indirectly prevented from invading their right to property which it could have invaded if it had not, in doing

so, also invaded their right to equality.'[75] This was the only ground
on which the Act was found unconstitutional – and it was openly
disclosed and discussed. The *Times of India*, for example, noted this
fact while reporting on the judgment on 14 March, when it stated,
'If the Supreme Court upholds the Bihar judgement, the remedy
might lie in amending the legislation so as to make compensation
uniform and to prescribe that all the estates would be taken over
by the Government.'[76] Yet no one seemed to press for this course of
action, and the reason was glaringly evident – such a course would
'arouse a storm within the Congress party which contained a large
element of small landlords'.[77]

The utter consternation in the corridors of power was thus not
simply about the immediate consequences of the Bihar judgment,
the hurdles of which could be surmounted relatively easily by
amending the requisite legislation. The government's panic was as
motivated by its fear of having to delay land reform legislation and
face the electorate with its promise unfulfilled as it was by a sense
of outrage over the fact that the courts had had the temerity to
create this delay in the first place. By this point, the government had
realized that an amendment was an easy way to constitutionally
ratify all of its policies and programmes that either were facing
or had the potential to face constitutional roadblocks in the near
future. This included both the nationalization programme and the
policy of caste- and community-based reservations. For all of its
troubles, from criticism by Opposition leaders to a disobedient
press and from the constitutional validity of land reform to the
legalization of reservations, an amendment was the simplest and
easiest of solutions.

In the end, however, the biggest motivation was the establishment's
quasi-vengeful desire to enforce its will and show the Constitution
and the judiciary their place in the pecking order, a desire borne
of its inability to truly and fundamentally accept constitutional
bounds on its own power. The government wanted to make the
unconstitutional constitutional, to demonstrate the primacy of
its power over the judiciary and such things as the Constitution
– hence why it refused to either seriously contemplate bringing
its legislation in line with constitutional provisions or wait for an
appeal to the Supreme Court, but enthusiastically plumped for the
idea of a constitutional amendment instead. The establishment, to
quote the legal scholar Sarbani Sen, was asserting an old conceptual

maxim: 'sovereign power, by its very definition, cannot be subjected to a constitution'.[78]

If there were any within the government that were still dithering on the need for a constitutional amendment to secure their social revolution, the necessary push was given by the Calcutta High Court on 22 March when it rejected the stand taken by the West Bengal government that compensation for land calculated on the date a property had been notified for acquisition in 1946 would still be valid when it was actually acquired in 1950.[79] Here, the government had acquired property to resettle refugees from East Pakistan, but declined to pay compensation at prevailing market rates, instead calculating compensation as on the date the acquisition had been notified in 1946. The court struck this skulduggery down, noting that the word 'compensation' carried within it a sense of being both just and fair, even if these words had not been pencilled out in the Constitution.[80]

What the court had held was this: apart from zamindari abolition, the government would have to provide appropriate compensation pegged at market rates for whatever property it acquired. Even if the Constitution had not specified that it had to be so, the word compensation by itself assumed justness and equity. Unlike zamindari abolition, there was no avenue for a presidential assent to allow ordinary legislation for property acquisition to elude the constitutional requirement to pay fair compensation. The government could no longer acquire property at whatever price it felt like, and even though this formulation was not applicable to zamindari abolition, the timing of the judgment caused tremendous heartburn. It was like the proverbial straw that broke the camel's back.

The Cabinet Committee met again at the end of the month in a sombre mood. On ways to secure reservations and zamindari abolition, differences were pronounced. Law Minister Ambedkar proposed that Article 14, guaranteeing equality before the law, be partially dismantled to constitutionally ring-fence community-based reservations and enable differential rates of compensation (that had proved to be the hurdle for Bihar's zamindari abolition law), once and for all. It would be desirable, he argued, for the state to 'preserve the power to treat different classes of citizens differently for the purpose of removing inequalities' – and this could be done by introducing a proviso placing corresponding limitations on the right to equality before the law in the Constitution itself.[81] It was a deceptively simple, but potentially deadly, idea.

He was countered by Attorney-General M. C. Setalvad who, recognizing how drastic the potential implications were, advised that '[it] would be best to leave Article 14 as it stands'. Any express provision overriding the principle of equality before the law, written into the Constitution in necessarily broad terms, Setalvad contended, would practically nullify the principle itself.[82] From the sparse minutes of the meeting, it is impossible to tell who supported the proposal and who opposed it, or indeed, how serious the threat to Article 14 was. Eventually, however, the attorney-general's arguments carried the day. Wary of opening a pandora's box, the committee decided against recommending any limitations on the right to equality.[83] Article 14 and the right to equality before the law survived unscathed.

With regard to freedom of speech, the tables were turned. Ambedkar and the law ministry were insisting that the word 'reasonable' be retained in all clauses in Article 19, and that it should be added before any restrictions on the freedom of expression. The inclusion of the word 'reasonable' would, they felt, prevent the state from gaining the draconian power of abridging or denying such a freedom in its entirety. Ambedkar's views were the diametric opposite of what the home ministry desired. The members of the committee disagreed with Ambedkar and agreed with Rajaji. They considered it expedient to leave the term 'reasonable' in other parts of Article 19 where it existed, but did not believe that any restrictions on freedom of speech ought to be so qualified.[84] They absolutely did not want the judiciary to sit in judgment over the reasonableness of their attempts to muzzle the press or throttle public criticism.

Members of the committee perhaps feared the political repercussions that might have followed the removal of the protection that 'reasonable' provided to the other freedoms in Article 19: the demonstrable ability of the judiciary to adjudicate on whether legislation abridging those rights could be considered 'reasonable'. Yet, in their opinion, criticism by Opposition leaders, brickbats from commentators and disparagement in the press represented such a great threat to the security of the republic and its friendly relations with foreign states – the latter an obvious euphemism for the government's policy vis-à-vis Pakistan – that the need for any possible restrictions on the freedom of speech to be reasonable was now redundant. The threat was so compelling, the need for protection so urgent, that all thought of waiting till August or September was also jettisoned, much like the need for reasonableness. The committee would now aim to prepare, present and pass the amendment within the current session.[85]

On his departure as India's last governor-general, C. Rajagopalachari had verbalized the establishment's desire to 'restore the unqualified reverence for the state that our ancients [had] cultivated ... reverence for law and discipline'.[86] As home minister, it was now apparent how literal he had been. What did this state of affairs say about 'the biggest liberal experiment in democratic government'?[87] And equally importantly, about those leading this experiment? A decade before independence, in a pseudonymous article, Jawaharlal Nehru had confessed to 'an intolerance of others and a certain contempt for the weak and the inefficient' and warned that one day, when he had executive authority, he could take advantage of his powers, 'sweeping aside the paraphernalia of a slow moving democracy'.[88] Could there have been a grain of truth in his statement? He already had near-complete dominance over the government and over the party – were the Constitution and the judiciary next?

5

The Clouds Burst

Public Proposition

Over February and March 1951, as hysteria over zamindari abolition and feverish preparation for an amendment had overtaken the Government of India and occupied the centre of its attention, in the precincts of the Supreme Court the hearings for two major cases had been drawing inexorably to a close. These were the cases that concerned the constitutional validity of caste- and community-based reservations. The first of these was the Tamil Nadu government's appeal against the Madras High Court's order invalidating its Communal GO and quashing reservations in educational institutions.[1] The second was the petition filed by B. Venkataramana against the operation of the Communal GO and the policy of reservations and quotas in selections for government employment.[2] The constitutional future of another pillar of the Congress party's social agenda was about to be decided.

Formal orders in both cases were reserved by the Supreme Court on 26 March. Though no one really knew what the court had decided, in light of the prevailing judicial winds, the press felt emboldened to speculate that the Madras government's appeal was likely to have been dismissed, and all signs indicated that the bench had found that its 'order fixing the number of candidates for admission to colleges conflicted with Article 29(2) of the Constitution'.[3] Such reports further unnerved the already apprehensive Tamil Nadu government, whose leaders, like their counterparts in Bihar, now desperately turned to Nehru for deliverance. Increasingly insistent appeals from Madras for a revalidation of communal representation streamed into Delhi, adding to the pressure on the Government of India and the Union Cabinet.

At its meeting, the Cabinet Committee parried such requests – for the moment at least. In principle, it accepted the need to amend Article 15 prohibiting discrimination in order to save the idea of caste-based reservations.[4] But members were hesitant about accepting the Madras government's demand for fixed community-wise quotas, which would require even more far-reaching constitutional chicanery. This had little to do with the intensity of the political pressure from Madras, which rivalled that from Bihar, and a lot to do with the prime minister's own reluctance in accepting the principles behind special quotas.

Many of the committee's (and the Cabinet's) views and recommendations were thus shaped as much by the opinions they thought Nehru expected of them or their beliefs about what Nehru wanted, as they were by political pressure from state governments. Nehru's biographer Sarvepalli Gopal – the son of India's first vice-president, Sarvepalli Radhakrishnan, and a founder of the JNU Centre for Historical Studies – termed it 'the eager subservience of mouldering mediocrities who claimed to be his [Nehru's] colleagues'.[5] The committee, like the Cabinet itself, looked to the prime minister for 'absolute leadership and direction'.[6] For his part, as Gopal[7] noted, Nehru had to 'curb his inclination to take all decisions and make out that they were the results of innumerable discussions. He had to disown the eagerness of his colleagues to leave all the policy making to him and insist on the cabinet seeming to function as reality.'[8]

Which bits of political pressure were amplified and which bits were abbreviated and resisted followed the vagaries of the prime minister's personal opinions, despite the often pedantic adherence to the use of deliberative mechanisms like committees and the idea of collective policymaking. India was, in Gopal's words, a 'one-man show' with Nehru as its 'thaumaturgic personality'.[9] If political pressure from Madras was being partially resisted, it was down to the prime minister himself rather than any particular desire on the part of the Cabinet. It was a measure of his suzerainty rather than any measure of the efficacy of political pressure from the states. Much of the decision-making in Delhi was now being driven more by the force of the prime minister's personality than by political pressures being brought to bear by his colleagues or chief ministers.

It was against this backdrop that detailed reports about the proposed amendments first appeared in the press. 'Five major amendments relating to fundamental rights in the constitution are proposed to be made by the Government of India,' reported the *Times of India* on 9 April:

> The amendments proposed are in respect of Article 14 guaranteeing equality before the law, Article 15 prohibiting discrimination on grounds of religion, Article 19 guaranteeing certain personal rights of the citizen such as freedom of speech, Article 31 relating to compulsory acquisition of private property and Article 32 regarding the right to move the Supreme Court for the enforcement of fundamental rights. Amendments to the Constitution became necessary as judicial interpretations of fundamental rights created difficulties in the execution of the policy of the Government.... The proposed amendments, it is suggested should be of a retrospective character ... (and) expected to be passed before Parliament adjourns towards the end of May.[10]

Other newspapers were even more scathing in their reportage. *The Statesman*, for example, described the proposed amendment in bold letters in its headline as a 'Move to Abridge Fundamental Rights of Citizens'.[11] Information that had so far remained a secret, contained within the top echelons of the government and the Congress party, or hinted at only cryptically in the press, now became public.

On the same day, as India woke up to news about the nature and extent of the government's offensive against fundamental rights, the Supreme Court announced its verdict on the Communal GO. In the first case, the judges upheld the Madras High Court's order holding the Communal GO inconsistent with Article 29(2) of the Constitution, which prevented discrimination in admissions to educational institutions. The Madras government had contended that its responsibilities to promote the welfare of backward classes via the Directive Principles of State Policy overrode its obligation to respect fundamental rights. A Constitution bench of the Supreme Court – Justices Harilal Kania, Saiyid Fazal Ali, M. Patanjali Shastri, Mehr Chand Mahajan, Sudhi Ranjan Das, B. K. Mukherjee and Vivian Bose – unanimously rejected this contention in its entirety.

'The chapter on Fundamental Rights is sacrosanct,' the bench reminded the Madras government,

> and not liable to be abridged by any Legislative or Executive Act or Order, except to the extent provided in the appropriate article in Part III. The Directive Principles of State Policy have to conform to and run as subsidiary to the Chapter of Fundamental Rights. In our opinion, that is the correct way in which the provisions found in Parts III and IV have to be understood.[12]

In the second case, the Supreme Court struck down the use of the principles of caste- and community-based quotas in the selection of candidates for employment by the state.[13] Unlike Article 29, however, which prohibited discrimination in admission to educational institutions, Article 16, which did the same for matters of employment by the state, did have a clause declaring that nothing in the said article would prevent the state from making special provisions in favour of backward classes. The court noted nevertheless that there was a schedule of such classes set out in the Madras Provincial and Subordinate Service Rules, and while reservations for these classes might be upheld on this account, they could not be upheld for any other communities, including Muslims, Christians and non-Brahmins. The bench found the Communal GO void, illegal and repugnant to the Constitution.[14]

The phrase 'repugnant to the Constitution' found a prominent place in newspaper reports about the judgments the next day, embarrassing and annoying the Madras government no end.[15] Equally importantly, however, it was observed by the court, and reported by the newspapers, that the Constitution explicitly enabled reservations for backward classes in matters of state employment, even if it made no such provision in the case of admissions to educational institutions.[16] In other words, reservation of posts for backward classes, based on some form of assessment, was not to be regarded as unconstitutional – but arbitrary communal rationing was. Reservations of all kinds in educational institutions were a constitutional anathema – but the Cabinet Committee had already caught on to that predicament and was seized of the matter.

Nonetheless, none of these nuances made any difference in Madras, where a panicked Chief Minister Kumaraswamy Raja again beseeched Nehru to amend the Constitution to retain the Communal GO in its entirety because it was necessary, in the interests of south India, to maintain the status quo with respect to both recruitment to services as well as admissions to colleges.[17] To his credit, the prime minister immediately shot Raja's request down and firmly suggested that the best course was to 'frame a new GO strictly within the terms of Article 16, keeping in mind that any special concessions can be made only for really backward classes of citizens and solely on that ground and not on the ground of equal distribution for all communities or on a basis of rationing for the several communities'.[18]

Nehru's prompt and firm denial of Kumaraswamy Raja's request, coupled with an equally firm directive to comply with constitutional provisions, was the plainest indicator that if push came to shove, the prime minister was in a position to withstand all manner of pressure from the party's state units. It was a clear sign that even more than political pressure from the provinces or the desires and inclinations of the Congress party, the narrative around the proposed amendments to the Constitution was being driven by the prime minister's own views and appetites. Tamil Nadu MLAs agitated and complained, ministerial delegations came pleading, but Prime Minister Nehru was having none of it and sternly ticked them off. This bit of political pressure, which did not agree with his own opinions, was not going to be amplified.

In his stand, he was encouraged and supported by the press. 'Local MLAs who regard themselves as custodians of caste interests rather than representatives of the people should not be allowed to devise other means of perpetuating the existing discrimination,' advised the *Times of India*. 'The State Government's legitimate solicitude for the backward sections can find better expression in the provision of free tuition, scholarships and free hostels. When it takes the vindictive form of Communal GOs, such crutches create vested interests hard to dislodge.'[19]

Inundation and Disapproval

News of the Supreme Court's stamp of approval on the Madras High Court's judgment declaring the Communal GO void, and its continuing tough stance on matters of constitutional liberty and individual freedom, coincided with the appearance of newspaper reports detailing the government's proposed changes to the Constitution. Together, they brought the issues of constitutional morality, civil liberties, fundamental rights and democratic propriety back to the centre of public discourse and resulted in an outpouring of thought and opinion on the matter.

Isolated reports about a plan to amend the Constitution had appeared in the press over the year, triggered either by an intemperate remark by someone in the government, or in the form of apocalyptic warnings of a threat to freedom and democracy by Opposition leaders like Jayaprakash Narayan and Shyama Prasad Mookerji. For the first time, men and women beyond the rarefied circles of power became aware of the government's plans and gained access to enough information to conduct appraisals. As political figures, commentators, editors, thinkers and ordinary citizens contemplated the nature and extent of the government's proposals, the government was inundated with a deluge of criticism – the fightback began.

'Should politics be allowed to play pranks with constitutional rights and guarantees?' asked one scathing editorial in the *Times of India*.

With an eye obviously on the coming electoral battle, the Government of India propose to introduce a Bill for amending Part III of the Constitution of India which embodies the fundamental rights guaranteed to the citizen. It is complained that certain judicial interpretations have created difficulties in implementing official policies, notably in the field of nationalization or state participation in industries and in the abolition of zamindaris. If the purpose of the amendments is to make these constitutional guarantees more concrete and practical and eliminate the possibility of individual rights being pushed to fantastic lengths, they will be welcomed by the public. But these changes seem animated more by a desire to conserve and consolidate the power and patronage of the executive and the government vis-à-vis the rights and liberties of the individual ... Particularly dangerous is the attempt to qualify freedom of speech ... Superficially these may seem innocuous provisos, but the country has good reason to remember the protean forms which arbitrary power takes in its efforts to maintain public order. Moreover, the relations between the State and the Fourth Estate are best left to convention and mutual understanding ... There are few spheres affecting public life and opinion where the letter of the circumscribing law can be more easily abused.[20]

'The State Governments have been betraying a most undemocratic and indeed thoroughly lawless temper in their eagerness to maintain their powers and enforce their pet policies,' complained another.

They not only encroach on public rights and liberties, regardless of the laws and constitutional guarantees, but at times proceed unabashedly to make new laws or twist old ones to suit their autocratic impulses. Now the infection appears to be spreading towards the Centre, to the very heart and core of our independent, sovereign, secular Republic, founded on the eternal democratic principles of Liberty, Equality, Fraternity, and Justice. An apprehension is created that the Government of India themselves propose to amend the Fundamental Rights out of existence ... But to tinker with the Constitution in its most vital and precious parts so soon after its inauguration can only mean one of two things, both equally humiliating: either that, with all our vociferous vaunts, we are not quite fit for self-government and the democratic order, or that the popular representative governments in the States and in the Centre are unable to govern within the framework of the Constitution which we have been flourishing in the face of an admiring world.[21]

'Apart from its expediency,' the commentator warned, 'an attempt to amend or alter the Constitution as soon as its principles are found inconvenient would be laying down a most unwholesome practice. It would justify tampering with the Constitution to suit the transient whims of every clique in power for the time being.'[22]

'The proposed amendments by the provisional Parliament must be viewed with alarm and [they] cannot be allowed to be hatched by the executive to be imposed on the country as a fait accompli,' declared Pran Nath Mehta of the Constitution of India Society. 'The chapter on fundamental rights is the pivot on which the whole Constitution revolves. To proceed to amend, alter and modify the very basis of the constitutional structure is an abuse of the amending right granted by Article 368.'[23] The society implored the Government of India to defer any amendments till after the first general election, and took the position that 'the freedom of speech and expression is a right of so fundamental a character that any attempt to further abridge it is tantamount to the repudiation of the Constitution'. In doing so, it warned, the government risked turning the Constitution into 'a poor, ambiguous, senseless, unmeaning adjective, for the purpose of accommodating any new set of political or administrative notions'.[24]

The lack of democratic legitimacy of a provisional parliament indirectly elected on a limited franchise was also brought up by P. R. Das – eminent jurist, former judge of the Patna High Court and founder of the Civil Liberties Conference – who called the approach of the governments of Bihar and UP 'disgraceful' and charged the Government of India with having 'no moral right to amend the Constitution without the verdict of the people'.[25]

Dr M. R. Jayakar, one of India's finest legal luminaries – the only Indian to be nominated to the Judicial Committee of the Privy Council and a member of the original Constituent Assembly – weighed in on the government's proposals and expressed his fear 'that those Articles which had been considered by judicial tribunals as most important guarantees of the rights of the people would be interfered with'.[26] The fundamental rights chapter in the Constitution was an assurance or guarantee to the public that the state would observe its foundational principles of liberty, justice and democracy, he argued, advising the prime minister that 'it would be unwise to create the impression that the Government are only too anxious to interfere with such public guarantees in the Constitution as soon as those guarantees are found inconvenient'.[27] Standing alongside Chief Justice M. C. Chagla of the Bombay High Court during his address – the same one who had rebuked the Congress party for its authoritarian impulses over freedom of speech – Jayakar entreated his listeners 'to be watchdogs of the Constitution' and entrusted them with the responsibility to be 'agents of the public weal'.[28]

Jayakar's rousing call struck a chord with the legal fraternity, which responded strikingly in defence of constitutional liberties. Determined to mark their objection to the government's domineering ways, the Bombay State Lawyers Conference recorded an emphatic protest against the proposed amendment of fundamental rights, and apprised the governments of their view 'that if it was found absolutely necessary to do so, any amendment should be undertaken

PLATE 1 *A Constituent Assembly meeting, 1949. B. R. Ambedkar, chairman of the Drafting Committee, sat in the centre.*

PLATE 2 *B. R. Ambedkar presenting the final draft of the Constitution to Rajendra Prasad, chairman of the Constituent Assembly, 25 November 1949.*

PLATE 3 *Legal luminaries, later cabinet colleagues: B. R. Ambedkar and C. Rajagopalachari, 1948.*

PLATE 4 *The Constituent Assembly in session, 1948.*

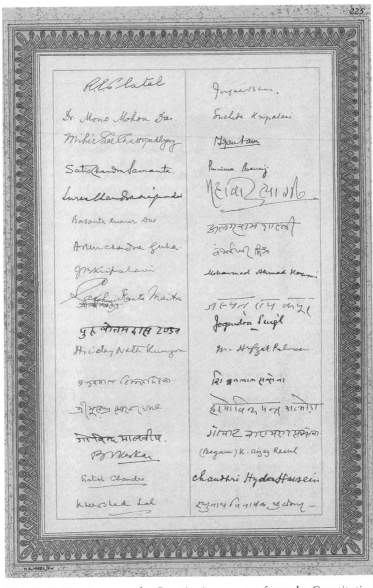

PLATE 5 *Signatories to the Constitution: a page from the Constitution bearing the signatures of (among others) J. B. Kripalani, Purushottam Das Tandon, Hriday Nath Kunzru, Govind Malaviya, Begum Aizaz Rasul, Sucheta Kripalani, Shibban Lal Saksena, Mahavir Tyagi, Mohanlal Gautam and Algu Rai Shastri.*

PLATE 6 *The first Cabinet of the Republic of India with the president, 31 January 1950. Seated L to R: B. R. Ambedkar, Rafi Ahmed Kidwai, Baldev Singh, Abul Kalam Azad, Jawaharlal Nehru, Rajendra Prasad, Sardar Patel, John Matthai, Jagjivan Ram, Amrit Kaur and Shyama Prasad Mookerji. Standing L to R: Khurshed Lal, R. R. Diwakar, Mohan Lal Saksena, N. Gopalaswami Ayyangar, N. V. Gadgil, K. C. Neogy, Jairamdas Daulatram, K. Santhanam, Satya Narayan Sinha and B. V. Keskar.*

PLATE 7 *A stamp bearing the portrait of the Anglo-Indian leader and educationist Frank Anthony.*

PLATE 8 *A stamp bearing the portrait of the liberal leader Hriday Nath Kunzru.*

PLATE 9 *Jawaharlal Nehru addresses a committee meeting, 1949. Rajendra Prasad and Sardar Patel are seated to his left.*

PLATE 10 *Jawaharlal Nehru addresses the Constituent Assembly, 1946.*

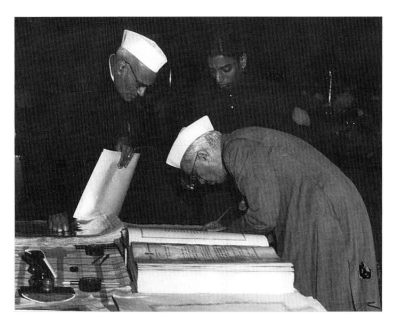

PLATE 11 *Jawaharlal Nehru signing the Constitution, 1950.*

PLATE 12 *Colleagues and competitors: (L to R) Shyama Prasad Mookerji, Jairamdas Daulatram, Govind Ballabh Pant, Jagjivan Ram and Jawaharlal Nehru.*

PLATE 13 *Founders of the Republic – Members of the Constituent Assembly, 1950. Among the figures in the front row: Baldev Singh (first from left), John Matthai (second from left), Amrit Kaur (fourth from left), Jawaharlal Nehru (fifth from left), Rajendra Prasad (seventh from left), Shyama Prasad Mookerji (first from right), Jagjivan Ram (third from right), Jagjivan Ram (third from right) and Sardar Patel (fourth from right).*

only after obtaining a mandate from the people after the General Elections'.[29] The views of the Bombay lawyers found wide echo among a large number of advocates and bar associations across the country, many of whom joined their Bombay compatriots to register their protest against the government's desire to abridge constitutional guarantees.

Not to be outdone by the lawyers, businessmen and industrialists also got on the protest bandwagon. The executive committee of the Federation of Indian Chambers of Commerce and Industry (FICCI) prepared a long representation to the law ministry urging the government to postpone all consideration of amending the Constitution until after the first general elections. 'The very fact that the General Elections are not far away', observed the committee, 'should be enough not to hustle through far-reaching changes in the Constitution, particularly when they are likely to be misunderstood as electioneering tactics by the party in power.' 'Arbitrary revision of such fundamental provisions designed to meet conflicting points of view', the representation pointed out, was 'in effect a breach of faith not calculated to inculcate much respect either for the Constitution or for the authors of such amendments'.[30]

Apart from organizations such as the zamindar associations, lawyers conferences and FICCI, large numbers of individual citizens who studied the reports on the amendment also responded to the government plans with an outpouring of criticism and scorn.

Concerned citizens wrote to the newspapers to express their consternation. 'Every time a decision given by the judiciary regarding the Constitution goes contrary to the policy of the party in power and is hence disapproved by them the Constitution cannot be amended,' wrote two angry citizens from Bombay, 'otherwise the sanctity of the Constitution would disappear ... Hence the Constitution of India should not be amended to suit the current policies of the party in power.'[31] Others conceded the government's and Parliament's legal power to amend the Constitution, but still advised against any hurried attempt to tamper with fundamental rights until the first election on a universal franchise had been conducted.[32]

An ambitious young lawyer from Delhi, appalled at the government's intended depredations against his rights and freedoms, wrote a letter to the editor of the *Times of India* denouncing the government's proposals in the most withering terms:

> In the garb of protecting the Zamindari Abolition Acts the Government are going to change Article 19 and make freedom of speech more restricted. The two restrictions on freedom of speech namely 'in the interests of foreign powers' and 'in the interests of public order' are full of dangerous possibilities. The second restriction has been interpreted to mean that the satisfaction of a junior official is considered enough to deprive me of my fundamental right. The interpretation that unless freedom of speech led to 'clear and present danger' no restriction could be placed is going to be thrown overboard. This will literally stifle all genuine opposition and criticism of the government. Can this be allowed?[33]

'A convenient handle is being obtained by the government to suppress all comments on their foreign policy,' the angry young lawyer continued. 'Why is Mr Nehru becoming so shaky about his policy by wishing to suppress all criticism of it?'[34]

The young lawyer's letter raised crucial, searching questions. The two restrictions were indeed full of the most dangerous possibilities: they represented a virtual desecration of the most pivotal parts, the 'heart and soul', of the republican Constitution. Was the government proposing to stifle all genuine criticism and suppress all opposition? Did criticism of Pakistan and the government's foreign policy really threaten the safety and security of the nation? Why was Mr Nehru shaky? What was the government terrified of? As a strong leader prepared to steamroll his way through, there were no answers forthcoming.

And who was the source of this bitterly caustic assessment of the Nehru government and its motives? None other than the future liberal icon, high court chief justice and civil liberties activist Rajinder Sachar. His letter graphically illustrated the unrestrained hauteur with which India's first government viewed the Constitution and the contempt in which it held the rights and liberties of individual citizens.

Much later in life, when he had become known for speaking his mind, Sachar wrote in a highly acclaimed article in 2016:

Wherever there is a written Constitution, the Supreme law is the law of the Constitution and for even the Parliament to accept that its powers are limited by the written Constitution is not in any manner to derogate from its sovereignty but only to accept that its sovereignty, like the sovereignty of the executive and the judiciary, is limited by the written Constitution.[35]

These views – the complete opposite of Nehru and the Congress party – had first been firmed up in 1951 when he had watched the Nehru government brazenly refuse to accept such limitations on its authority. He had been saying much the same thing in 1951 as he had in 2016, to little avail and even less concern. A landmark precedent was in the process of being set.

A Presidential Objection

The deluge of criticism that appeared in the press seemed to the government, however, like water off a duck's back. Neither the charge that the Constitution was being vandalized to place the Congress party on a stronger footing in the upcoming general election, nor the accusation that the amendment was a power grab by the executive in order to muzzle critical opinion – and not even grave questions of democratic legitimacy and allegations of breach of faith – perturbed the prime minister. Calls to set a positive precedent, seek a democratic mandate, uphold constitutional morality or simply avoid hustling through the amendment and wait for a general election were equally blithely brushed aside.

Unfazed by the continuing stream of criticism that was appearing in the press and being voiced by the intelligentsia, the Cabinet Committee reported in mid-April with further recommendations. It wanted to leave Article 31 as it currently stood, but, the main aim being to protect current and future legislation related to zamindari abolition and land acquisition, it desired the addition of a new Article 31A 'saying that nothing in the fundamental rights could be used to invalidate laws for the taking of estates or rights in them'.[36] The committee also awoke to the potential risks that the right to practise any profession or carry on any occupation might entail for the government's plans for nationalization of industry and the exclusion of private enterprise. It recommended that Article 19(6), which qualified the right to practise any profession or carry on any business, be amended to the effect that the said right would not 'affect the operation of any existing law for the carrying on by the government of any trade, business, industry, or service to the exclusion of citizens'.[37]

Mindful of the need to avoid an electoral backlash in Madras and revalidate caste-based reservations, the committee also advocated amending Article 15 – the right to freedom from discrimination – to read that nothing in the said article would prevent the state from making any special provisions for the advancement of any socially or educationally backward class of citizens, as well as any Scheduled Castes or Scheduled Tribes.[38] The committee's recommendations fulfilled most of the prime minister's requirements, and none of his demands were resisted. The Tamil Nadu government's requests to ensure that the amendment supported the Communal GO's reservation policy based on communal rationing was firmly turned down, but the demand to make reservations constitutionally invulnerable was enthusiastically upheld, as the prime minister desired. As a courtesy, a copy of the report was sent to President Rajendra Prasad.

On 19 April, the Constitutional Changes Committee of the Congress party conferred with the Cabinet Committee to apprise them of their views, including, incidentally, their desire to curtail Article 14, the right to equality, a request the Cabinet Committee emphatically turned down, noting that the government 'did not think any curtailment or modification of Article 14 ... desirable or necessary'.[39] In light of what transpired at the meeting, it was suggested in newspaper reports that 'only amendments to Article 19 and 31 will be sponsored since only those clauses would be touched which needed imminent change'.[40] This view, being given out to the press by government and party sources, was mainly misdirection and obfuscation meant to lull the public and the Opposition into a sense of complacency. 'Informed circles suggest,' one report read, 'that the Government of India will not embark on any large-scale modification of the Constitution just at present.'[41] Establishment sources kept harping on about how the changes were 'limited in number and scope',[42] even as they realized full well that it would radically change the relationship between the state and the citizen.[43]

Tremendously agitated at the Cabinet Committee's refusal to revalidate the Communal GO in its entirety, Chief Minister Kumaraswamy Raja led a ministerial delegation to Delhi on 27 April to 'hold discussions on the situation arising from the Supreme Court's order on the Communal GO'.[44] Their request was denied. Another ministerial delegation led by the finance minister came calling a week later to again demand, in the words of a major newspaper, the revalidation of 'the twenty-year-old tradition of doling out privileges and preferences on a communal basis'.[45] 'It is sad that the Congress Ministry in Madras,' commented an editorial, 'agitated over losing support from the castes and sub-castes which thrive on the Communal GO, has failed to imbibe the spirit and to respect the provisions of India's democratic and secular constitution.'[46] Nehru sent them packing again – demonstrating again his mastery of the situation and testifying to the fact that rather than any political pressure from below, the amending process was now being driven by his own will.

Meanwhile, President Rajendra Prasad, who had examined the Cabinet Committee's report as well as the draft amendment prepared by the law ministry, wrote to the prime minister on 30 April with his comments. Conversant with the law, well equipped to understand legal and constitutional nuances, well informed about the political situation and supremely knowledgeable about the intentions of the Constituent Assembly over which he had presided, Rajendra Prasad was not pleased with what he read. Unlike members of the Cabinet and the party, Prasad considered himself Nehru's equal in stature. They might have pandered to Nehru's will; he was having none of it.

'The Constitution has a sanctity which does not attach to ordinary laws enacted by Parliament or the Legislature of a State,' the president wrote bluntly, 'and should not ordinarily be sought to be amended unless and until every other method available for dealing with any problem that has arisen has been tried and found to be inadequate.'[47] He was greatly dismayed by the cavalier disdain with which the democratic government was treating the provisions for fundamental rights and individual freedom – the most pivotal part of the entire Constitution. 'Part III of the Constitution which lays down the Fundamental Rights has a special importance and significance of its own,' he added indignantly. '... It is an irony of fate that this Part which stands above every other Part of the Constitution is the first to be assailed.'[48]

The present Parliament, he argued, was provisional in nature and acting under the transitory provisions of the Constitution until a new bicameral legislature came into being – 'and although it has all the powers of Parliament and anything it does cannot be questioned on the ground of lack of competence, expediency and propriety ought to dictate caution'.[49] Since this was already the fag end of a long session on the eve of the general election, Prasad opposed any precipitate action to tamper with the Constitution without giving full time not only to members of Parliament but also to the public and the country at large to consider and comment on the implications of the amendment.[50]

Turning to the substance of the proposed amendment, Prasad took Nehru and the Cabinet to task for the offhand manner in which they were treating so serious a subject. As far as Sections 124A and 153A of the Indian Penal Code and other public security legislation to curb the freedom of speech were concerned, the president had 'an impression that the Supreme Court has not gone to that extent [of giving any extreme decisions] and the extreme decisions of the High Courts have not been affirmed by the Supreme Court'.[51] 'If I am correct in my reading of the extent to which decisions have been finalized,' he forcefully asserted, 'I venture to think that no case for amending the Fundamental Rights Articles has arisen.' 'We must test the correctness of the extreme decisions of the High Courts by bringing them in appeal or otherwise before the Supreme Court,' he advised the Cabinet. 'If on the other hand, the decisions have been finalized by the Supreme Court the first attempt should be to bring the impugned provisions of law in conformity with the Constitution.'[52]

President Prasad was equally irked by the proposed addition of Article 31A, which he considered ill-thought-out and malicious. The Bihar Land Reforms Act may have been invalidated by the Patna High Court, but a similar land reform bill had been upheld by the high court in Nagpur after the decision in Bihar, indicating that zamindari abolition as such was not prohibited by the Constitution. If any particular Act had been held to be invalid, he noted, it was not because there was anything wrong with the Constitution but that the Bihar legislation contained wrong provisions which might be changed to make it conform to the Constitution.

'I would therefore suggest,' he brusquely counselled Nehru,

[T]hat instead of taking the very serious step of amending the Constitution, the first step should be to get a verdict of the Supreme Court on the correctness or otherwise of the Patna decision. Simultaneously the impugned Act should be examined by the Government with a view to so amending it as to bring it into conformity with the Constitution.[53]

Like most dispassionate observers, the constitutional head of the republic objected to both the content and the timing of the amendment, which ravaged the fundamental rights of individual citizens and violated the norms of democratic conduct. Prasad was perceptive to both – the need to establish positive democratic conventions, and the need to display moral and constitutional rectitude in these situations – and warned the prime minister to tread cautiously and avoid any hasty action. Any changes to the Constitution, he felt, should be made in the most proper and democratic way possible, or else it would undermine India's nascent constitutional democracy and create a terrible precedent for the future. 'On the whole,' the president presciently concluded, ' … the amendment will create more problems than it will solve and the objective of preventing further litigation … is not likely to be achieved.'[54]

The Edge of the Precipice

In the reckless, impetuous bid to establish the government's supremacy and open the constitutional doors to the Congress's social revolution, however, all caution had been thrown to the wind. The creation of the Nehruvian state demanded constitutional blood – and the prime minister and his acolytes were willing to spill it. Smug in the knowledge that he commanded overwhelming public adulation, enjoyed near-undisputed supremacy over the Congress Parliamentary Party and had an unchallengeable majority in Parliament,[55] the prime minister had little reason to engage with his critics or moderate his approach. Not even at the insistence and urging of the president of the republic, the highest constitutional authority in the land. Much like the prime minister's other critics, Rajendra Prasad found his views contemptuously disregarded.[56]

Undeterred by the storm of criticism swirling around him and dismissive of the president's objections, Nehru wrote to his chief ministers to inform them that a constitutional amendment was now imminent. 'In the course of this amendment we shall endeavour to get some lacunae filled,' he declared. 'But the main purpose of the amendment is two-fold: one to remove certain difficulties owing to judicial interpretations of fundamental rights ... The other ... relates to social measures relating to land which various State Assemblies have passed and which have been held up by judicial decisions.'[57] Having come this far, the prime minister was now set on his course, and neither the reluctance of the president, nor the disapproval of the press, nor the displeasure of the intelligentsia was going to dissuade him. The Government of India now went into overdrive to make sure the amendment was tabled in Parliament as soon as possible.[58]

As this frenetic preparation continued in the background, on 10 May, the Allahabad High Court finally pronounced its judgment on the UP Zamindari Abolition and Land Reform Act. Contrary to the expectations of many lawyers and major zamindars, a full bench of the high court held 'that the Zamindari Abolition Act did not contravene any of the provisions of the Constitution and was not invalid on that account'.[59] The applications of over 4,000 zamindars were dismissed without costs. The decision came as a huge reprieve for the UP government, and especially for Govind Ballabh Pant, who had personally put his considerable shoulders to the wheel to get the Act drafted and passed through the assembly. Prime Minister Nehru and the Government of India, however, were put in an immense quandary.

The judgment took the wind out of the sails of Nehru's arguments and made clear, once and for all, that there was little to negligible risk of the Constitution standing in the way of properly conceived and executed legislation for land reform and zamindari abolition. It was now apparent to anyone who cared that the problem lay not so much with constitutional provisions and fundamental rights, as with the legislation prepared in Bihar and the posture and sensibilities of Congress leaders. President Rajendra Prasad was proven to be right: the courts were not holding up zamindari abolition, and amending the offending Act to make it conform to the Constitution should be the first step in this situation.

Over the preceding months, Prime Minister Nehru had been harping on about the necessity of an amendment in light of the danger the Constitution posed to the Congress party's dreams of social revolution: the binary choice between saving zamindari abolition and respecting the fundamental rights provisions in the Constitution. The Allahabad High Court's judgment demonstrated the conspicuous falsity of these claims. The prime minister had consistently claimed that the judicial pronouncements on zamindari abolition were the prime reason that the amendment had to be hurried through as soon as possible. It was now evident that this was mostly a smokescreen for a power grab by the executive. Now that the major cause of its annoyance was taken away, one might have thought the government would pause and relent, take stock of the situation and avoid a frontal assault on the Constitution. But Nehru and his government were not to be dissuaded.

The latent, barely suppressed authoritarianism that had characterized India's new democratic rulers was now given open expression. As the sole inheritors of the British Raj, India's post-colonial leaders had assumed the same sense of entitlement: to stifle dissent, to censor adverse opinion and muffle all opposition. Throughout the nationalist struggle, Congress leaders had claimed to be the only true representatives of the Indian people, and the only ones entitled to speak for them, laying claim, in the name of the nation, to possession of the state and its territory.[60] The exclusion of other parties from a seat at the political high table had been as much a Congress goal as the orderly transfer of institutional power into its own hands. Congress leaders, as a contemporary observer remarked, equated political freedom with political agreement – with themselves and their opinions.[61] The creation of the new democratic republic forced them to theoretically end this position.

India's new democratic leaders had now to contend not only with the representative claims of other groups and criticism by ideological opponents, but also the pre-eminent constraining power of the Constitution. To their surprise, they realized that unlike their colonial predecessors, they could not do as they felt and would be forced to endure their opponents. Furthermore, they would have to submit to and be bound by constitutional restrictions. Having enjoyed disproportionate and unchecked power since 1947, however, this 'cluster of notables', as the constitutional historian Harshan Kumarasingham referred to them,[62] was not going to cede ground so easily. The rush to amend the Constitution, then, was a part of what Kumarasingham described as 'the executive struggle and search for constitutional pre-eminence … conducted without the involvement or the open knowledge of the electorate'.[63] Through it, India's leaders were effectively defining their own roles within the constitutional scheme, while simultaneously seeking to redefine their relationship with the nation's citizens and shape the future expectations and powers of constitutional offices.[64]

Few thus doubted what the amendment was truly about. The headline in *The Statesman* of 11 May 1951 said it all: 'Provision Against Sedition to Be Made in Constitution: Mr. Nehru Might Introduce Bill This Week'.[65] 'Firmly rejected during the discussion in the Constituent Assembly as an anachronism in Free India,' read the report,

> sedition is to be introduced into the Constitution through an official amendment. Contrary to earlier reports that the intention to amend Article 19, relating to personal freedoms had been abandoned, the final draft of the amending bill, it is learnt, imposes substantial restrictions on the freedom of speech and expression … the exceptions that Parliament by legislation may enforce are to be extended by the addition of sedition and activity which may endanger foreign relations.[66]

The same evening, the evening before the amendment was introduced in Parliament, Alladi Krishnaswamy Aiyyar – the very person who had argued against reservations in court and had the Communal GO invalidated – advised Law Secretary K. V. K. Sundaram that Article 29(2) prohibiting discrimination in admissions to educational institutions be altered in the manner of Article 15 to completely protect the government's reservation policy.[67] On that hot summer evening of 11 May 1951, the nation, its constitutional future and the liberties and freedoms of its citizens teetered at the edge of a precipice. It was the government's penultimate chance to step back from the edge. It chose not to.

On the morning of 12 May 1951, at exactly 9.31 am, Prime Minister Jawaharlal Nehru interrupted the long-running debate on the Representation of the People Bill and introduced the Constitution

(First Amendment) Bill in Parliament. Till that moment, the government had provided no official intimation of what exactly it was planning to do; few had known the precise form the amendment would take. First on his feet was Hussain Imam, the Muslim League leader from Bihar, who, like his compatriots Chaudhary Khaliquzzaman and Hussain Shaikh Suhrawardy, would also one day end up in Pakistan.

'What is to be amended? What is to be amended? This is a very unusual thing,'[68] he sputtered as other similarly agitated Opposition members rose in support. 'Let us not deal with it at this stage,' retorted an equally surprised Speaker G. V. Mavalankar. 'The Bill will be made available to study.'[69] Fifteen months after the inauguration of the new republic, the first battle to protect the original Constitution and the constitutional vision of the founding fathers, the first battle to defend civil liberties and fundamental rights – indeed, the first battle of Indian liberalism – had begun.

The Battle Begins

The official introduction of the amendment in Parliament gave the press and the public their first glimpse of the specific clauses that made up the amending bill. It acted as a lightning rod for criticism and galvanized the Opposition. 'Nehru Introduces Bill to Amend Constitution: Further Curbs on Freedom', blared the headline in *The Statesman*.[70] 'The Constitution Amendment Bill is legally bad and subversive of the Constitution,' declared P. N. Mehta, general secretary of the Constitution of India Society. He lambasted Nehru for his duplicity:

> Only a few months ago the Prime Minister, while addressing the All India Newspaper Editors Conference at Delhi, categorically and emphatically announced that the Government had absolutely no intention to abridge the Freedom of Speech and Expression. Is not the country now entitled to know what immediate and present danger has arisen during this short interval which is endangering 'public order' and 'foreign relations' that such a drastic curtailment is necessary?[71]

One of India's most respected lawyers, the man who had defended Bhagat Singh in the Lahore Conspiracy Case, then issued his clarion call: 'The destruction of Freedom of Speech and Expression would be an event so evil in its consequences that the country for decades together may remain bound hand and foot. This invasion of our liberty must be repelled. The Constitution must be saved.'[72] His words electrified the legal fraternity. In Delhi, over fifty senior advocates led by N. C. Chatterjee (the father of future communist leader Somnath Chatterjee) and Gopi Nath Kunzru (brother of the liberal parliamentarian Hriday Nath Kunzru) issued an appeal 'to all fellow lawyers and in particular all bar associations throughout India to protest against the proposal to abridge the fundamental rights embodied in the Constitution of India'.[73]

The *Times of India* published a damning editorial, in which the government and the prime minister were raked over the coals:

An air of indecent haste pervades the Prime Minister's efforts to amend the constitution ... and it is an illuminating commentary on the democratic workings of the Centre and the States that they should so soon have found it difficult to accommodate themselves within the framework of the constitution. This monumental piece of legislation has been operative for barely fifteen months. Conventions and judicial interpretations ordinarily govern the growth of constitutional practice, and for a government to seek amendment even before the first general election of a newly independent country is probably unprecedented ... Though it is proper that such freedoms should not degenerate into licence what is the provocation or justification for so hedging in the right of expression as to make it perilous for the press to comment freely on foreign affairs or such expansive subjects as public order?[74]

'Too many dictatorships have been reared in the sacred name of public order,' warned the commentator, 'and to leave the interpretation of this term to the tender mercies of officialdom is to barter away a precious privilege.'[75] It was now unmistakable: Nehru's amendment represented an outright repudiation of the powerful and expansive vision of republican freedom and individual rights that had been envisioned in the original Constitution and articulated by the judiciary. It was the first step towards the creation of the Nehruvian state, with its odious state apparatus, its prescriptive dominance of a personality-driven social agenda, its overwhelming primacy of executive authority, and its grim, resolute suppression of alternative ideological positions – all precariously balanced against a pedantic dedication to democratic procedure and collective policymaking.

The amendment radically reconceived the relationship between the government and the citizen in direct contradiction to the imagination of the Constituent Assembly. It was a victory for the supporters of the quotidian injustices that the state and its democratic helmsmen meted out to their critics and opponents using the arbitrary powers they had inherited from their colonial forebears, a tool to strengthen their hands and cement the grip of the Congress party on institutional power, unfettered by constitutional constraints. In the words of the *Times of India*: 'the bulk of Congress members now feel that the time for action – drastic action – is here and now and that no impediments to progress can be allowed to take root in the soil of constitutional obscurantism.'[76] The translation of fundamental rights into constitutional obscurantism was a grim reminder of how far attitudes within the establishment had shifted since the heady days of January 1950.

The main question that everyone, from the president downwards, was asking was 'why' – what was the need for this tearing hurry? What was the prime minister thinking? As a major newspaper reported:

> The urgency with which this measure is being canvassed has itself been the subject of considerable comment. Large sections of the press and other independent bodies like the Supreme Court Bar Association have written and spoken in terms of varying disapproval of what they fear might be construed as indecent haste and immoral precedent ....[77]

The prime minister answered in Parliament. On 16 May 1951, debate began on the Constitution (First Amendment) Bill. Prime Minister Nehru opened proceedings by tabling a motion to refer the bill to a twenty-one-member Select Committee led by himself for consideration, with the report expected in five days. The committee was to include leaders from the Opposition like Shyama

Prasad Mookerji, Hriday Nath Kunzru and Prof. K. T. Shah,[a] whereas Congress nominees included C. Rajagopalachari and B. R. Ambedkar, among others. Another member of the committee gaining first-hand experience in constitutional subversion was the young Congress leader (and future Congress president) Dev Kant Barooah,[b] who would set a new benchmark of sycophancy during the Emergency with the slogan 'India is Indira and Indira is India'.

By this time, it had also been openly reported in the press that Congress members had been discouraged from making any critical speeches, and a strong party whip was expected to cover any genuine misgivings.[78] Convinced that he was in command of the situation, the prime minister rose to commence his seventy-five-minute-long address. 'The Bill is not a very complicated one, nor is it a big one,' he began. 'Nevertheless, I need hardly point out that it is of intrinsic and great importance.'[79]

Parliamentary Encounter I:
Nehru Takes the Stage

First, the prime minister took up the points raised by his critics. There had been no haste, he insisted; the bill had been brought forward 'after the most careful thought to the problem'.[80] Even the early date set for the Select Committee to report back was not due to any desire to hurry, but because he could not 'see how a prolongation of this date for a relatively simple bill, however important, enables us to give greater thought to it'.[81] In fact, his government had no desire to seek the powers that the amendment

---

[a]Khushal Talaksi Shah (1888–1953) was a lawyer, economist and socialist politician. An alumnus of the London School of Economics and Gray's Inn, he was appointed a professor of economics at Mysore University when only 30, served as the general secretary of the National Planning Committee set up by the Congress in 1938, and was elected to the Constituent Assembly in 1946.

[b]Dev Kant Barooah (1914–96) was a Congress politician from Assam. He was elected to the Constituent Assembly in 1948, and later to the Lok Sabha and the Assam Legislative Assembly. He was president of the Congress during the Emergency (1975–7) and is now chiefly remembered for his sycophantic slogan 'India is Indira. Indira is India.'

was creating at all, and was unlikely to take advantage of them; what they really wanted to achieve, instead, was to 'leave something for the succeeding parliaments and the younger generation ... that they can wield and handle with ease for the advancement of India'.[82]

Just how restrictions on free speech were a gift to the younger generation to be used for the advancement of India, Nehru refused to divulge. But he did tell his audience why they were necessary: 'We live at a time of grave danger in the world, in Asia, in India. No man can say what the next few months, or if you like the next year, may bring. I am not thinking of the election, but rather of other happenings that are bigger than elections. Now at this moment when great countries ... think almost of a struggle for survival, when they think that in spite of their greatness and power they are in danger, all of us have to think in terms of survival.'[83] He could not, of course, tell his colleagues what these grave happenings were, or, indeed, what steps he was going to take to avert this danger – only that grave international issues were involved and that things said and done repeatedly may lead to the gravest consequences with regard to foreign countries.[84]

The press came in for a savage verbal flaying:

It has become a matter of great distress to me to see from day to day some of these newssheets which are full of vulgarity and indecency and falsehood, day after day, not injuring me or this House much, but poisoning the mind of the younger generation, degrading their mental integrity and moral standards. It is not for me a political problem but a moral problem. How are we to save our younger generation from this progressive degradation and the progressive poisoning of their mind and spirit?[85]

Fake news, which undermined the morale of the armed forces and corroded the nationalist sentiment of the youth, was also a major concern:

From the way untruth is bandied about and falsehood thrown about it has become quite impossible to distinguish what is true and what is false. Imagine our younger generation in schools and colleges reading this, imagine, I ask this House, our soldiers and our sailors and our airmen reading this from day to day. What kind of impression do they carry? ... when there is no sense of responsibility and obligation, what are we to do? How are we to stop this corroding influence?[86]

The amendment was not only necessary but eminently desirable, he told Parliament, because if these changes were not made, the whole purpose of the Constitution 'may be defeated or delayed' – and it was their duty to see that the Constitution was correctly interpreted to reflect the 'will of the community'.[87] The whole purpose of the Constitution, Nehru apprised the assembled members, was a dynamic movement towards certain objectives. How was this purpose of the Constitution being defeated? By the courts of the land laying more stress on justiciable fundamental rights, which represented a 'static element', than on the non-justiciable Directive Principles of State Policy, which truly represented this dynamic movement.[88]

In other words, the enforcement of fundamental rights was defeating the Constitution. Nehru was telling Parliament that directive principles – which included instructions on sundry matters ranging from reduction of inequality and provision for maternity benefits to protection of cows and the organization of animal husbandry, and included the still contentious direction to create a Uniform Civil Code – reflected the true purpose of the Constitution and trumped the chapter on fundamental rights, the supposed 'heart and soul', which in reality was actually hindering the Constitution from fulfilling its purpose. The whole conception of fundamental rights and the protection of individual liberty, he argued, was an old nineteenth-century idea drawn from the French Revolution, an idea that had now been superseded by the dynamic ideas of the twentieth century as represented by the directive principles: ideas of social justice, economic and legal reform, cow protection and animal husbandry.

The state and the Constitution, rather than protecting the rights and freedoms of the individual, were to champion these ideas. In the normal course of events, such issues were resolved through the development of conventions and the slow process of judicial interpretation, which, as Nehru stated, other countries with written constitutions had gone through. But because we lived in rapidly changing times, he declared, India could not wait for judicial interpretation or the development of conventions. Neither could the Congress party's social agenda. 'You, I and the country [*sic*] has to wait with social and economic conditions ... and we are responsible for them,' he thundered.

> How are we to meet them? How are we to answer them? How are we to answer the question: for the last ten or twenty years, you have said we will do it. Why have you not done it? It is not good for us to say: We are helpless before fate and the situation we have to face at present.[89]

Nehru's views were an audacious and extraordinary inversion of the foundational principles of the constitutional order, deploying the standard authoritarian tropes of vague threats against the state and the constitutional imperatives of a social revolution. He had been saying much the same thing to his colleagues and chief ministers over the year. Only now, in Parliament, with recent events having demonstrated the complete inaccuracy of most of his claims, they were far more insidious, unsettling Congressmen and Opposition figures alike. They were, equally, a statement of his power and a confession of his fears. He had promised his people a social revolution, and neither his critics, nor the lawyers kidnapping and purloining his magnificent Constitution,[90] nor the judiciary, nor indeed the magnificent Constitution itself, were going to come in his way.

Parliamentary Encounter II: Mookerji Replies

Shyama Prasad Mookerji, the unofficial leader of the Opposition, rose to reply immediately after Nehru finished speaking. Unlike Nehru's long, rambling declamation, Mookerji's speech was sharp and hard-hitting. His careful and eloquent deconstruction of Nehru's explanations, which he termed weak, halting and unacceptable,[91] electrified his audience and led to repeated thumping of desks by appreciative non-Congress members.

'What is the sad picture that we present to the country today?' he asked the House with his trademark rhetorical flourish.

> Within a year and a half of enacting the Constitution we have come forward, and however much the Prime Minister might

attempt to say that the changes are simple, that there is no
controversy about it, he knows it in his heart of hearts ... that
what he is going to do is nothing short of cutting at the very
root of the fundamental principles of the Constitution which he
helped, more than anybody else, to pass only about a year and
a half ago. This is the challenge he has deliberately thrown to
the people of India. I do not know why he has thrown up this
challenge. Is it due to fear? Does he feel that he is incapable today
to carry on the administration of the country unless he is clothed
with more and more powers to be arbitrarily utilized so that his
will may be the last word on the subject? Or is it his doubt in the
wisdom of the people whose champion he has been all his life?
Does he feel that the people of India have run amuck and cannot
be trusted with the freedom that has been given to them?[92]

Mookerji proceeded to calmly and clinically take Nehru's claims
apart, repeating many of the criticisms that had been aired in the
press. He called the restrictions on the freedom of speech a ruse
to penalize the government's political opponents, reminding the
prime minister that action against a small group spreading venom
and vulgarity did not require a change in the Constitution; the
powers provided to Parliament and the state legislatures were
broad enough.[93] He admonished the prime minister for taking
away rights that had deliberately been given only a year and a half
ago,[94] and emphasized the need to set good democratic precedents
and create good democratic conventions while decrying the desire
to constantly arm the executive with new and arbitrary powers.[95]
He believed that the 'dangerous' qualifier on relations with foreign
states was targeted at his criticism of Pakistan and his desire to annul
Partition, arguing that democratic freedom necessarily implied that
any viewpoint be allowed to circulate in the country so long as it
did not advocate violence and chaos.[96]

He echoed the views of President Rajendra Prasad that the Patna
High Court judgment had only recognized the flaws in the Bihar
legislation rather than indicating any problems with zamindari
abolition. On the principle of zamindari abolition with fair
compensation, there was unanimous approval of the House – and
such legislation was anyhow protected in the Constitution. The
inability of the government to create a set, uniform formula for
such legislation was down to its own incompetence and could not

be blamed on the Constitution. The only 'logical, fair and equitable procedure' in this situation, Mookerji argued, was to approach the Supreme Court and wait for its judgment. In his opinion, only if the Supreme Court came to a conclusion that invalidated the fundamental principle of zamindari abolition could there be any justification for amending the Constitution.[97]

The Ninth Schedule – the repository of unconstitutional laws – became the subject of a ferocious attack:

> What you say is that particular laws which are mentioned in a schedule to the Constitution, no matter whether they infringe any provision of the Constitution or not, are deemed to be valid. Is that any way in which the Constitution should be amended? … By this amendment you are saying that whatever legislation is passed, it is deemed to be law. Then why have your Constitution? Why have your fundamental rights? Who asked you to have these fundamental rights at all? … You passed the fundamental rights deliberately and you clothed the judiciary with certain powers not for the purposes of abusing the provisions of the Constitution but for giving interpretations and generally acting in a manner consistent with the welfare of the people. If the Supreme Court has gone wrong, come forward and say that the Supreme Court has come to such and such conclusions which are repugnant to the basic principles on which the Constitution was based. But the Supreme Court has not had a chance to consider this matter and you come forward with this hasty proposal that any law mentioned in the schedule would be deemed to be valid. Not only that. I can even understand your considering the laws before you, but you are saying that in future if any law is passed in regard to these subjects, it would be deemed to be valid notwithstanding the provisions of the Constitution. Can anything be more absurd and more ridiculous?[98]

Mookerji went after Nehru with a vengeance. 'For a period of so-called emergency,' he sarcastically advised the prime minister,

> you can pass a law and say that the entire task of framing, interpreting and working the Constitution will be left in the hands of Pandit Jawaharlal Nehru, assisted by such people whom he may desire to consult. Pass a simple amending bill. And then

declare that for the next two years nothing more need be done in India ...But do not have a camouflaged Constitution ...You are treating this Constitution as a scrap of paper....[99]

The leader of the Opposition cautioned Nehru against the headlong rush to enforce his will, encouraging him to reflect on the future and the dangerous precedent he was setting. 'Maybe you will continue for eternity,' he warned, 'in the next generation, for generations unborn; that is quite possible. But supposing some other party comes into authority? What is the precedent which you are laying down?'[100]

Concluding his gripping, exhilarating oration, Mookerji exhorted his fellow parliamentarians to stand up for the Constitution and resist 'this encroachment on the liberty of the people of Free India' with the stirring words: 'For the saddest epitaph which can be carved in memory of a vanished liberty is that it was lost because its possessors failed to stretch forth a saving hand while yet there was time.'[101]

Parliamentary Encounter III

Mookerji's rousing words triggered protracted applause from all quarters, including several senior Congress members. So compelling was his oratory that the next speaker, Congress stalwart (and future Swatantra Party luminary) N. G. Ranga, described it as 'one of the most powerful and eloquent speeches' he had ever heard, and called Mookerji 'the Indian Burke' after the great British parliamentarian and conservative philosopher.[102] 'I began to think', gushed Ranga, 'how the British Parliament must have reacted to that other great man as he was reeling out his great eloquence.'[103] Reporting on one of the greatest verbal duels in Indian parliamentary history, the *Times of India* approvingly noted, 'Mr Nehru's sentiment was more than outmatched by the impassioned logic of Dr Mookerjee.'[104]

For a moment, even the government's strongest supporters wavered in their commitment to their party manifesto and their subservience to the party agenda. Both Ranga and Thakurdas Bhargava, the second Congress speaker of the day, only offered their qualified support to the measure. Both backed the need for a constitutional amendment, particularly with reference to Article 31 and zamindari abolition, but both demanded that some of the concerns raised by Mookerji regarding civil liberties and the right to freedom of speech be addressed, and the government examine the amendment's potential for misuse.[105] Bhargava repeatedly pressed the government to introduce the word 'reasonable' before any restrictions on free speech that were written into the Constitution and questioned the appropriacy of giving the amendment retrospective effect.[106]

Maharaja Kameshwar Singh, the man who had spearheaded the legal fight against the Bihar Land Reforms Act, accused Nehru of 'sowing the seed of executive despotism' and 'playing with the supremacy of the Constitution for party advantage'.[107] He again reiterated his commitment to zamindari abolition with a fair and uniform rate of compensation and recommended that any such laws be made to conform to the Constitution. 'Let it not be said', he implored the prime minister, 'that the champion of democracy is following dictatorial methods.'[108] Halfway across the world, Kameshwar Singh's sentiments were mirrored by *The New York Times*, which reported that the bill 'imposing severe restrictions on the freedom of speech and expression' was being defended by the prime minister 'in the teeth of almost universal opposition in the country'. 'Nehru is adamant on curbing press' ran the scalding headline.[109]

The prime minister had begun the amending process certain that in light of a Congress majority, the bill would have easy passage. The sharp words from the unofficial leader of the Opposition and the hesitation visible on the treasury benches, combined with the burgeoning tide of criticism in the press, left him troubled and disturbed. 'The Bill for amendment of the Constitution is meeting with a good deal of opposition in the press and elsewhere,' a daunted Nehru wrote to his chief ministers as the day ended. 'We hope to get it through, even though that requires a two-third majority....'[110]

6

The Battle Rages

A Vigorous Defence

On the evening of 15 May 1951, the evening before fireworks began in Parliament, Speaker G. V. Mavalankar wrote to Prime Minister Nehru to express his objections to the proposed amendments. Echoing the critics outside the Congress, Mavalankar thought the amendment ill-timed and unnecessary in the present circumstances. Like the president, he didn't believe there was any pressing need to curb free speech, and even if there was, the amendment must not be pushed through without soliciting a wide range of public opinion. He also found the changes to Article 31 a grave infringement which would effectively deprive the individual of all fundamental rights in relation to property, on which, he argued, most peaceful progress and social reorganization depended.[1]

'We have felt the urgency of having some such amendment because the situation in the zamindari areas is becoming increasingly difficult,' replied Nehru. 'We are on the eve of what might be called a revolutionary situation … It is in our opinion, very important that rapid effect should be given to the Zamindari Abolition Acts.'[2] 'Any attempt to postpone this measure rather indefinitely may well lead to very serious consequences,' he admitted to the Speaker. 'For the Congress it would be fatal, because they would have failed in their primary objectives. I feel therefore that any circulation of the Bill involving long delays would be unjustified and possibly dangerous.'[3] Coming straight from the metaphoric horse's mouth, it was a remarkably candid admission about the cause of the prime minister's frenzied rush towards an amendment, and confirmation of the Opposition's charge that the Constitution was being changed to suit the Congress party. Much like the president, the Speaker ultimately also found his objections curtly brushed aside.

Compared to the Speaker, *Blitz*, the widely read tabloid news magazine published in Bombay and frequently critical of the government (though generally considered progressive and Nehruvian in its outlook),[4] was far more vituperative. Commenting on the amendment, it carried a sensational full-page article titled 'Nehru – Sponsor of Civil Liberties Union 1936 – Destroyer of Our Four Freedoms 1951'.[5] 'There is as much deterioration in the moral fiber of Nehru as there is in the moral strength of the so-called Congress,' it raged. '[T]he sponsor of civil liberties in 1936 has become the sucker of liberties in 1951.'[6]

Of the continuing parliamentary debate over 17 and 18 May, the *Times of India* reported:

> Whatever of the Prime Minister's imperative to Parliament to amend the Constitution survived the incisive logic of criticism yesterday was today well and nigh totally demolished by the formidable tide of argument that flowed from Congressmen and Independents alike, which not one supporter of the Bill was able to adequately answer.'[7]

Despite supportive speeches from Congress leaders like Renuka Ray, Krishna Chandra Sharma and M. P. Mishra – who even contended that there was no need to elicit any public opinion because 'no public opinion can be more weighty than the will of the Members of this Parliament'[8] – Nehru was eviscerated by his opponents, who, according to press reports, 'decimated the force' of his arguments.[9] Such opponents included not only independent members like H. N. Kunzru and Ramnarain Singh and Opposition figures like Hussain Imam, but also – to Nehru's surprise and discomfiture – renegade Congressmen like Deshbandhu Gupta, H. V. Kamath and Syamnandan Sahay.

Kunzru declared that Articles 19 and 31 were not being amended, they were effectively being repealed, and if passed, the new article would extinguish freedom of speech and expression almost entirely.[10] There was only one reason for this extraordinary course of events: the upcoming general election.[11] H. V. Kamath suggested 'that what needed amending was not the Constitution, but the

policies of the Government'. The blanket validation of land reform
legislation and the creation of the Ninth Schedule constituted, in
his opinion, 'nothing short of midsummer madness'.[12] Hussain
Imam described the amendment as 'laying the foundations of an
authoritarian state', and Syamnandan Sahay thought it tragic
that the Constitution was being reduced to the level of ordinary
legislation. Deshbandhu Gupta charged the prime minister with
showing little faith in the people of the country, who, according to
the Preamble to the Constitution of India, more than any Parliament,
had given themselves the Constitution as a charter of freedom.[13]

The government found itself struggling to answer the simplest
questions: if they did not desire to use any of the enabling provisions
of the amendment, then what was the hurry? If the Supreme Court
hadn't pronounced any verdict on zamindari abolition, where was
the need to change the Constitution? Why was the government so
keen to circumscribe freedom of expression? What was the imminent
threat that Nehru kept referring to? Why were they so disinclined to
set a positive example and create exemplary democratic traditions?
Unable to face the heat, the government wheeled out Law Minister
B. R. Ambedkar to mount a vigorous defence.

In a nearly two-hour-long speech, Ambedkar assured the House
that the government did not intend to misuse any of the powers
it was acquiring, and the amendment was only meant to arm
Parliament with the power to pass certain legislation when necessary
rather than enact any specific laws in the immediate future. He
reiterated Nehru's spiel that judicial pronouncements were 'utterly
unsatisfactory' and not in consonance with the Constitution –
especially the invalidation of the Communal GO and the policy
of quotas – and that the government was committed to fulfilling
its obligations as enumerated in the directive principles. New
restrictions on free speech were necessitated by the refusal of the
Supreme Court to interpret into the Constitution the doctrine of
'inherent police powers'[14] like the United States, he argued. In order
to secure itself from threats and fulfil its obligations, he maintained,
it was vital that the Constitution be amended.[15]

Keen critics of the proposed Article 31B, which created the
Ninth Schedule as a constitutional vault for land reform legislation,
Naziruddin Ahmed, Syamnandan Sahay and H. V. Kamath questioned
Ambedkar on the need for such an outrageous constitutional device
to provide blanket protection to bad and possibly unconstitutional

laws. 'Just imagine the amount of burden that would be cast upon myself, on the Law Ministry, the Food and Agriculture Ministry and other Ministries involved if we were to sit here and examine every section of each of these Acts to find out whether they deviate,' came Ambedkar's terse reply.[16] A more graphic revelation of the government's unending search for shortcuts and its apathetic and lackadaisical attitude would have been hard to find.

In his closing speech requesting MPs to refer the bill to the Select Committee, Nehru too spoke with fervour in defence of the amendment to Article 15 and continued to dwell on the confusion caused by the contrary judgments of the Allahabad and Patna High Courts – an obviously disingenuous turn of phrase. 'This business of equality before the law,' he exclaimed,

> ... [is] a dangerous thing ... and it is completely opposed to the whole structure and method of this Constitution and what is laid down in the Directive Principles ... I am not changing the Constitution by an iota ... I am merely giving effect to the real intentions of the framers of the Constitution and the wording of the Constitution.[17]

An overwhelming majority of MPs did in the end vote to send the bill to the Select Committee, with instructions to report back on 23 May. Only two votes were cast against Nehru's motion, demonstrating yet again the prime minister's firm grip on the Congress Parliamentary Party.[18] The measure clearly had the support of a substantial number of Congress MPs. But the ferocity of the debate, the equivocation from several Congressmen – particularly with regard to freedom of speech – and outright hostility from others, also brought home to Nehru that he was in for stormy days ahead, even if Congress MPs remained subservient for the moment.

The dramatic resignation of Acharya Kripalani from the Congress amid the ongoing parliamentary combat heightened this sense of tension.[19] Declaring war on the government, Kripalani announced his intention to bring all Opposition forces into one fold.[20] Some even speculated that another high-profile resignation from Communications Minister Rafi Ahmed Kidwai, a member of Kripalani's dissident Democratic Front, could soon follow. Eventually, no such schism surfaced and Kidwai and other supposedly dissident members remained loyal to Nehru.

When the Congress Parliamentary Party met two days later on 20 May, however, a formal motion to drop the proposed amendment to Article 19 was moved by Deshbandhu Gupta. It was easily defeated.[21] But the fact that it was suggested and voted on at all was an unambiguous indication to the 'high command' that it could not rely blindly on the support of all its MPs, that many of them were getting restive about the assault on the freedom of speech and on the constitutional ideals that they themselves had helped shape. The unceasing criticism was also getting to Nehru. 'I think much of the criticism is misconceived,' he wrote to his chief ministers. 'There is a strange fear in the minds of some that Parliament might misbehave and therefore should not have too much power given to it.'[22] None bothered to tell him that such a robust fear of excessive executive power was the bedrock of liberal democracy.

A twelve-member delegation of the All India Newspaper Editors' Conference (AINEC), led by its president – the same renegade Congress MP Deshbandhu Gupta – also met the prime minister on 20 May to press its demand that the government drop the proposed amendment in the present circumstances or postpone it to a later date so that 'public opinion may be fully elicited on the subject'. The doyens of the press were told by the prime minister that while the government was not prepared to meet either demand, it would nevertheless try to modify the amendment to try and mitigate their concern.[23] Many wondered, was the unrelenting pressure forcing him to soften his stand?

Whether AINEC would be convinced by this softened stand, however, remained open to question. An editor, who had attended AINEC's deliberations prior to its deputation meeting the prime minister, had recorded:

> The feeling against Mr. Nehru ran so high … that some members suggested setting up immediately a 'direct action' committee to prepare a program of effective protest against what was described as the 'high handed' action of the Nehru government. Direct action, if it is decided upon, will take the form of asking all newspapers to launch a country-wide campaign to persuade the people not to vote for Congress and Mr. Nehru.[24]

Could Nehru succeed in conciliating an incandescent fourth estate? Or would India's leading journalists and editors launch an unprecedented electoral campaign? Many within AINEC, it seemed, were now prepared to raise the stakes and lock themselves into an eyeball-to-eyeball confrontation with the government.

The Interlude

From Parliament, the Constitution (First Amendment) Bill now made its way to the Select Committee. Much like Parliament itself, the Select Committee was dominated by the Congress party. Having weathered the torrid debate in the House, Congress members were confident of passing this hurdle with relative ease. Opposition leaders Shyama Prasad Mookerji, H. N. Kunzru, Sardar Hukam Singh,[a] K. T. Shah and Naziruddin Ahmed, who made up a small but vocal and vociferous minority, were equally determined to mount a strenuous defence of fundamental rights and civil liberties. Both supporters and detractors of the bill now waited with breathless anticipation for the Select Committee's report to appear and settled down to a brief interlude.

Meanwhile, outside the corridors of power, the emotionally charged debates in Parliament provoked an ever-growing torrent of adverse opinion. As the committee deliberated on the clauses of the amendment, vehement criticism from pressmen, businesses, lawyers, civil society groups and political figures alike continued to flood the pages of newspapers and the government's undue haste and lack of respect for democratic propriety became a common topic of public discussion.

The Supreme Court Bar Association took the lead by denouncing the amendment and demanding that the executive function within the limits prescribed by the Constitution. Assembled lawyers appealed to all 'public bodies who believe in civil liberties and particularly freedom of speech and expression' to 'mobilize public opinion and express themselves in unequivocal

---

[a]Sardar Hukam Singh (1893–1983) was a politician from Punjab and a member of the Shiromani Akali Dal, a party closely identified with Sikh religious interests. He was elected to the Constituent Assembly in 1948, and to the Lok Sabha in 1952. Later, he switched sides and joined the Congress, becoming Speaker of the Lok Sabha in 1962.

terms'.[25] Following in its footsteps, the Nagpur High Court Bar Association 'passed a resolution expressing its emphatic view that the proposed amendments were improper, unjustified, highly undemocratic and opposed to the fundamental rights of the citizens of India'.[26] Former judges like N. C. Chatterjee of the Calcutta High Court and S. P. Sinha of the Allahabad High Court also inveighed against the measure and gave public statements castigating the government.[27]

The Progressive Group, Bombay – a liberal organization consisting mostly of Muslims and Parsees – challenged the competence of a provisional parliament elected on a limited franchise and opposed any amendment of the Constitution before a general election.[28] The All India Newspaper Editors Conference, unconvinced by Nehru's assurances to its delegation, restated its demand for the complete withdrawal of the proposed amendment to Article 19 and the freedom of speech and expression.[29] The Standing Committee of AINEC 'placed on record its considered opinion that the proposed amendment (was) unwarranted and uncalled for, and hoped that the representations made by the President would persuade the Government to reconsider their attitude'.[30]

Nehru, concerned at the reactions in the press, invited major editors and correspondents – Devadas Gandhi of *Hindustan Times*, Ramnath Goenka of the *Indian Express* and Shiva Rao of *The Hindu* – for a briefing with him.[31] It did little to stem the tide of disapproval. In private correspondence, Deshbandhu Gupta informed the prime minister that his verbal assurances lacked any constitutional validity and, to give concrete form to them, suggested the inclusion of a new clause in the Constitution guaranteeing the freedom of the press – something akin to Article 1 of the American Constitution.[32] 'These wide powers [which the government was appropriating via the amendment]', Gupta maintained, 'were an open invitation to parliamentary majorities to abridge the freedom of the press.'[33] Nehru promptly rejected Gupta's suggestions out of hand.

In Kanpur, the tremendously well-respected elder statesman Sir Jwala Prasad Srivastava, former Cabinet minister, former member of the Viceroy's Executive Council and former member of the original Constituent Assembly, stated that the proposed amendments 'were ill-timed, inept and ill-advised' and warned that they 'sought to take away the guarantees in the Constitution'.[34] An interesting aside: Srivastava's son-in-law Minocher 'Minoo' Masani would one day found the Swatantra Party and become one of Nehru's fiercest critics, leading the liberal fightback against Congress dominance.

Within the fourth estate, reactions to an amendment that placed 'the press literally at the mercy of bureaucratic whims'[35] were universally condemnatory and vituperative, with open declarations that the 'press will and must organize its resources to fight this encroachment on fundamental freedoms'.[36]

One writer railed:

> Public order is the foundation of a stable state. But to empower governments with the expansive right to abridge freedom of expression in matters pertaining to public order is surely to strike at the roots of democratic rule and life … Tomorrow a communist government under cover of the proposed amendment to restrict free comment on foreign affairs might dragoon the press into bowing to the behests of the Kremlin … In the name of public order a dictatorial administration … may scotch all opposition to itself by a blanket ban on criticism against the Government on the ground that this is likely to undermine public order. These are the dangers to democracy and democratic rule inherent in the new amendments.[37]

'The whirling of time has indeed brought forth its revenges', mused another senior commentator.

> Those who in former times championed most vociferously freedom of speech and expression, having now settled down in the seats of power, see no incongruity in themselves proposing to impose more rigid restrictions upon them. Clearly they show no understanding of the nature of freedom.[38]

'If further restrictions are to be imposed,' he asked the government,

> [it] must surely be shown that because of the absence of these restrictions our friendly relations with foreign governments have been imperilled, public order has been endangered and there has been widespread incitement to offences. So far as one can make out from the debates, there has been no attempt to show that throughout the country conditions have been such as to

necessitate these changes. All we find is mention of a few judicial pronouncements – occasionally even judicial *obiter dicta* – from which it is argued that the changes are necessary.[39]

Without the amendments of Articles 15 and 31, 'certain inconveniences will undoubtedly be caused to the party in power, certain policies sponsored by the party will not show all the results expected from them, and this may cause the electorate in certain areas to be not too enthusiastic in its support,' he argued. 'But surely these furnish no reasons for forcing through fundamental changes'.[40]

The legal correspondent for the *Times of India* accused Law Minister Ambedkar of trying to be too clever by half in censuring the Supreme Court for refusing to support his doctrine of 'implied police powers' and published long extracts of his speeches to the Constituent Assembly in 1948 to demonstrate how he had gone back on his own claims. In 1948, Ambedkar had categorically asserted before the Constituent Assembly that instead of formulating fundamental rights in absolute terms and depending on the Supreme Court to invent the doctrine of 'police powers' and read limitations into them (as happened in the United States), they were going to directly write such restrictions into the Constitution itself, forestalling the need or the ability of the Supreme Court to invent any doctrines. Having made such a statement in the Constituent Assembly, in the correspondent's opinion, for the law minister to now demand 'implied police powers' was nothing short of dishonesty.[41]

'In supporting the Constitution (First Amendment) Bill the prime minister stated, inter alia, "it was not to be used by the present Government but will be handed down as a legacy to future parliaments,"' wrote an irate citizen from Bombay in a letter to a major newspaper. 'Then what is the necessity of introducing it in the present Parliament? If, as Mr Nehru admits, "nothing could be static or unchanging" and the situation may alter radically, it is hardly fair to act presumptuously towards the next Parliament.'[42]

The spate of criticism and adverse opinion, incessant and implacable, momentarily shook the prime minister. Within the Select Committee, he came under increasing pressure on the issue of freedom of speech and expression, on which a growing number of Congressmen disagreed with him. Many supporters pressed him to include the phrase 'reasonable restrictions' to allow any of the restrictions placed to be justiciable rather than grant the government blanket and arbitrary powers to curb free speech and completely exclude any possibility of judicial review. Nehru, who self-confessedly wanted to circumscribe the judiciary's power and show the judges their place in the pecking order,[43] recoiled at this advice.

'I confess I do not like the word "restriction" or "reasonable" added to it,' he wrote to T. T. Krishnamachari, Congress MP from Madras and former member of the Drafting Committee in the Constituent Assembly.

> So far as I can see, the courts have always had the right to consider any legislation .... It is true that if this amendment is passed, they will be somewhat restricted in their interpretation. But I feel that putting in the word 'reasonable' would be an invitation for every such case to go to the courts with ensuing uncertainty.[44]

In the prime minister's own words, he did not want the restrictions on the freedom of speech to need to pass any test of reasonableness. He wanted to exclude the courts from adjudicating on them altogether. The word or the idea of restrictions may not have appealed to him very much, but the idea of them being reasonable appealed to him even less. It was a strangely contradictory position to take: to dislike restrictions but want them to be overarching and non-justiciable when written into the Constitution. Between the fundamental rights of the country's citizens and the prime minister's single-minded devotion to remaking India in his own image, the latter was the undeniable victor.

Resistance, Rebellion and Sleight of Hand

The Select Committee finished its deliberations on the evening of 22 May 1951. By Nehru's own account, Opposition figures forced extensive discussions on every single issue, often compelling the committee to meet both in the morning and in the afternoon to complete its work. Article 19 and the freedom of speech remained a major bone of contention. 'I feel quite exhausted,' the prime minister confessed at the end of four days of deliberations.[45]

Outside, the storm of criticism refused to abate. Under fire from the press, the commentariat and the Opposition, large numbers of Congress MPs began to vacillate on the extent of their support for Nehru's line, particularly the attack on Article 19. When the Congress Parliamentary Party met on 23 May to take stock of the situation, the prime minister was presented with a petition signed by seventy-seven MPs asking for a free vote when the amendment was discussed in Parliament.[46] Nehru was taken aback by the move and surprised by the rapid slide in support. From a near-unanimous majority in favour of the amendment to Article 19 in the meeting on 20 May to the demand for a free vote on 23 May, the deterioration in the party's mood was swift and, for Nehru, dangerous.

The prime minister sensed the precariousness of the situation. The party might have been in his thrall and there may not have been any open rebellion, but there were enough doubters and dissidents to deny him his victory over the Constitution if he did not moderate his stand. By the time the Union Cabinet met in the evening, Nehru was already under significant pressure from rebellious MPs and probably mulling his options. Within the Cabinet, several ministers now started to insist that the word 'reasonable' be included in the amending bill to safeguard judicial oversight of restrictions on fundamental rights. Many perhaps realized that without it, the amendment constituted a near-existential threat to Part III of the Constitution. Support for Nehru's draconian vision of emasculating the courts was now fading at an alarming rate.

The surprising turn of events shocked the prime minister and convinced him of the need to pedal back. It brought home the limits to which both the Cabinet and the Congress Parliamentary Party were willing to obey his diktats. Hemmed in on the issue, Nehru conceded ground and accepted the inclusion of the word 'reasonable' in order to prevent a split in the Cabinet and ensure that there were fewer avenues for internal dissent when trying to muster a two-thirds majority.[47] 'The cabinet is understood to have decided to meet the mounting criticism against the proposed amendment to Article 19(2) of the Constitution, relating to "restrictions" on the freedom of speech and expression by accepting a modification that will render it justiciable,' reported a correspondent. 'The clause in question is to be amended by limiting to "reasonable restrictions" the proposed unfettered right of the State to impose restrictions in the interests of public order and maintaining friendly relations with foreign states.'[48]

It was a very limited concession, extracted much against the prime minister's own will and volition. But it served to dilute the absolute worst part of the proposed amendment and placate the agitated members of the Cabinet. Whatever restrictions the government might legislate on the right to freedom of speech, they would have to submit to a judicial determination of their reasonableness. The unrestrained ability of the state to curtail fundamental rights, the most extreme of Nehru's ideas, was negated. Unbeknownst to the participants in that momentous Cabinet meeting, their rearguard action had just warded off one of the gravest threats the Constitution ever faced, or was likely to face in the future. A handful of doubters and dissenters, having built up the conviction to stand up to a larger-than-life prime minister that towered over them in the public eye, had just saved the foundations of Indian democracy and its constitutional order.

Whether the concession would be enough to mollify restive Congress parliamentarians, of course, was another question altogether. The sobering experiences of 23 May left Nehru unsettled and disturbed. Could he rely on his MPs to fall in line behind him as in the past? Suddenly he was not so sure. 'You can have no idea whatever of the tremendous difficulties we have had with this Bill and we are not out of the woods yet,' he confided to West Bengal Chief Minister Bidhan Chandra Roy. 'Till the last moment I shall not know whether we can have the requisite two-thirds number for passing these clauses.'[49]

While the effects of the concession on the Congress Parliamentary Party remained a matter of conjecture, it distinctly failed to impress the doyens of the press. Now decidedly nervous, the All India Newspaper Editors Conference resolved to hold a special plenary session 'to consider the steps which should be taken to protect the liberties of the press now threatened by the proposed amendment to Article 19(2) of the Constitution'.[50] In an attempt to embarrass Nehru into reconsidering his stance, correspondence between Deshbandhu Gupta and the prime minister was made public. It had little effect.

On the question of reservations and Article 15, however, there was much more consensus within the Cabinet. Insistent requests had continued to pour in from Madras arguing that the proposed alteration of Article 15 was insufficient to protect reservations for the backward classes and 'hence a new clause should be added to the article to the effect that nothing in the article or in Article 29(2) should prevent special provisions for the educational, economic, and social advancement of the backward classes'.[51] Cabinet ministers, and Congress members in the Select Committee, accepted this demand to bring Article 29 – which prohibited discrimination in admissions to schools and colleges – into the ambit of the amending bill. They were now of the view 'that this provision is not likely to be, and indeed cannot be, misused by any government for perpetuating any class discrimination against the spirit of the Constitution, or for treating non-backward classes as backward for the purpose of conferring privileges on them'.[52]

In a new twist, they also recommended that all references to 'economic' and 'economically' be dropped and the language be limited to 'socially and educationally backward classes'.[53] Through this sleight of hand, the Cabinet sought to achieve two objectives. First, it would remove any prospect of economic criteria coming in the way of calculating the backwardness of a class based on their 'social and educational' standing. Second, it would pre-empt and negate any demands for special provisions or reservations for those who could be termed economically backward without the corresponding status of social or educational backwardness. In other words, they wanted to acquire the power to legislate for caste- and community-based reservations – what the Constitution scholar Granville Austin called 'compensatory discrimination'[54] – while preventing the creation of any affirmative action mechanisms based on economic criteria.

The exclusion of economic backwardness from the ambit of India's reservation and affirmative action policies – either as a test for community-based reservations or as a criterion in and of its own accord – would open up a new political fault line that has endured to this day. Today, the debate around this fault line is expressed either in terms of demands for reservation for 'economically weaker sections' among the forward castes or demands for exclusion of the 'creamy layer' in reservations for Other Backward Classes. But few recall just where the race to social backwardness first began. Much before V. P. Singh and Mandal in 1990, much before the ninety-third amendment and Arjun Singh in 2006, it was in this dimly remembered Cabinet meeting that the constitutional groundwork for this debate was first laid.

President Rajendra Prasad, who had been keeping a close eye on proceedings as the debate raged in Parliament and outside, now made a final, eleventh-hour effort to persuade the government to

abandon the reckless course it had set itself on. In a note to the prime
minister, Prasad reminded him of his view that the amendment was
'premature and uncalled for', and of the need to lead by example
by establishing good conventions.[55] He again cautioned Nehru
against an attempt to overrule judicial pronouncements through
a constitutional amendment, admonishing him that it would raise
fundamental issues related to the separate functions of the legislature
and the judiciary.[56] Nehru, already irritated by what he thought was
Rajendra Prasad's propensity to exceed his brief, was incensed.

'As you are aware, the Bill for the amendment of the Constitution
has been discussed with great thoroughness both in Parliament and
the Select Committee, as well as in the Press and by the outside
public,' came the prime minister's terse response to the substance of
the president's objections.

> Before the Bill took shape, the matter was considered by a sub-
> committee of the Cabinet and a committee appointed by the
> Congress party in the Parliament. The two committees held
> consultations together. We consulted also eminent lawyers,
> including the Attorney-General and Shri Alladi Krishnaswamy
> Aiyyar. Both of them were clearly of the opinion that it was
> within the competence of Parliament to consider and pass this
> measure ... After this very full consideration of this subject
> from every point of view, the Cabinet have come to certain firm
> conclusions, which are now embodied in the Select Committee's
> report ... The Government is convinced of the necessity as well
> as the validity of the amendments proposed.[57]

'It would be exceedingly unfortunate if the public became aware
that the President held a contrary opinion to that of the Cabinet
in such a matter and was pressing for its adoption by the Cabinet,'
he reprimanded Rajendra Prasad. 'I shall certainly place your note
before the Cabinet as desired by you ... I do not propose to circulate
this for fear of leakage and undesirable publicity. I trust also that
your office has not sent copies of this note to anyone else.[58]

For the second time, the president of the republic found his advice
spurned and his views treated as unworthy of serious consideration.
Committed to the constitutional order and the maintenance of
decorum, Rajendra Prasad, despite his strong feelings on the matter,
followed Nehru's advice and scrupulously avoided publicizing his
opposition.

'Not Enough'

On 25 May 1951, the new draft of the Constitution (First Amendment) Bill emerged from the Select Committee. Along with the draft, the report from the Select Committee was submitted to Parliament the same morning. After several days of intense deliberations, the twenty-one members produced an eighteen-page-long report.[59] Recommendations from the committee took two pages; scathing minutes of dissent by Opposition members filled sixteen. As the press prominently noted, 'All the five non-Congress members of the committee recorded minutes of dissent, some of them including Dr Shyama Prasad Mookerjee and Pandit Hriday Nath Kunzru doubting the very advisability of amending the Constitution in such haste after it had been in operation for only sixteen months.'[60]

In his minute of dissent, S. P. Mookerji strongly questioned the need for any further restrictions on the freedom of speech and expression, cautioned against undermining the independence of the judiciary and issued a warning about the potentially dangerous implications of retrospective legislation.[61] 'The onus of proving the need for changes has not been satisfactorily discharged,' he argued. 'The main reason advanced was that the judiciary had pronounced its opinion on certain laws which were disfavoured by the government.' 'The existing restrictions on the right to free speech and expression were more than sufficiently restrictive and there should be no fresh additions to these restrictions,' he urged, and 'the word public order must be subject to the "clear and present danger" test, namely that the substantive evil must be extremely serious and the degree of imminence extremely high.'[62] 'Nothing has as yet happened to justify the taking away of the jurisdiction of the judiciary in this sweeping manner,' he wrote, castigating the government for its scramble to amend Article 31 and create a schedule of unconstitutional laws.[63] 'Instead of amending the lawless laws and making their provisions consistent with fundamental rights, the Government are following a strange procedure of adhering to such reactionary laws and changing the fundamental rights.'[64]

'If we have a written Constitution and Fundamental Rights, as indeed we have solemnly and deliberately chosen to have,' Mookerji sagely observed, 'we have to abide by their provisions. No government can brush them aside or hurriedly seek their alterations simply on the plea that judicial interpretations and decisions are not to its liking.'[65]

'Restrictions like the pre-censorship of news and the banning of the entry of a newspaper into a state were imposed during the war under the Defence of India Rules,' read the excoriating observations of H. N. Kunzru, challenging the Congress to explain 'why the Government in a free India should be allowed to exercise such powers as were not exercised even during the British regime in peacetime'.[66] Turning his attention to the revalidation of Sections 124A and 153A of the Indian Penal Code – sedition and causing enmity between groups respectively – Kunzru wrote: 'The history of Section 124A is well known. It was passed in its present form in 1818 to curb the activities of Indian patriots ... Now that India is free, it should find no place in a statute book in its existing form.'[67]

K. T. Shah, Sardar Hukam Singh and Naziruddin Ahmed produced a joint minute of dissent asserting their opinion 'that the experience gained under the Constitution was insufficient to justify an amendment, they did not have the texts of the laws to be validated [laws that would be placed in the Ninth Schedule] and there was no evidence at all to justify this wholly gratuitous and unwarranted restriction on civil liberties'.[68] 'We have grave doubts and misgivings as to the wisdom, propriety and justification of the Bill,' the trio concluded, flagging their reluctance to support the government's invasion of individual freedom and its failure to enact legislation in conformity with the Constitution.[69]

We must therefore record our conviction that there is neither foundation nor justification adduced by the sponsors of this measure for attempting to effect such radical changes in our Fundamental Rights, limiting, if not denying, them in material particulars ... we find that the individual clauses of the Bill offend against our basic convictions ... there is no justification for thus limiting the most important of the civil liberties, characteristic of a modern, progressive, free democracy.[70]

Unlike many of the amendment's other critics, K. T. Shah, Hukam Singh and Naziruddin Ahmed also chose to place on record their objection to caste- and community-based reservations. 'The clause [amendment to Article 15] ... leaves out economic considerations and speaks of "educationally and socially backward classes", which would needlessly rivet attention upon one of the most deplorable features of our social system,' the trio contended. 'We consider that to be ... incompatible with the letter and spirit of the Constitution.'[71]

In the new democratic republic, however, the views of the Opposition, no matter how well reasoned or how well intentioned, counted for little in the eyes of the country's new regime. Opposition leaders, much like the president and the Speaker, found themselves sidelined and their views treated with indifference and scorn. This was to become a norm. In this Nehruvia India, 'there were numeroud committees and consultation was frequent,' wrote Sarvepalli Gopal, '... the deficiency was in spirit and animation'.[72]

If ever more evidence was needed, the Select Committee report convincingly demonstrated the complete and utter lack of consensus on the matter and the absence of any respect for the Opposition's views. There was little doubt left that the amendment of the Constitution was a Congress project driven by the prime minister with no support from Opposition figures – not even from those who conceded the principles of land reform and affirmative action.

Despite the passionate arguments put forward by Opposition figures, the majority of the Select Committee felt otherwise. Fervent appeals to Nehru's sense of democratic propriety and the need for the 'provisional parliament' to show moral uprightness by waiting for a general election fell on deaf ears – all warnings that a dangerous precedent was being created went unheeded. The only major changes the committee recommended were the use of the word 'reasonable' before restrictions to make justiciable any legislation on the subject in respect of Article 19, a limitation of the language to 'socially and educationally backward' and the removal of all reference to economic backwardness, and the inclusion of Article 29(2) within the ambit of the qualification to be added to Article 15. In all other respects, including the alteration of Article 31 and the creation of the hugely controversial Ninth Schedule, the committee ignored the intense resistance of the Opposition and placed its stamp of approval on the bill drafted by the government.

Newspapers had been optimistically speculating on the concessions that Nehru might agree to in a bid to propitiate his critics and assuage his restive MPs. The recommendations of the Select Committee left them disappointed and angry. 'Except for a grudging concession to the press and certain other modifications for elucidating other provisions the Bill to amend the Constitution has emerged unscathed from the 21 member Select Committee,' lamented a report in a major newspaper.[73] Having ruminated on the changes suggested by the committee for several days, another correspondent reaffirmed the stand of the press by stating that 'the so-called concessions to popular demand are no adequate substitutes for existing safeguards'.[74]

In a muscular editorial evocatively titled 'Not Enough', the *Times of India* contended that phrases such as 'reasonable restrictions', meant to be safeguards against the heavy hand of the government 'can at best constitute only a partial check on the executive's abuse of powers. Experience shows that terms such as "reasonable compensation" can carry a multitude of meanings. Moreover, those who may be victims of the new repressive laws are not always likely to have the means to seek legal redress.'[75] 'A more pernicious feature of the new amendment is that the scope of the permitted restrictions remains as wide as the original draft,' raged the writer. 'As for the new restrictions allowed in the sacred name of public order, these can only help unscrupulous regimes to identify their own safety with the "security of the state" and to stifle all organized protest.'[76]

'Why are "economically backward" people less deserving of help than "socially and educationally backward classes"?' the editorial fumed. 'As for securing special rights for Backward Classes, Clause 4 of Article 15 as redrafted does not prevent the treating of non-Backward Classes as Backward for the purpose of privileges on them.'[77] Positively seething, the writer of the editorial warned Nehru: 'At the root of democratic progress is the belief that the heterodoxies of today may become the orthodoxies of tomorrow and that the opposition of today may in the course of time achieve the majesty of government.'[78] It was a warning that was apocalyptic and oracular in equal measure. Nearly seventy years on, facing the full force of the amendment, the Congress party, Nehru's ideological descendants and co-travellers and the one-time cheerleaders of the Nehruvian offensive, live on to testify to the veracity of the unknown writer's prophetic warning.

Nevertheless, at that moment in May 1951, so far-fetched did the possibility of the Opposition achieving the majesty of government seem that none bothered to take it seriously. Small in number, limited in electoral appeal and lacking any party organization, the threat of the Opposition one day using Nehru's own stick to beat him with carried near-negligible weight as a deterrent. But what the

Opposition lacked in numbers and electoral appeal, it made up for in its strength of purpose and its dedication to the defence of the Constitution. Having failed to convince the government to heed their opinions in the Select Committee, Opposition leaders now prepared to make a last-ditch stand in Parliament.

'The Opposition' noted one journalist,

> [M]ay be numerically small in view of a strong Congress Party whip, and many doubters have certainly been satisfied by the change rendering justiciable the restrictions that might be imposed on freedom of speech and expression. But for all that, the Opposition will be intense and will probably be speaking for more than those who might care to walk out of the 'noes' lobby ... Members of the former Democratic Front [Kripalani's group of dissident Congressmen] have taken counsel together on this measure ... they are expected to oppose tooth and nail the very principle of a constitutional amendment at this stage.[79]

As the amendment bill and the debate around it moved inexorably towards a conclusion, Opposition figures from across the political spectrum, few and far between as they were, now braced themselves and prepared for a fateful parliamentary confrontation. Much like the warriors of yore, woefully outnumbered and comprehensively outgunned, these intrepid defenders of constitutional freedoms unsheathed their verbal swords and rode out to battle.

Parliamentary Encounter IV: Storm over Parliament

The battle was joined on 29 May 1951, as Prime Minister Nehru moved the bill as amended by the Select Committee for Parliament's consideration. Even before Nehru began speaking, he was interrupted by H. V. Kamath objecting to the 'vitiated' proceedings in the Select Committee.[80] He was quickly shouted down by the Speaker to allow Nehru to begin proceedings. The mood was sombre – this time, there would be no niceties.

'We live in a haunted age,' Nehru informed his colleagues.

I do not know how many members have this sense ... of ghosts and apparitions surrounding us, ideas, passions, hatred, violence, preparations for war, many things you cannot grip, nevertheless which are more dangerous than other things ... Hon. Members tell me that this Constitution has been in existence for sixteen months. Can any member tell me what the fate of the world will be in another sixteen months?[81]

The apocalyptic imagery was fitting.

In his seventy-minute address, the prime minister justified the amendments to Article 19 by vague allusions to a grave danger to the state and repeated the allegation that fundamental rights were now an obsolete idea. The addition of the word 'reasonable' made anything done under the Act patently justiciable, he continued, admitting that they had avoided using that word earlier 'to avoid an excess of litigation about every matter, everything being held up and hundreds, maybe thousands, of references constantly made by odd individuals or odd groups thereby holding up the work of the state'.[82]

The brazen admission by the prime minister that he considered individuals fighting for their constitutional rights to be odd and had wanted to prevent them from knocking on the doors of the judiciary provoked an indignant reaction from H. V. Kamath about the sacrosanct nature of fundamental rights. Nehru remained unfazed. 'I wish the House would be clear about this and realize the times we live in,' he sneered, 'in this country and other countries, and not to quote so much some ancient script or ancient thing that was said at the time of the French Revolution or the American Revolution. Many things have happened since then.'[83]

'It is not merely a question of what words you put in the Constitution' he glowered.

It is a question of dealing with the situation ... of saving the country from going to pieces, as some people want and try to make it ... Are we going to fight it with these words, to be told that this word comes in the way and that word prevents you from doing this? No word will be allowed to come in the way because the country demands it ... Do you think any Constitution will prevent me from dealing with such a situation? No. Otherwise the whole Constitution goes ... I want to be perfectly clear in declaring that

if I am responsible and this Government is responsible, anything
that goes towards disrupting the community ... will be met with
the heavy hand of the Government. There has been enough loose
talk about this. It is for this country and this House to have
or not to have this Government. But these are the terms of this
Government, no other terms.[84]

If the exposition of his repressive and near absolutist vision for
the new republic needed further elaboration, Nehru proceeded
to delineate it while giving the press a piece of his mind. 'I know
something of the press, and I have been connected with the Press
too somewhat, and can understand their apprehensions,' he insisted.

Yet I say that what they have said is entirely unfair to this
Government. And I say that the Press, if it wants that freedom –
which it ought to have – must also have some balance of mind
which it seldom possesses. They cannot have it both ways –
no balance and freedom. Every freedom in the world is limited.[85]

As for why the government had included relations with foreign
states as a ground to restrict fundamental rights, Nehru's reasoning
was equally outlandish. He only wanted to cover incitement to
war and defamation of foreign heads of state, he claimed, but it
was phrased to say friendly relations with foreign states because it
was a friendly way of saying this and nice from the literary point
of view.[86] Exactly what amounted to a danger to friendly relations
with foreign states, as usual, Nehru declined to specify. None
bothered to point out that constitutional provisions were unlikely
to be judged on literary merit. But the grim prognosis of the heavy
hand of government and the limits of freedom evoked lusty cheers
from Congress MPs.[87]

The prime minister mounted a spirited defence of the amendment
to Article 15, which, he contended, had been necessitated by the
events in Madras. 'The argument of the Courts was valid from one
point of view,' he insisted, 'namely that communities as such could
not be discriminated against. But for a variety of historical reasons,
all manner of socially, educationally and economically backward
classes existed and in order to encourage their progress "something
special" had to be done for them.'[88]

'Some apprehensions had been expressed that this amendment might be used to perpetuate class discrimination,' reported an eyewitness, 'but Mr Nehru assured the House, this power would not be misused.'[89] Some critics such as K. T. Shah and H. V. Kamath had pointed out that 80 per cent of the people were backward in those terms, regardless of their caste or community. Any special provisions should thus cater for all of them. 'It is no good saying that,' Nehru replied disdainfully.

Much of this was, of course, a reiteration of what the prime minister had previously argued – an elaboration of his views and an outline of his perspective on democracy. They were the standard tropes: the Constitution needed to be flexible and follow the curves of life; it could not be allowed to ossify around ancient slogans from the French Revolution and archaic ideas about fundamental rights; the press and his critics were out of control and needed to be disciplined; the Constitution could not be allowed to come in the way of the Congress manifesto; the judiciary was overreaching itself by preventing the government from ignoring the Constitution and doing whatever it wanted to, which of course was obviously for the security of the nation. It was the most articulate depiction of the premises that underpinned Nehru's conception of the democratic state, premises that progressively became principles of the new post-colonial order.

Opposition leaders K. T. Shah and Naziruddin Ahmed, who were the next to speak, both ripped into Nehru's contention. 'Prof. K. T. Shah threw ridicule on this (the PM's) argument by stating that the Constitution already made adequate provision for grave emergencies,' reported a newspaper. 'By a declaration of emergency, the President could suspend the entire Constitution and Government would be armed with unfettered power to take any measure that might be necessary.'[90] Naziruddin Ahmed maintained that if any laws had been invalidated,

the fault lay not with the Courts, which had interpreted the Constitution correctly, but with the Government, who had failed to adapt such laws as was enjoined upon them by Article 372 of the Constitution ... (much) as the British Government had adapted a whole series of enactments to the 1935 Act by a single consolidated measure.[91]

The gods now decided it was their turn to communicate their displeasure. Claps of thunder rolled across the sky. As Naziruddin Ahmed savaged the amending bill, a sudden thunderstorm broke over the national capital. 'The gale and accompanying thunder showers came upon New Delhi so suddenly,' reported the *Times of India*, that even before windows and skylights could be closed, many MPs on the Congress benches were drenched in the rain. On a more portentous note, power went out and the lighting inside Parliament failed, plunging the chamber into gloom.

The darkness was an unmistakable omen for the new republic, a moment of delicious irony. 'Freedom of Speech is being taken away,' remarked H. V. Kamath to general guffaws, 'and there is a storm over it.'[92]

Parliamentary Encounter V: No Holds Barred

As the debate over taking the bill into consideration played out over 30 and 31 May, Parliament witnessed a fierce war of words on the subject as a spirited Opposition continued to confront the government. 'As an obvious result of yesterday's party whip, Congress members abandoned all criticism in the House and this only brought into sharp relief whatever opposition came from independent members,' noted *The Statesman*.[93] Having weathered tremendous criticism, several proponents of the amendment were pressed into service to give speeches supporting the government's stand. Yet, even here, support was either lukewarm or often driven by ulterior motives or general frustration.

Reverend Jerome D'Souza, Congressman and Jesuit priest, was enthusiastic about the restoration of the Madras Communal GO because it was impossible to overlook the fact of backwardness, but he was more concerned with extending caste-based reservations for Christians so that socially backward classes could freely convert to Christianity without losing their backward status. He wanted race and culture as well as caste and community to be recognized to determine such backwardness, but insisted that religious differences should be ignored,[94] presaging the modern demand for recognition of Scheduled Caste and Backward Class Christians. As for freedom of speech as given and practised in England, he professed his condescending belief that since Indians did not possess the 'phlegmatic' English character distinguished by its stolidity and balance, it was necessary to restrain the organs of public opinion.[95] The statement was greeted by widespread cheering across the treasury benches.[96]

The famous Anglo-Indian educationist Frank Anthony,[b] venting his frustration over the conundrum the bill represented, declared that he was not 'prepared to accept the argument that these amendments are only an amplification, a clarification ... They are a revolutionary, radical change in the original Article 19(2).'[97] 'The only way to stop the inevitable, ultimate dictatorship, communist dictatorship is a dictatorship of Jawaharlal Nehru,' he lamented. 'But because I believe that a dictatorship today is the only way to prevent a later dictatorship, I am prepared to give blanket powers to Jawaharlal Nehru. That is my only reason for supporting these amendments completely.'[98] He continued with his complaint:

> Our leaders are incapable of thinking and practising in terms of democracy. The British occupation taught us ... respect for the forms and trappings of democracy but the spirit and content of democracy have escaped the people and they have escaped our leaders ... If the Constitution is largely dead, if it is largely still-born, why worry about making an excision?[99]

On the Opposition side, the charge was led by Shyama Prasad Mookerji and Acharya Kripalani.

Mookerji reminded the House that they had deliberately chosen a written Constitution incorporating a chapter on fundamental rights. They could well have decided not to create a chapter on fundamental rights in writing, but having done so, they necessarily had to admit the corollary that their powers to legislate on such matters were limited by the Constitution they themselves had

---

[b]Frank Anthony (1908–1993) was an Anglo-Indian lawyer and educationist. An alumnus of the Inner Temple, he was a member of the Central Legislative Assembly from 1942 to 1946 and a member of the Constituent Assembly from 1946 to 1950. He was instrumental in negotiating two reserved seats in Parliament for Anglo-Indians, to be nominated by the president.

created. Fundamental rights 'were so many checks on the hasty and tyrannical action of the majority and served to protect the liberty of individuals and minorities,' he stressed. 'And if fundamental rights were enumerated in writing, that was in order to withdraw them from the arena of political controversy.'[100] 'You cannot pass or amend a Constitution to fight with ghosts,' he warned Nehru, likening him to the Prince of Denmark fighting imaginary troubles in Shakespeare's *Hamlet*.[101]

In spite of the opponents of the bill being in a minority, Mookerji argued vehemently against the revalidation of repressive laws originally created to stifle Indian freedom under colonial rule, warning that they were 'sounding the death-knell of democracy'.[102] 'We are giving more powers to Parliament to enact more laws restricting freedom,' he censured his colleagues. 'I submit that this is a completely wrong approach to the problem.' 'But in any case,' he remonstrated with the government,

'the power which you are now taking is not power which is necessary for any emergency that has arisen in the country, but for perpetuating certain lawless laws which our British masters had forged for the purpose of curbing freedom in India. That is what we are doing.'[103]

'Let me exhort and conjure you never to suffer an invasion of your political constitution, however minute the instance may appear, to pass by without a determined persevering resistance,' he fervently entreated the House, quoting the *Letters of Junius*, a tranche of open letters written by an anonymous eighteenth-century British polemicist critical of King George III. 'They soon accumulate and constitute law. What yesterday was fact, today is doctrine.'[104]

Acharya Kripalani, veteran Gandhian, erstwhile Congress president and a leading light of the struggle for independence, was vitriolic in upbraiding the government. The country was pledged to zamindari abolition, he argued, and the population's views on the subject were well known. It was perfectly reasonable to change the Constitution to effect this, 'but the country was also solemnly pledged to the freedom of speech and expression, especially in light of the restrictions imposed on these freedoms by an alien government. Yet these freedoms were now to be abridged.'[105] Public order and incitement to offence were undefinable terms, the Acharya opined. *Satyagraha* was an offence, all processions and demonstrations disturbed public order. Were all these to be stopped by using the might of the state against its own citizens?[106]

There were no replies. Kripalani, one of Gandhi's most ardent disciples, spoke slowly and with a bite to his voice, relishing the opportunity to take his former party apart. Sidelined, ignored and humiliated by his one-time colleagues, he now laid into them with bitter acerbity. The chamber, which had emptied out as Congress leaders dutifully extolled the virtues of the amendment, rapidly began to fill as Kripalani continued.[107] 'It is superfluous to speak at this stage. Government seem to have made up their mind and they have a solid majority behind them; whatever is proposed will be carried out,' he acknowledged with unsentimental frankness. 'But sometimes, it becomes one's duty to raise a voice of protest when things that we never imagined before are done.'[108]

'We are accused of being idol worshippers,' he claimed. 'By whom are we accused? I am sure the greatest beneficiary of this idol worship is our Prime Minister and also, may I add, his government. But for this idol worship this government would have fallen at least twenty times during the course of the last three years.'[109] 'I know from experience that when people who are weak are given power, they use their power to their own injury,' he apprised the prime minister, his voice gleaming with glacial sarcasm.

> A government that cannot dismiss a peon in office wants to clothe itself with extraordinary powers! I submit, these extraordinary powers will be used to your injury; and who will use them? It will be they that will come after you. You are not going to be eternal. No government is going to be eternal .... More power will only injure you. So please be satisfied with limited power, because your capacity is very limited indeed.[110]

* * *

Meanwhile, outside Parliament, political observers, commentators and ordinary citizens alike continued to fulminate against the government and the prime minister. 'Mr Nehru's apologia for the Constitution Amendment Bill as it emerged from the Select Committee fails to convince,' wrote the *Times of India*. '... [T]he prime minister urged that a Constitution has to be flexible and move with and adapt itself to the curves of life. If Governmental reactions to the Constitution could be traced in a graph, they would be more curvaceous than a scenic railway.' 'We might be living in the arid days of the tired thirties,' it snidely remarked, 'when foreign bureaucrats spoke thus to the representatives of the people.'[111]

Another commentator tartly observed:

> How can we have a straight, stiff, stable constitution, eternally hugging the dead distant slogans of obsolete revolutions – Liberty, Equality, Fraternity, Justice – the crude claptrap with which politicians create imaginary utopias? ... It is good to be reminded now and then in the midst of canting moral and political platitudes that our life and the Constitution which moulds it are of such insubstantial and delusive stuff.[112]

'Though in the interests of the Fundamental Rights, the Constitution itself cannot be taken as sacrosanct,' reasoned an angry citizen in a letter to a newspaper, 'legislation by a constant clash with the Constitution should not render it chimerical by passing amendments to suit the purposes of the administration. Any attempt to recast the Constitution with the needs of the Government would be a mockery of democracy.'[113] In Lucknow, the socialist leader Jayaprakash Narayan, who had spent much of the year targeting the Government of India for its dictatorial tendencies and holding Nehru personally responsible for them, gave a long statement outlining his views:

> It is a great tragedy that in a single-party Parliament the ruling party should take advantage of its majority to tamper even with Fundamental Rights. The very purpose of defining the Fundamental Rights in the Constitution is to place them beyond the interference of parliamentary majorities. Pandit Nehru's repeated reference to the security of the State was itself a pointer to a grave danger that has been created for the future of Indian democracy. Except those in power, no one else in the country seems to be aware of any threat to the security of the State and yet these crippling amendments are sought to be made in the name of this danger.[114]

Inside Parliament, however, an unruffled Prime Minister Nehru continued to rail against the press, its descent into 'obscenity and vulgarity applied to politics' and 'the whole nature of the development of mechanical civilisation', due to which the mind of the people was becoming mechanized.[115] He was ashamed to see the cartoons that were printed in the newspapers, he denounced their degradation of public life and fretted about the effects of such 'freedom of speech' on the morale of poor villagers and soldiers. He even raged about the low quality of human beings in India. He was thinking neither of the press nor of the upcoming election when he brought this amendment, he piously affirmed, and repeatedly asked his colleagues to trust his words.[116]

Given his own views as previously expressed both in his private correspondence and in his public statements, many of these pious affirmations were little short of outright lies. Neither Nehru nor his colleagues cared. Such moral edicts had already been consumed in the fiery birth of the post-colonial order.

On 31 May 1951, at 2.00 pm, the Speaker called for a division on the motion for Parliament to take the bill into consideration. With 246 ayes to fourteen noes, the motion was passed. Twenty-nine members abstained. The announcement of the result was greeted with loud cheers.[117] 'Big Majority for Nehru Motion,' read headlines the next morning.[118] The final, decisive phase of the parliamentary battle had begun.

Parliamentary Encounter VI: The Guillotine Is Applied

Reporting on the terminal debate on the amendment, one prominent newspaper wrote, 'The Bill will be taken up for detailed consideration for the next two days and the guillotine will be applied at 1 p.m. on Saturday.'[119] It was a decidedly apt turn of phrase. For what was happening, as the liberal MP Hriday Nath Kunzru frequently and persistently proclaimed in Parliament, was nothing short of an amputation of some of the most vital fundamental rights provisions in the Constitution, the same ones that Prime Minister Nehru openly derided as ossified, archaic remnants of the ideas that fired the French and American Revolutions. The right to freedom of speech and the right to property were effectively being repealed.

On the evening of 31 May, Prof. K. K. Bhattacharya, Congress MP from UP, wrote to Nehru seeking a free vote on the bill. 'If you do not give me this freedom,' he informed the prime minister, 'it will be my painful duty to leave the Congress Party in Parliament so as to be free to vote in accordance with the dictates of my conscience.'[120] Nehru refused, and as Parliament convened on Friday, 1 June, Bhattacharya resigned from the Congress party and joined the ranks of the amendment's opponents. Nonetheless, even with this late defection, Opposition leaders knew that there was little they could do: their loss was already preordained. Nothing they said, nothing they did could alter the unshakeable majority the Congress commanded. Still, they decided to fight to the last man. And the last two days witnessed fearsome verbal combat.

As each clause of the Constitution (First Amendment) Bill was taken up for discussion over 1 and 2 June, Opposition figures moved dozens of amendments to each clause. In the amendment to Article 15, H. V. Kamath attempted to add a proviso that special provisions for backward classes would not impose unreasonable restrictions upon the right to equality guaranteed to all citizens.[121] Congress mutineer Shibban Lal Saksena pressed to include the word 'economically' in the description of 'socially and educationally backward classes'. 'If the amendment is allowed to pass in its present form,' he averred, 'it will mean that any class which has entrenched itself in power may use this clause to advance its own particular class.'[122] Congress members such as M. A. Ayyangar from Madras remained unyielding in their claim that after the Scheduled Castes and Tribes, backward classes must be the first charge on the attention of the state.[123]

When the amendments to Article 19 were taken up for discussion, Shyama Prasad Mookerji forcefully demanded that if the freedom of speech had to be curtailed, then the amendment should provide for such power to be vested solely in Parliament and not in the state legislatures to achieve uniformity across the country and minimize the chances of misuse.[124] On this issue, Mookerji traded lengthy, heated arguments with Home Minister C. Rajagopalachari and Law Minister B. R. Ambedkar. In impassioned, animated exchanges, both sides pointedly accused each other of obstinacy and irresponsibility. Prime Minister Nehru was charged with suppressing news from China that was critical of the communist regime,[125] to which he replied that the news of communist atrocities in China and Tibet was grossly exaggerated.[126]

On the amendments to Article 31, Naziruddin Ahmed, Syamnandan Sahay and Shibban Lal Saksena again took the lead in criticizing the government. The new Article 31B, creating the Ninth Schedule, was severely criticized, and the government was accused of 'drifting away from a policy of respect for private property' and establishing a terrible precedent.[127] In an ultimate appeal, H. N. Kunzru again warned of the dangers of the amendment: the revalidation of sedition and revival of censorship.

Yet, argue as they might, the bill's opponents were only succeeding in delaying the inevitable. None of their amendments to the bill were accepted. In vote after vote, when the House divided, Opposition amendments were voted down and the government's version of the bill carried through with large majorities. 'There was fearful slaughter of over a hundred non-official amendments of varying importance,' noted press reports, and only three changes were accepted: two verbal clarifications to 19(2) and 31A and the addition of the Hyderabad (Abolition of Jagirs) Regulation in the Ninth Schedule.[128] Even the most controversial and emotionally charged clause related to freedom of speech and expression was carried by an overwhelming majority of 228 votes to nineteen. Most of the journalist members abstained. All Opposition amendments were voted down, just as they were when changes to Article 15 and Article 31 were considered.[129]

As the debate neared its conclusion, tempers within the chamber ran high. There were tempestuous exchanges between Shyama Prasad Mookerji and H. V. Kamath on one side and Speaker G. V. Mavalankar and Law Minister B. R. Ambedkar on the other over voting procedures on amendments. The doughty old socialist Shibban Lal Saksena again requested the prime minister to take the House into confidence and explain the grave difficulties that had compelled him to curtail fundamental rights and resurrect sedition as a major crime.[130] 'It is shameful for all of us to resurrect all such obnoxious laws by the back-door,' he bewailed. 'I am very sorry that this Bill is being passed by this House. We cannot help it but certainly we can record our protest against the enactment of this measure.'[131]

Congress support for the bill remained untempered. Joachim Alva, Tribhuvan Narayan Singh, Renuka Ray, Seth Govind Das and

Mohanlal Gautam spoke extensively on the usefulness of the bill as the clock wound down towards 6.00 pm. Drawing the curtains on the case for the Opposition, Mookerji castigated Parliament for failing to establish a healthy convention by refusing to elicit public opinion and giving retrospective effect to constitutional changes.[132] He described the new amended Article 31 and the Ninth Schedule as a 'constitutional monstrosity' and accused the prime minister of deliberately curbing the rights of the citizens without giving adequate reasons.[133]

'The answer to popular discontent is not by passing repressive measures,' he pleaded with Nehru.

> I would therefore appeal to the Prime Minister even at this stage – of course you have got your majority; you will carry this Bill through; you carry it through – but in giving effect to it you must not be guided merely by a sense of intoxication of the power that is in your hands because you have 240 supporters inside the House. Outside the House, there are millions who are against you and you will have to remember how to placate them properly....[134]

Several days of bruising debates and devastating criticism had got to Nehru. Recalling the debate, he would say, 'Listening to constant accusations and denunciations was too much for my patience.'[135] 'I say this opposition is not a true opposition, not a faithful opposition, not a loyal opposition. I say it deliberately,' an infuriated prime minister responded.[136] 'Yours is not a true Bill,' came Mookerji's sharp retort, further stoking Nehru's temper.[137] The prime minister and the leader of the Opposition now hurled insults across the floor of the House.

Nehru, shaking his fists in fury, charged Mookerji with making false statements and scandalous speeches. 'Because your intolerance is scandalous,' came Mookerji's riposte. 'It has become the fashion in this country for some people to go about in the name of nationalism and in the name of liberty to preach the narrowest doctrines of communalism,' growled Nehru. 'You are an arch-communalist, responsible for the partition of this country,' replied Mookerji.

Writing in the *Times of India* the next morning, a reporter described the verbal duel as 'an intemperate and impassioned slanging match between the prime minister and Dr Shyama Prasad Mookerjee'.[138] Parliamentarians sat glued to their seats as two of India's finest orators traded barbs across the chamber. Both Nehru and Mookerji declared that the other was going to hear many truths before the debate was finished. Tempers frayed and passions were aroused. 'For ten minutes,' an eyewitness observed, 'the chamber was treated to the furious political oratory of the hustings with its challenges and replies.'[139]

'We here have had to put up with much from a few Members in this House who have challenged ... ' seethed Nehru. Even before he could finish, Mookerji cut in: 'This is dictatorship and not democracy.'[140] When an anxious and exasperated Govind Malviya – son of the Congress stalwart and educationist Madan Mohan Malviya – complained about the constant interruptions of the prime minister's speech, Nehru sneered: 'I have invited them ... I only wanted to see how much restraint Dr. Mookerjee has ... ' 'What restraint have you shown?' Mookerji snapped back. 'What restraint have you shown?'[141]

In the heat of the moment, Prime Minister Nehru challenged his opponents to combat, 'combat everywhere, intellectually or any other kind of combat on this issue and every other issue'.[142] 'It is we who have brought about these major changes,' he thundered,

> and not these petty critics of the Government and it is we who are going to bring about major changes in this country. We are not going to allow petty critics and others to stop changes. They advance arguments which might have had some relevance some hundreds of years ago but which have no relevance now.[143]

At 6.40 pm, the guillotine was finally applied and the emotionally charged and bitterly acrimonious debate came to an end – a stormy conclusion to a debate described by a major newspaper as 'the lowest level of parliamentary dignity witnessed this session'.[144] The Speaker rang the bell for the House to divide. Opposition figures S. P. Mookerji, H. N. Kunzru, Naziruddin Ahmed, Acharya Kripalani, Ramnarain Singh, K. T. Shah, Hussain Imam and Sardar Hukam Singh were joined in the noes lobby by conscientious Congress rebels H. V. Kamath, K. K. Bhattacharya, Sarangadhar Das, Shibban Lal Saksena, Damodar Swarup Seth and Sucheta Kripalani. Another prominent face among them was the tribal leader Jaipal Singh, the man who had captained the Indian hockey team to a gold medal in the 1928 Olympics.

The final count was taken. There were 228 ayes, twenty noes. Close to fifty members had abstained. 'The motion is adopted by a majority of the total Membership of the House and by a majority of not less than two-thirds of the Members present and voting,' announced the Deputy Speaker solemnly. 'The Constitution (First Amendment) Bill, as amended, is passed.'[145] Indian democracy, dubbed as top dressing on undemocratic soil even at the moment of its birth, would never be the same again.

7

The Aftermath

I

The passing of the Constitution (First Amendment) Bill marked the end of the first battle of Indian liberalism. The provisions on fundamental rights in Part III – the heart and soul of the entire Constitution according to Ambedkar – had been vandalized. The judiciary had been publicly emasculated, civil liberties deliberately and extensively curtailed. A new precedent of retrospective constitutional amendments to nullify judicial pronouncements had been set. The true post-colonial Indian state was born. The Nehruvian revolution was underway. None were left oblivious as to what had happened. *The Leader*, an influential nationalist newspaper published from Allahabad, described the immediate aftermath in its headline: 'Fundamental Rights Restricted: Parliament Approves Amendments'.[1]

'We have been accused of curbing and throttling the press and of trying to behave in an autocratic manner in regard to it,' a relieved Nehru wrote to his chief ministers. 'The press campaign against these amendments has gone on and some foreign papers have eagerly taken advantage of this to condemn us ... I can understand a certain apprehension in the minds of the press ... But I confess that I have been surprised at the vehemence of this opposition.'[2] Nevertheless, even the passage of the bill with a humungous majority failed to completely quell all dissidence. For a short while, firm, principled criticism as well as determined rearguard action continued.

Speaking in Bombay, Supreme Court Chief Justice Harilal Kania wrung his hands and appealed to the nation's honest and independent citizens to ensure that the independence of each of the three limbs of the state was maintained, warning that the weakening of the judicial limb 'can only result in chaos and the breakdown of society'.[3] Few doubted what the chief of the Indian judiciary was hinting at. 'When the Court decided a matter, it laid down whether a particular action was or was not in accordance with the law,' Kania averred.

When a citizen challenged a particular piece of legislation it was the duty of the Supreme Court to state whether the legislation was right or wrong. If the courts did not know what their function was, there would be dictatorship. While law was necessary for the upkeep of society, equally essential were courts to determine whether the legislature passed the law within the written word of the Constitution.[4]

'The All India Newspaper Editors Conference supported by a large and responsible section of the Indian Press has been carrying on an agitation against the amendments to the Constitution,' wrote S. A. Sabavala, a senior editor of the *Free Press Journal*.

This... has been treated with contempt by the Prime Minister and our one-party Parliament ... I understand that AINEC is meeting in Bombay in the third week of June to consider further action ... I would like to suggest that the editors now consider something more positive than verbal and written protestations of their faith in the need for unqualified freedom of the press subject to the checks already written into the Constitution ... The Prime Minister has by his very words and deeds challenged the very existence of a free and democratic press in this country. Faced with this situation, are we to go on passing resolutions?[5]

At a press conference on 11 June, Prime Minister Nehru was questioned on how the amendment was going to affect the press. 'I do not think that, in spite of the heat raised in the recent debates, it affects the Press much', he replied in his typically offhand manner.

You will forgive me if I say we talk so much of the freedom of the Press, but more and more I see that that freedom might as well be exercised by anyone who has money enough to buy up a paper.

Recently, it is rather an odd experience for me to see a newspaper
... within a week or ten days completely change its policy, tone
and everything except in regard to one matter and that was its
rather extreme dislike of the Government and me ... That is the
freedom of the Press![6]

President Rajendra Prasad, who was as unhappy at the turn
of events as the chief justice, was not allowed the luxury of
publicly expressing his displeasure. He did, however, write to
Alladi Krishnaswamy Aiyyar to ask for his opinion. He now
raised substantial legal objections. The problem as he saw it was
twofold. First, the provisional parliament only had one House,
whereas Article 368, which gave Parliament the power to amend
the Constitution, required a two-thirds majority in both Houses.
Was a single chamber provisional Parliament, then, competent to
amend the Constitution?

Second, the government had got around this difficulty by
adapting Article 368 to temporarily refer to Parliament rather
than two separate Houses by using the Constitution (Removal of
Difficulties) Order No. 2 – issued by the president on 26 January
1950 (under powers granted to him by Article 392) to make minor
adaptations to the Constitution in order to remove any procedural
difficulties that arose before a full Parliament was elected. Could this
adaptation itself be ultra vires, since, under the guise of removing
difficulties, it effectively (albeit temporarily) amended Article 368
without adhering to the amending procedure as the article itself
required?[7]

'If any or both of the above contentions are correct and the
amendments are ultra vires of the Parliament,' Prasad queried
Aiyyar, 'is it the duty of the president to assent to the Bill even when
he knows them to be ultra vires, particularly in view of Article
60 whereby he is required by his oath of office to the best of his
ability to preserve, protect and defend the Constitution?'[8] In other
words, what the president was asking was whether the government
could use a presidential order to change the procedure to amend
the Constitution that Article 368 detailed without following that
very procedure in the first place. Could it then use the amended and
changed procedure to make significant amendments to something
as cardinal as fundamental rights, when Article 13(2) prevented
Parliament from making any law to abridge them? Was this not

a textbook example of the misuse of the powers granted to the president under Article 392?

Aiyyar's response, as Granville Austin notes, is not on record. 'But earlier, when Prasad had addressed him with such concerns, Aiyyar had told him he must give his assent.'[9] Unwilling to risk a public confrontation with the prime minister and mindful of the need to maintain the constitutional order, Rajendra Prasad assented to the bill on 18 June 1951. And just like that, some of the most precious individual rights that the citizens of the new republic had enjoyed under the new Constitution were seized by the state, never to be returned to its citizens again. In a conversation with AINEC President Deshbandhu Gupta after signing the bill into law, Rajendra Prasad noted:

> So far as the Prime Minister was concerned, he had given them [the press] an assurance that the Government was not going to fetter freedom of the Press, but what they apprehended was that once the power was taken by the Government, they could not be sure it wouldn't be used against the Press later on. The best safeguard was contained in the Constitution and if the Constitution itself is amended, the Press is left to depend upon the goodwill of the Government for the time being.[10]

Unbowed, AINEC picked up the gauntlet by declaring that publication of the nation's newspapers would be suspended on 12 July as an unparalleled mark of protest against the 'unwarranted and uncalled for encroachment on freedom of expression'.[11] And each day thereafter, to impress on the public the enormity of what had just unfolded, India's editors resolved to emblazon a slogan on the front pages of their newspapers: 'Freedom of expression is our birthright and we shall not rest until it is fully guaranteed by the Constitution.'[12] The move made news the world over, with multiple newspapers, including *The New York Times*,[13] the *Guardian*,[14] *The Telegraph*, the *Chicago Daily Tribune*[15] and *The Washington Post*,[16] reporting on it.

Invoking the words of Bal Gangadhar Tilak,[17] whose pugnacious slogan 'freedom is my birthright and I shall have it' they were borrowing from, however, did not give AINEC the steely determination of the late nationalist leader, famously jailed in Mandalay for sedition in 1909. Several editors argued that suspension of newspapers even for a day 'might be taken advantage of by Pakistan in a manner inimical to India's interests'.[18] With dissension within its ranks, AINEC's proposed 'hartal' had to be postponed,[19] first for a short while and then, despite strident opposition to such postponement from some quarters, indefinitely.[20] Without its opening battle, AINEC's proposed war of attrition, begun with a bang and lauded the world over, ended – to paraphrase the poet T. S. Eliot – in a whimper. Even before its first gesture of defiance, India's press, unlike Tilak, quickly buckled.

Concerned zamindars and lawyers, still entertaining hopes of fighting the government, took the matter to the Supreme Court in a final effort to block the amendment – raising many of the same contentions that President Prasad had raised with Alladi Krishnaswamy Aiyyar. In its judgment on the matter, delivered on 5 October 1951, the Supreme Court threw these contentions aside and upheld the amendment on the ground that it had been enacted validly and that Parliament had unlimited power to amend the Constitution without any exception whatsoever.[21]

The judgment only confirmed what had now been known for several months. The original provisions for individual freedom and civil liberties had been deformed and diminished. What remained was a vastly enfeebled imitation of what the Constituent Assembly had first drawn up; so much so that India's pre-eminent legal scholar, Prof. Upendra Baxi, termed it 'the Second Constitution'.[22] Even before the first democratic election had been held, even before the teeming millions of the new republic had been given a chance to elect their representatives and voice their political preferences, the nation's new democratic rulers had already launched an egregious and far-reaching attack on the rights of their subjects – the effects of which would reverberate through time.

The All India Civil Liberties Conference made a final appeal, imploring 'all political parties in the country to exert themselves to the utmost to undo the mischief that has been done by the Constitution (Amendment) Act and [to] restore the Constitution to a form in which freedom of speech and press would be fully protected and placed beyond the reach of fleeting majorities in the legislatures'.[23] Its pleas fell on deaf ears. India – its leaders, its citizens, its institutions, its political parties – had already moved on.

II

The immediate ramifications of the amendment, which had already been delineated over the course of the debate and commentary that had surrounded the passage of the bill, were full and fearsome. Sections 124A and 153A of the Indian Penal Code were revalidated and made operational again by the addition of new grounds for restricting freedom of speech and expression, making 'sedition' and 'promoting ill-will between communities' into major criminal offences. Ditto for public order and public safety regulation. With the revalidation of such laws, the government reclaimed the coercive powers that its colonial predecessor had once had, and which the Constitution had originally denied it. As Deshbandhu Gupta told President Rajendra Prasad,

> All those repressive laws which were inconsistent with or contravened the fundamental rights had become void. This amendment of the Constitution revives them all by a stroke of the pen ... all that had been achieved by the joint efforts of the Press and the Congress within the last forty years or more had now been nullified.[24]

Parliament soon passed The Press (Objectionable Matter) Act penalizing the publication of material it did not like, giving concrete shape to Gupta's fears.

Article 31, which had restrained the state from acquiring property except by the authority of law for a public purpose and on payment of compensation, was swept aside. The additional Article 31A now declared that no law providing for acquisition of landed estates shall be deemed void on the grounds that it contravened Article 14, the right to equality, or Article 19, Clause 1(f) of which guaranteed to citizens the right to acquire, hold and dispose of property as they saw fit. The new Article 31B created the Ninth Schedule, and declared that no law specified in the schedule 'shall be deemed to be void, or ever to have become void' on the grounds that it takes away or abridges any of the rights conferred by the Constitution – and no contrary judicial pronouncement could prevail. It was a provision 'directly opposed to the scheme, structure and spirit of the Constitution'.[25]

In this way, a constitutional vault was created to store certain laws and give them blanket protection from the Constitution – and at the same time, a mechanism was devised to emasculate the courts and exclude the possibility of judicial review entirely. The Ninth Schedule became, for all acts and purposes, a repository of potentially unconstitutional or actually unconstitutional laws and regulations beyond the purview of the courts. Any legislation declared void by the courts, once it received the protection of the Ninth Schedule, became legal and constitutional again. As one legal scholar observed, 'Even if any of the Acts had driven a coach and pair through the fundamental rights guarantees, it could not be questioned and if it was unconstitutional, it became constitutional.'[26] In effect, the schedule granted constitutional protection to the Constitution's abusers, 'a legitimization of constitutional illegitimacy'.[27] Through such constitutional skulduggery, under the guise of Nehru's social revolution, India's political class was given the green light to ride roughshod over both the Constitution and the judiciary.

Similarly, Articles 15 and 29, which prohibited discrimination on grounds of race, sex, caste, religion, etc., were made ineffective by the introduction of the caveat that nothing in those Articles would prevent the state from making special provisions for the advancement of socially and educationally backward classes of citizens. Reservations for (the yet to be identified or demarcated)[a] 'backward classes' (above and beyond Scheduled Classes and Scheduled Tribes) was made constitutionally permissible, laying the groundwork for a tectonic shift in Indian social and political life – making a mockery of the idea of individual rights while producing and reinforcing the seductive idea of collective rights. For all intents and purposes, an individual became constitutionally defined by and subsumed into their community-based identity.

---

[a]The First Backward Class Commission (the Kaka Kalelkar Commission) was only created in 1953, and so in 1951 no one knew what this category meant, how it was to be defined and who it was to include. Unlike Scheduled Castes, which are a strictly caste-based legal category to which a caste group can be added by presidential notification, the backward classes are supposed to theoretically be a dynamic administrative category assessed and defined by a 'backward classes commission'. In practice, however, caste became the criteria for assessing backwardness as well – exemplified by both the First and the Second Backward Class Commissions (the Kaka Kalelkar Commission in 1953 and the BP Mandal Commission in 1979).

The explicit removal of any reference to economic criteria ensured that all benchmarks of backwardness would remain focused on caste, religion and community; other personal circumstances were made irrelevant and redundant. Reservations for 'backward classes' were made constitutionally permissible, regardless of economic standing. Reservations for 'forward classes' were made constitutionally impermissible, regardless of economic standing – a setup only partially undone by the creation of the new category of 'Economically Weaker Sections' via the 103rd Amendment in 2019. Enduring resentment ensued. 'Social backwardness' became a defining feature of Indian public life, launching a race to be defined as 'socially and educationally backward'.

Of course, many argue that given the powers that Nehru had appropriated from the Constitution, and the consequent capacity for mischief and malevolence that legislation under it possessed, the amendment's effects were fairly limited over most of his rule. In other words, in proportion to the quantum of power he appropriated, Nehru made use of a comparatively limited portion of it.[28] The various legal instruments that the amendment gave birth to, despite their strong wording, supposedly did not suppress critical opinion as much as they might have. This is only partly true. Nehru made use of many of the powers the amendment granted, even if in moderation, and never considered returning the rights and powers he had unceremoniously seized from the people and the judiciary.

For example, he twice wrote to his chief ministers expressing the view that 'any interference with the freedom of the press has to be avoided'[29] and 'none of us wants, for instance, the old sedition law to continue on the statute book'.[30] Like many of the pious affirmations in Parliament during the debate, these sentiments were honoured only in breach. The sedition law continued on the statute books, as did Sections 153A and 295A of the Indian Penal Code. To these was soon added the Press (Objectionable Matter) Act. Nehru himself may have made only limited use of them – but he bequeathed them intact to his successors as a stick to beat India's people with, to do with as they willed. He did so after having been warned repeatedly about the consequences by his opponents both within Parliament and outside. His contempt for the Opposition and his faith in his righteous superiority was such that he failed to take heed. The constitutional infrastructure he provided, and never repealed, outlived him, providing a building block for the legal armouries of his successors, to be unleashed on the country's hapless citizens whenever they step out of line.

III

In her work on the relationship between constitutionalism and popular sovereignty, the legal scholar Sarbani Sen argued that Article 368 and the power of amendment it conferred opened up 'the possibility of legalising through the use of constitutional law, future constitutional transformations that seek to reject some elements of past constitutional traditions'.[31] Yet, the First Amendment went much further than simply rejecting some elements of past constitutional traditions. There was precious little by way of constitutional tradition to reject in 1951 anyway, apart from the institutional memory of the colonial state that much of the post-colonial government had absorbed by osmosis and imitation. Not even the founders, the vast bulk of whom also sat in the provisional parliament, had ever imagined a constitutional transformation in fifteen months, even before the first election had taken place.

The First Amendment thus did not just legalize a constitutional transformation that rejected past traditions. If anything, it was, in fact, the lack of these traditions that demanded the creation of 'instant conventions'[32] and, as per Kumarasingham, provided an opportunity for executive actors to shape both the future functions and expectations of their offices, and the demarcation of power within the country's institutional structure.[33] As the first of over 100 amendments, the First Amendment thus created major precedents both legally and politically, inaugurating certain traditions and crystallizing other tendencies already present in the nation's political sphere. In the immediate term, it effected certain changes such as the revalidation of sedition and blanket security for land reform legislation. But in the longer term, it was, as Granville Austin noted, 'consequential far beyond its immediately visible content'.[34] The immediate ramifications of the amendment had already been delineated over the debate and commentary that surrounded the passage of the Constitution (First Amendment) Bill. Longer-term consequences, many unfolding to this date, came to light much later, proving many of the bill's opponents to have been correct.

Foremost among the precedents Nehru created was the precedent of amending the Constitution to overcome and overturn judicial pronouncements. By retrospectively amending the Constitution to overcome adverse judicial pronouncements supposedly impeding the fulfilment of certain government policies and programmes, Nehru established a new template of using constitutional amendments to overcome court judgments and to render constitutional actions that at the time of their commission had been patently and apparently unconstitutional. As he wrote to his chief ministers:

> A Constitution must be held in respect, but if it ceases to represent or comes in the way of the spirit of the age or the powerful urges of the people, then difficulties and conflicts arise. It is wise therefore to have not only stability and fixity of purpose, but also a certain flexibility and pliability in the Constitution. A rigid Constitution may well come in the way of change in a transitional age.[35]

This became a maxim, institutionalizing and promoting the view that the Constitution, rather than being the foundation of the nation's social contract, was a legal document to be amended and abridged at will whenever it suited the government or came in the way of the supposed urges of the people. By extension, it was implied that executive power had to subdue the judiciary; in every conflict between the two, the will of the government and of the legislature must prevail. The amendment did not merely make it easier to pass laws, as the legal philosopher Arudra Burra observed, it was an assertion of right, 'a signal to the courts about who was boss when it came to the Constitution'.[36] In Parliament, Mookerji had warned that treating the republic's foundational document as a scrap of paper would only encourage others to disrespect it even further. Over a hundred amendments later, he has been proven right. Fundamental rights, which started out as permanent guarantees, became – to quote Chief Justice Hidayatullah – 'the plaything of special majorities'.[37]

Worse, the reasons Prime Minister Nehru used to justify the amendment – fundamental rights as obsolete remnants of the ideas of the French Revolution, the superiority of the directive principles over fundamental rights, the state's obligations to collective rights and community identity – represented a complete inversion of the very basis of the constitutional order. With these, Nehru rationalized and condoned a profoundly illiberal vision that was strikingly at odds with the moral imagination that had animated the original Constituent Assembly.

'Each restriction of individual rights in this [the First] amendment,' noted the JNU political scientist Nivedita Menon,

[s] ought to empower a different subject – the first a cultural community, the second the state, and the third a class. Clearly if the individual is understood to be the cornerstone of modern liberal democracies, then the first amendment can be understood to have further disabled what Sunil Khilnani calls Indian liberalism.[38]

It was a debilitating blow from which Indian liberalism is yet to recover.

The constant affirmation of the primacy of the Congress party's manifesto over the Constitution, the repetition ad nauseam of the argument that the courts should not be allowed to get in the way of government policies, the recurrent references to unseen dangers and the use of a brute parliamentary majority to push through a constitutional amendment exposed the latent authoritarianism that lurked beneath the republican exterior of India's new democratic government and its leaders. The open disregard for democratic propriety and the need for establishing healthy democratic traditions on the part of India's first independent government only legitimized and normalized a spirit of authoritarianism, majoritarianism and constitutional subversion – a spirit that, like the amendment itself, would outlive Nehru and continue to cast a long shadow over the history of independent India. The passing of a major constitutional amendment curbing fundamental rights by a provisional parliament elected on a limited franchise, in the face of vociferous criticism and against the advice of the president and the Speaker, in furtherance of a party agenda, was nothing short of a constitutional travesty.

A precedent both novel and terrible was thus established by the First Amendment. From then, each precedent has only built on the one preceding it, civil liberties and fundamental rights being progressively watered down, leaving the Constitution – to paraphrase the historian Sunil Khilnani – as an edifice that continually looms over public life as a permanently embarrassing monument, representing an ideal of legality and procedural conduct regularly ignored by state and society alike.[39] Step by subversive step, the executive has acquired vast coercive powers, diminishing both the citizen and the judiciary. Fundamental rights, civil liberties – indeed, the very concept of the judiciary and the Constitution as checks on the government – have been unfortunate but easy casualties in this assertion of executive power, reinforcing precisely those traits and powers of the state that Indian nationalists had struggled against when they had been ruled by their colonial masters.

No single piece of legislation has encapsulated those traits and powers as comprehensively as Section 124A of the Indian Penal Code (IPC) which dealt with the crime of sedition. The grounds added to Article 19 for enabling restrictions on the freedom of speech and expression – public order, the interest of the security of the state, relations with foreign states and incitement to an offence – provided the constitutional architecture for this, and a whole host of coercive and repressive legislation. The simple change of grounds on which the right could be legally abridged from 'any matter which undermines the security of or tends to overthrow the state' to 'in the interest of the security of the state', combined with the addition of public order, opened the floodgates for drastic and oppressive laws. From Sections 124A, 153A and 295A of the IPC – sedition, promoting enmity between groups and outraging religious feelings, respectively – to penal provisions of the Information Technology Act to draconian legislation like the National Security Act, the Maintenance of Internal Security Act and the Unlawful Activities Prevention Act, it is the First Amendment that has provided the constitutional groundwork for them to exist.

Through the years, such legislation has been routinely used by governments to stamp their power while playing fast and loose with the rights guaranteed by the Constitution. Many such legal provisions, used to stifle free speech and critical opinion by banning books, arresting journalists, jailing activists and harassing political opponents, owe their continued survival to the First Amendment and the sledgehammer it took to the fundamental rights provisions guaranteed by the Constitution. They are not, as is often believed, simply a remnant of colonialism but a consequence of the drive for power displayed by India's post-colonial elite. Opposition figures such as Shyama Prasad Mookerji demanded that any restrictions on fundamental rights in the name of the security of the state must meet the test of 'clear and present danger' – but to little avail. Far from being remnants of colonialism, then, laws like sedition are the outcome of the Nehruvian state.

And nothing has exemplified Nehru's social revolution as much as the Ninth Schedule, the infamous repository of unconstitutional laws, acknowledged as a 'very extraordinary provision' even at the moment of its conception.[40] 'Neither Nehru nor others recognized the genie they had loosed: that the Schedule would be used for the protection of land laws regardless of their quality or legality, for laws other than land reform laws; for laws regulating business; and for laws to serve the personal interests of the powerful,' Granville Austin argued.[41] That, again, is only partly true, for both inside Parliament and outside, critics and opponents had requested the prime minister to tread with caution. He chose to ignore those warnings. 'Nehru's actions,' noted Gopal Sankaranarayanan,

> though probably justified at the time, showed a lack of prescience, because with one fell blow, he created two mechanisms by which the supremacy of Parliament would be emphasized: a) the power of the Constitutional Amendment to nullify the judgments of the courts, used for the first time in this instance and b) the Ninth Schedule, by which the very power of judicial review of legislative action (one accorded by the Constitution itself) would be excluded. In the years to come, these two instruments more than any other would be used by less responsible governments to trammel the judiciary and muzzle the electorate.[42]

By excluding the power of judicial review from a whole class of legislation and granting constitutional protection to unconstitutional laws, solely in the pursuit of the Congress party's social agenda, Nehru emasculated the judiciary and emphasized the power of the executive and the legislature – and by extension, himself and the Congress party. Once it became easy for Parliament to validate any piece of unconstitutional legislation by putting it in the Ninth

Schedule, where its constitutionality could not be challenged, India's democratic politicians jumped at the opportunity to have their own way, indulging in all forms of constitutional chicanery.

Over the years, the repository of unconstitutional laws continued to overflow as his successors, following in his footsteps, continued to draft, pass and secure unconstitutional legislation. Originally framed as a repository for land reform legislation, in 2006 the number of potentially or actually unconstitutional laws placed in the Ninth Schedule stood at 284. Laws relating to industrial development, nationalization, foreign exchange and economic offences; laws relating to elections, reservations and representation – all found a cosy home. In the words of the jurist A. G. Noorani, '... an incongruity, introduced as a result of sheer neglect became an obscenity created by wilful resolve'.[43]

With its judgments in *Kesavananda Bharati*[44] – which established the doctrine of 'basic structure' – and *I.R. Coelho*[45] (which clarified the doctrine vis-à-vis the Ninth Schedule) the Supreme Court has, of course, partially taken back many of the worst powers that Nehru had wrested from it in 1951. But it has been unable to reverse the damage that the fundamental rights provisions in the Constitution have sustained. In fact, the judiciary itself has occasionally been guilty of upholding the validity of draconian legislation by relying on the constitutional immunity granted by inclusion in the Ninth Schedule.[46] Even more troublingly, the illiberal, authoritarian tendencies within India's ruling dispensations, of which the First Amendment was an early manifestation – with the consequent disdain for civil liberties, prioritization of the needs of the state and offhand dismissal of the norms of democratic propriety – have only grown, each executive power grab begetting one greater than the last.

Moreover, this (theoretically democratic) pattern for the violation of constitutional norms came to be regularly revisited in subsequent years. This reached its apogee during the rule of Nehru's daughter, Indira Gandhi, whose fifteen years in power saw an unprecedented twenty-nine amendments to the Constitution. The 24th Amendment, for example, enabled Parliament to dilute fundamental rights through further amendments and abrogated a Supreme Court ruling[47] curtailing that power. The 25th Amendment, by way of illustration, exempted any law giving effect to Article 39(B & C) of the directive principles from judicial review, even if it violated fundamental rights. And the notorious 42nd Amendment, passed during the Emergency, excluded judicial review of constitutional amendments altogether, introduced new directive principles and gave them primacy over fundamental rights, barred high courts from pronouncing on the constitutionality of parliamentary legislation and even added an entirely new chapter of 'Fundamental Duties'.[48] Each, to a greater or lesser extent, purported to secure the 'social revolution' and the Directive Principles of State Policy against pesky citizens claiming their rights.[49]

Of course, the most egregious of these have since been overturned or constrained, either by following amendments or judicial pronouncements – and it is certainly unlikely that Nehru's intention had been to pave the path to the excesses of the 1970s. But a direction had certainly been illuminated.

'[T]he choice of a social revolution from above', wrote Gyan Prakash, had effectively placed 'a heavy reliance on the leaders' commitment to democratic procedures.'[50] It was a commitment that Nehru and his successors found difficult to live up to. Like its detractors predicted, the amendment only proved to be the start of a slippery slide towards authoritarianism.

IV

If, on the one hand, the passage of the amendment exposed the despotism that lurked below the surface of the new democratic republic, on the other, it also testified to the pusillanimity and lack of commitment to any democratic or republican values on the part of the first generation of independent India's leaders – to quote Sarvepalli Gopal, the subservient mouldering mediocrities who comprised the Nehru Cabinet. Many of these luminaries would soon be exposed by events.

'Since Mr. Rajagopalachari assumed the office of Home Minister,' observed the *Times of India* a few days after the passage of the amendment,

> there has been a severe curtailment of fundamental rights both within the framework of the Constitution and in the day to day business of administration. The Home Ministry's proposed move

to clothe the military with certain powers to cope with civil disorders is yet another manifestation of the authoritarian trend creeping into government.[51]

Having presided over the desecration of the Constitution's fundamental rights provisions and laid the foundations of repression and coercion, a few years later, Rajaji would found the Swatantra Party to make the case for liberalism and civil liberties and fight against the Nehruvian state. By then, it was much too late. Coercive powers, once usurped, were never going to be surrendered.

Law Minister B. R. Ambedkar did not even have to wait as long as Rajagopalachari. Within months of the amendment, failing to get Nehru to bend on the Hindu Code Bill, facing the obduracy of the conservative wing in the Congress, feeling utterly dissatisfied with the prime minister and finding himself lonely and isolated within the government, he would be forced into resigning from the Cabinet. Again, having drafted and helped pass the drastic changes to Article 31 and the effective curtailment of the right to property, including the exclusion of judicial review, Ambedkar would now appear in the Supreme Court on behalf of the zamindars of Uttar Pradesh and Bihar to argue against the very Zamindari Abolition Acts he had helped secure against the Constitution.[52] There he would bleat on about the 'spirit of the Constitution' and argue that 'the Constitution being avowedly one for establishing liberty, justice and equality and a government of a free people with only limited powers, must be held to contain an implied prohibition against taking private property without just compensation and in the absence of a public purpose'.[53] It was, again, too little, too late.

Congress MPs, significant numbers of whom had been on the verge of revolt on the eve of the vote on the amendment – seventy-seven of them having pointedly asked for a free vote on it – had also quickly fallen in line. Why had they done so? 'If the Treasury benches ultimately carried the day,' a commentator observed,

'it was not because the House was with them but because the elections hold a Damocles' sword over the head of every Congress Member ... there was much tumult and shouting on the part of Congressmen but the same spirit was not evident in the lobby. How else is one to explain the strange spectacle of scathing criticism of the Constitution Amendment Bill and the opposition of a bare handful when the division bell rang?'[54]

It was capitulation on a breathtaking scale: hesitancy and scepticism quickly driven out by the desire for party tickets and the need to keep on the right side of the party bosses.

It might be useful at this point to briefly speculate about what such a capitulation really meant. As Nehru's anxious letters bore out, the prospect of a backbench rebellion had not been an idle threat; the failure of the restive MPs to move beyond abstentions thus implicitly implicated them in the amendment's legal and political consequences. Did this indicate a pre-existing belief in Nehruvian socialism, already present in the doubters and dissenters, that manifested itself at crunch time? Or a commitment to communitarianism that captured the zeitgeist of the times to such an extent that doubts could be overpowered? Or was it a quasi-theistic submission to 'Nehru's judgment'?[b] Few MPs ever forthrightly set out their views about it, so we may never know for certain. All are possibilities, albeit highly improbable ones – and to admit any of them would necessarily imply that these acts of resistance had been intended to be mostly performative. What it did imply, however, and unequivocally so, was that freedom of speech and individual liberty were not – for most Congress figures – the hills they were prepared to die on.

Much of this was in a sense symptomatic of a broader contradiction within the Congress and, inevitably, in India's transition to democracy and republicanism. Before independence, the Congress imagination had been divided between Gandhi's vision of self-rule and village republics, Nehru's vision of socialism and a third incoherent idea of Hindu revivalism. Divided between these strands, liberal democracy was an outlier with little serious thought behind it, with what could only be described as a 'troubled relationship' with wider Indian society.[55] Liberty was understood not in terms of individual rights and freedoms but solely as a nation's collective right to self-determination. In nationalist thought, the idea of democracy and individual freedom was only posited as a counterweight to colonial rule; it enjoyed no firm backing in practice. The Congress 'could not pretend to any developed meditation on democracy, though it did embody a formidable will to power'.[56]

---

[b] I borrow the term 'Nehru's judgment' from my former supervisor Christopher Bayly, who used it to refer to an amalgam of policies and sentiments that constituted Nehru's political stances. See C. A. Bayly, 'The Ends of Liberalism and the Political Thought of Nehru's India', *Modern Intellectual History*, 12 (3): 605–26.

From its earliest days, the Congress party had claimed to speak for the entirety of the nation and to represent all Indians. The party was as committed to denying every other group or party a seat at the political high table as it was to gaining control of the levers of power. As the self-declared representative of the nation, the Congress laid claim to possession of the colonial state and all of its territory.[57] With the advent of democracy and the inauguration of the Constitution, this position – incompatible with any idea of constitutional democracy – was strained to breaking point. When its collectivist moorings and intolerance of opposing ideologies clashed with an expansively liberal Constitution, the Congress party, instead of defending the normative foundations of democracy and the fundamental rights enshrined in the Constitution, instinctively turned on its own creation.

A good example of the party's inability to deal with challenges to its claims of possessing the colonial state is the Congress stalwart Govind Ballabh Pant, then chief minister of UP and later home minister in the Nehru Cabinet, schooling a crowd in Mathura:

If you have any complaints against the present Government, you should not use the same methods for redress of grievances which you did in the days of the British. You should approach the proper authorities and place your suggestions before them. It is not proper to criticise your own ministers on the public platform. Making defamatory statements about the Government, ministers and officials on the basis of false or distorted stories is not a good tendency ... Loose talk about the Government, ministers or officials should cease. In countries like England, America, Germany and France you will not find people talking in streets, shops and bar associations against the government or ministers.[58]

In such a setting, 'individuality as a way of social being was a precarious undertaking'.[59] It was because of these reasons that Sunil Khilnani – the originator of the phrase 'the idea of India' – described Indian liberalism to be 'crippled from its origins: stamped by utilitarianism and squeezed into a culture that had little room for the individual'.[60] Yet, for a brief period between 26 January 1950 and 18 June 1951, Indian liberalism enjoyed a blooming of sorts. The liberal, enlightened and progressive Constitution that the

Constituent Assembly had framed was given free rein, vigilantly upheld by the judiciary and vigorously backed by the Opposition. The idea of fundamental rights as a judicial dyke against the caprice and high-handedness of executive power was forcefully defended, and India's new democratic rulers were compelled to come to terms with their reduced status in the new republic.

Indian democracy may have been established in a fit of absent-mindedness,[61] but there was nothing absent-minded about its functioning in its first year. The original Constituent Assembly had articulated an expansive new republican vision. Through this period of sixteen months, the judges of the high courts and the Supreme Court, liberal parliamentarians like H. N. Kunzru and H. V. Kamath, Hindu nationalists like K. R. Malkani and S. P. Mookerji, Gandhians like Kripalani, as well as disparate figures from all sides of the political spectrum – editors, writers, businessmen alike – advocated and doggedly defended this vision in the face of a determined onslaught by the government. It was to this vision that the First Amendment dealt a crippling blow.

The legally and constitutionally sanctioned ability of the government to censor and prosecute dissenting voices and critical opinion, the vanished right to property, an enduring and endemic political fault line over 'backward class' reservations, the regularity of constitutional subversion and the legitimacy of constitutional subterfuge, the naked disregard for civil liberties, the apparent lack of commitment to the Constitution and open contempt for democratic propriety – these are the legacies of the First Amendment. So are the steady marginalization of classical liberal thought as represented by men like Kunzru, the utter evaporation of a moderate, liberal strand of Hindu nationalism represented by men like Mookerji and Malkani and the steady degradation of the norms of democratic conduct represented by conscientious objectors like Kamath, Kripalani and Bhattacharya.

India has often been said to be flirting with authoritarianism. Yet, this was not always so. There was once a time, before authoritarianism became enshrined in its Constitution, when India also flirted with liberalism. At that moment, Mookerji had warned Nehru to stick with the original Constitution, that he was creating legal tools that would one day be wielded by his opponents, that his rule or that of his ideological co-travellers would not be eternal. It is a warning that every government and every citizen would do well to remember.

APPENDIX 1

Articles 15, 19, 31 of the Constitution: 1950 v. 1951

Article 19

Original Constitution 1950

19. (1) All citizens shall have the right—

   (a) to freedom of speech and expression;

   (b) to assemble peaceably and without arms;

   (c) to form associations or unions;

   (d) to move freely throughout the territory of India;

   (e) to reside and settle in any part of the territory of India;

   (f) to acquire, hold and dispose of property; and

   (g) to practise any profession, or to carry on any occupation, trade or business.

(2) Nothing in sub-clause (a) of clause (1) shall affect the operation of any existing law in so far as it relates to, or prevent the State from making any law relating to libel, slander, defamation, contempt of court or any matter which offends against decency or morality or which undermines the security of, or tends to overthrow the State.

[…]

(6) Nothing in sub-clause (g) of the said clause shall affect the operation of any existing law in so far as it imposes, or prevents the State from making any law imposing, in the interests of the general public, reasonable restrictions on the exercise of the right conferred by the said sub-clause, and, in particular, nothing in the said sub-clause shall affect the operation of any existing law in so far as it prescribes or empowers any authority to prescribe, or prevent the State from making any law prescribing or empowering any authority to prescribe, the professional or technical qualifications necessary for practising any profession or carrying on any occupation, trade or business.

Article 19

First Amendment 1951

19. (2) Nothing in sub-clause (a) of clause (1) shall affect the operation of any existing law, or prevent the State from making any law insofar as such a law imposes reasonable restrictions on the exercise of the rights conferred by the said sub-clause in the interests of the security of the state, friendly relations with foreign states, public order, decency or morality, or in relation to contempt of court, defamation or incitement to an offence.

19. (6) Nothing in sub-clause (g) of the said clause shall affect the operation of any existing law in so far as it relates to, or prevent the State from making any law relating to—

The professional or technical qualifications necessary for practising any profession or carrying on any occupation, trade or business, or

  (i) The carrying on by the State, or by a corporation owned or controlled by the State, of any trade, business, industry or service, whether to the exclusion, complete or partial, of citizens or otherwise.

Article 15

Original Constitution

15. (1) The State shall not discriminate against any citizen on grounds only of religion, race, caste, sex, place of birth or any of them.

(2) No citizen shall, on grounds only of religion, race, caste, sex, place of birth or any of them, be subject to any disability, liability, restriction or condition with regard to—

- (a) access to shops, public restaurants, hotels and places of public entertainment; or
- (b) the use of wells, tanks, bathing ghats, roads and places of public resort maintained wholly or partly out of State funds or dedicated to the use of the general public.

(3) Nothing in this article shall prevent the State from making any special provision for women and children.

Article 15

First Amendment

15. (4) Nothing in this article or in clause (2) of Article 29 shall prevent the State from making any special provision for the advancement of any socially and educationally backward classes of citizens or for the Scheduled Castes and the Scheduled Tribes.

Article 31

Original Constitution

31. (1) No person shall be deprived of his property save by authority of law.

(2) No property, movable or immovable, including any interest in, or in any company owning, any commercial or industrial undertaking, shall be taken possession of or acquired for public purposes under any law authorising the taking of such possession or such acquisition, unless the law provides for compensation for the property taken possession of or acquired and either fixes the amount of the compensation, or specifies the principles on which, and the manner in which, the compensation is to be determined and given.

(3) No such law as is referred to in clause (2) made by the Legislature of a State shall have effect unless such law, having been reserved for the consideration of the President, has received his assent.

(4) If any Bill pending at the commencement of this Constitution in the Legislature of a State has, after it has been passed by such Legislature, been reserved for the consideration of the President and has received his assent, then, notwithstanding anything in this Constitution, the law so assented to shall not be called in question in any court on the ground that it contravenes the provisions of clause (2).

(5) Nothing in clause (2) shall affect—

   (a) the provisions of any existing law other than a law to which the provisions of clause (6) apply, or

   (b) the provisions of any law which the State may hereafter make—
       (i)   for the purpose of imposing or levying any tax or penalty, or
       (ii) for the promotion of public health or the prevention of danger to life or property, or
       (iii) in pursuance of any agreement entered into between the Government of the Dominion of India or the Government of India and the Government of any other country, or otherwise, with respect to property declared by law to be evacuee property.

(6) Any law of the State enacted not more than eighteen months before the commencement of this Constitution may within three months from such commencement be submitted to the President for his certification; and thereupon, if the President by public

notification so certifies, it shall not be called in question in any court on the ground that it contravenes the provisions of clause

(2) of this article or has contravened the provisions of sub-section

(2) of section 299 of the Government of India Act, 1935.

Article 31

First Amendment

31A. Saving of laws providing for acquisition of estates, etc.

(1) Notwithstanding anything contained in Article 13, no law providing for—

(a) the acquisition by the State of any estate or of any rights therein or the extinguishment or modification of any such rights, or

(b) the taking over of the management of any property by the State for a limited period either in the public interest or in order to secure the proper management of the property, or

(c) the amalgamation of two or more corporations either in the public interest or in order to secure the proper management of any of the corporations, or

(d) the extinguishment or modification of any rights of managing agents, secretaries and treasurers, managing directors, directors or managers of corporations, or of any voting rights of shareholders thereof, or

(e) the extinguishment or modification of any rights accruing by virtue of any agreement, lease or licence for the purpose of searching for, or winning, any mineral or mineral oil, or the premature termination or cancellation of any such agreement, lease or licence, shall be deemed to be void on the ground that it is inconsistent with, or takes away or abridges any of the rights conferred by Article 14 or Article 19: Provided that where such law is a law made by the Legislature of a State, the provisions of this article shall not apply thereto unless such law, having been reserved for the consideration of the President, has received his assent: Provided further that where any law makes any provision for the acquisition by the State of any estate and where any land comprised therein is held by a person under his personal cultivation, it shall not be lawful for the State to acquire any portion of such land as is within the ceiling limit applicable to him under any law for the time being in force or any building or structure standing thereon or appurtenant thereto, unless the law relating to the acquisition of such land, building or structure, provides for payment of compensation at a rate which shall not be less than the market value thereof.

31B. Validation of certain Acts and Regulations without prejudice to the generality of the provisions contained in Article 31A, none of the Acts and Regulations specified in the Ninth Schedule nor any of the provisions thereof shall be deemed to be void, or ever to have become void, on the ground that such Act, Regulation or provision is inconsistent with, or takes away or abridges any of the rights conferred by, any provisions of this Part, and notwithstanding any judgment, decree or order of any court or tribunal to the contrary, each of the said Acts and Regulations shall, subject to the power of any competent Legislature to repeal or amend it, continue in force.

APPENDIX 2

Timeline of Major Events

1 26 January 1950 – The Republic is inaugurated; new Constitution comes into force.

2 1 March 1950 – Madras government bans circulation of *Cross Roads* magazine using the Madras Maintenance of Public Order Act.

3 2 March 1950 – The *Organiser* is subjected to a pre-censorship order under the East Punjab Public Safety Act.

4 8 April 1950 – S. P. Mookerji and K. C. Neogy resign from Nehru Cabinet in opposition to Nehru–Liaquat Pact.

5 22 April 1950 – Bihar Land Reforms Bill passed by the Legislative Assembly.

6 26 May 1950 – Supreme Court overturns restrictions on *Organiser* and *Cross Roads*, declares relevant sections of the public safety acts as unconstitutional.

7 1 June 1950 – John Matthai resigns from Nehru Cabinet after differences with Nehru over the Planning Commission and the government's Pakistan policy, accuses the prime minister of 'undue authoritarianism'.

8 6 June 1950 – Patna High Court declares Bihar Management of Estates and Tenures Act unconstitutional; Champakam Dorairajan files a suit against the Communal General Order (community-based reservations) in the Madras High Court.

9 27 July 1950 – Madras High Court strikes down the Communal General Order, finding it violative of the right to freedom from discrimination.

10 4 August 1950 – Uttar Pradesh Zamindari Abolition Bill
    passed by the Legislative Assembly and forwarded to the
    Legislative Council.

11 2 September 1950 – Purushottam Das Tandon elected as
    Congress president with Sardar Patel's support, defeating
    Acharya Kripalani, who had been supported by Nehru.

12 11 September 1950 – President certifies Bihar Land
    Reforms Act.

13 24 September 1950 – Bihar government issues a notification
    under the Bihar Land Reforms Act vesting the estates
    of Maharaja Kameshwar Singh of Darbhanga, Raja
    Vishweshwar Singh of Darbhanga and Raja Kamakhya
    Narain Singh of Ramgarh in the state.

14 26 September 1950 – Patna High Court grants an injunction
    restraining the state from acquiring the notified estates.

15 13 October 1950 – Patna High Court declares parts of the
    Indian Press (Emergency Powers) Act to be unconstitutional.

16 15 October 1950 – Bihar Chief Minister Sri Krishna Sinha
    writes to Nehru pleading for central intervention with
    regard to zamindari abolition.

17 19 October 1950 – Nehru replies, confirming that he is
    seriously considering an amendment to the Constitution,
    and then writes to law minister B. R. Ambedkar stating that
    constitutional provisions related to subversive activities,
    law and order, zamindari abolition and nationalisation of
    industry needed amending.

18 21 October 1950 – Cabinet meets and directs law ministry
    to prepare draft amendments to the Constitution.

19 28 November 1950 – Punjab High Court orders the release
    of Akali leader Master Tara Singh, jailed for sedition;
    reiterates that Section 124A of the Indian Penal Code was
    unconstitutional, as it contravened the right to freedom of
    speech and expression.

20 10 January 1951 – Uttar Pradesh Zamindari Abolition Act
    passed by the Legislative Assembly including amendments
    introduced by the Legislative Council.

21 24 January 1951 – President Rajendra Prasad assents to the

abovementioned act; over 4,000 petitions challenging its validity are filed in the Allahabad High Court.

22 25 January 1951 – Allahabad High Court issues interim injunctions restraining the government from taking possession of the estates.

23 12 March 1951 – Patna High Court declares the Bihar Land Reforms Act unconstitutional.

24 14 March 1951 – Ambedkar writes a memorandum sketching the outline of a constitutional amendment.

25 9 April 1951 – Supreme Court upholds Madras High Court's voiding of the Communal General Order.

26 30 April 1951 – Rajendra Prasad writes to Nehru criticising the proposed amendment and warning that it will create more problems than it will solve.

27 10 May 1951 – Allahabad High Court upholds the Uttar Pradesh Zamindari Abolition Act.

28 12 May 1951 – Nehru introduces the Constitution (First Amendment) Bill in Parliament.

29 15 May 1951 – Speaker G. V. Mavalankar writes to Nehru expressing his objections to the proposed amendment.

30 16 May 1951 – Parliamentary debate on the Amendment begins.

31 18 May – The Amendment Bill is referred to a Select Committee; Acharya Kripalani resigns from the Congress.

32 23 May 1951 – Congress parliamentary party meets. Nehru is presented with a petition signed by seventy-seven MP's asking for a free vote on the amendment.

33 25 May 1951 – A new draft of the Constitution (First Amendment) Bill and the Report of the Select Committee are tabled in Parliament.

34 2 June 1951 – Constitution (First Amendment) Bill is passed.

35 5 October 1951 – Supreme Court dismisses petitions challenging the amendment and upholds the validity of the Constitution (First Amendment) Act.

NOTES

Introduction

1 Jawaharlal Nehru, 16 May 1951, *Parliamentary Debates*, Part II, Vol. XII (New Delhi: 1951), p. 8832.

2 Ibid., 8822.

3 The imperatives of a modernist vision for India as Menon described them. See Nivedita Menon, 2004. 'Citizenship and the Passive Revolution: Interpreting the First Amendment', *Economic and Political Weekly*, 39:18: 1812–1819.

4 Bidyut Chakrabarty, 1992. 'Jawaharlal Nehru and Planning, 1938–1941: India at the Crossroads', *Modern Asian Studies*, 26:2: 275–87.

5 *Brij Bhushan v. State of Delhi*, AIR 1950 SC 129.

6 *Romesh Thappar v. State of Madras*, AIR 1950 SC 124.

7 *Kameshwar Singh v. State of Bihar*, AIR 1950 Pat. 392.

8 *Chintaman Rao v. State of Madhya Pradesh*, AIR 1951 SC 118.

9 'Communal G.O. Not Constitutional', *Times of India*, Bombay, 27 March 1951, p. 5; *State of Madras v. Champakam Dorairajan*, AIR 1951 SC 226.

10 *B. Venkataramana v. State of Madras*, AIR 1951 SC 229.

11 Jawaharlal Nehru to Chief Ministers, 18 February 1951, G. Parthasarathi, ed., *Letters to Chief Ministers, 1947–1964*, Vol. 2 (New Delhi: Jawaharlal Nehru Memorial Fund, 1986), p. 337.

12 Jawaharlal Nehru to Chief Ministers, 1 February 1951, Ibid., p. 325.

13 Jawaharlal Nehru to Chief Ministers, 21 March 1951, Ibid., p. 363.

14 Jawaharlal Nehru, 16 May 1951, *Parliamentary Debates*, Part II, Vol. XII (New Delhi: 1951), p. 8821.

15 Upendra Baxi, 'The Judiciary as a Resource for Indian Democracy', http://www.india-seminar.com/2010/615/615_upendra_baxi.htm (accessed on 20 November 2018).

16 A. G. Noorani, 2007. 'Ninth Schedule and the Supreme Court', *Economic and Political Weekly*, 42, 9: 731.

17 Dr Shyama Prasad Mookerji.

18   Dr S. P. Mookerji, 16 May 1951, *Parliamentary Debates*, Part II,
      Vol. XII (New Delhi: 1951), pp. 8838, 8856.
19   'Nehru Introduces Bill to Amend Constitution: Further Curbs on
      Freedom', *The Statesman*, 13 May 1951, Calcutta, p. 1.
20   'Lawyers Criticise Proposed Measure', *The Statesman*, 17 May
      1951, Calcutta, p. 5.
21   Justice Rajinder Sachar was a noted lawyer who later became a
      judge. He served as the chief justice of the Delhi High Court, and in
      the early 2000s headed the Rajinder Sachar Committee to study the
      condition of the Muslim community in India.
22   Letter to the Editor, *Times of India*, 30 April 1951, Bombay, p. 4.
23   'Heated Debate on Bill to Amend Constitution', *Times of India*, 3
      June 1951, Bombay, p. 7.
24   Ibid.
25   Jawaharlal Nehru to Chief Ministers, 17 May 1951, G.
      Parthasarathi, ed., *Letters to Chief Ministers, 1947–1964*, Vol. 2
      (New Delhi: Jawaharlal Nehru Memorial Fund, 1986), p. 397.
26   Jawaharlal Nehru to B. C. Roy, 25 May 1951, S. Gopal, ed.,
      Selected Works of Jawaharlal Nehru, Vol. 16/1 (New Delhi:
      Jawaharlal Nehru Memorial Fund, 1994), p. 191.
27   Granville Austin, 'The Expected and the Unintended in Working a
      Democratic Constitution', in Eswaran Sridharan, Zoya Hasan and
      R. Sudarshan, eds, *India's Living Constitution: Ideas, Practices,
      Controversies* (London: Anthem Press, 2005), p. 323.
28   *State of Madras v. Champakam Dorairajan*, AIR 1951 SC 226.
29   Jawaharlal Nehru to Chief Ministers, 21 March 1951, G.
      Parthasarathi, eds, *Letters to Chief Ministers, 1947–1964*, Vol. 2
      (New Delhi: Jawaharlal Nehru Memorial Fund, 1986), p. 363.
30   'First Amendment to 17-Month Old Constitution Passed', *Times of
      India*, 3 June 1951, Bombay, p. 1.
31   So much so that not a single book or major paper on the subject
      is available. Nivedita Menon, 2007. 'Citizenship and the Passive
      Revolution: Interpreting the First Amendment', *Economic and
      Political Weekly*, 39 (8): 1812–19 is the honourable exception.
      Arudra Burra provides an overview from the legal side, but there is
      little information about the broader historical context and political
      implications in his interpretation. For his overview, see: Arudra
      Burra, 'Freedom of Speech in the early Constitution: A Study of
      the Constitution (First Amendment) Bill', in Udit Bhatia (ed.),
      The Indian Constituent Assembly: Deliberations on Democracy
      (Abingdon: Routledge, 2018), pp. 319–381.
32   Drafted by a committee under the chairmanship of Sir Tej Bahadur
      Sapru. Mahatma Gandhi, Sarojini Naidu and Bipin Chandra Pal
      were also members of this committee. The bill was presented in the

British Parliament by Labour MP George Lansbury, where it didn't progress beyond the first reading.

33   The Nehru Committee was set up by the Indian National Congress under the chairmanship of Motilal Nehru to draw up a plan for *swaraj*, or self-rule, for India. The British ignored the report.

34   At the Lahore session of the Congress in 1929, the party declared its goal of *purna swaraj*, or complete independence. The independence pledge was taken on 26 January 1930, which date the Congress continued to celebrate as 'Independence Day' until 1947. That very date, 26 January, was thus chosen as the date to enact the new Constitution as a symbolic fulfilment of that pledge.

35   Jawaharlal Nehru to Chief Ministers, 18 January 1950, G. Parthasarathi, ed., *Letters to Chief Ministers, 1947–1964*, Vol. 2 (New Delhi: Jawaharlal Nehru Memorial Fund, 1986), p. 3.

36   'Message to the Nation', *National Herald*, 25 January 1950, New Delhi, p. 1.

37   Later to be minister of revenue and expenditure in the Nehru government.

38   *Constituent Assembly Debates*, Vol. IX, 16 September 1949.

39   Ibid., Vol. I, 11 December 1946.

40   'The Republic of India', *Times of India*, 26 January 1950, Bombay, p. 8. See also *Constituent Assembly Debates*, Vol. VII, 24 November 1948.

41   'Observance of Constitutional Morality: Dr. Ambedkar's Views', *Times of India*, 11 June 1950, Bombay, p. 14.

42   *Constituent Assembly Debates*, Vol. VII, 4 November 1948.

43   'The Republic of India', *Times of India, Republic Day Special*, 26 January 1950, Bombay, p. 8.

44   Ibid.

45   'Hail, Our Sovereign Republic: A Day of Great Significance and Fulfilment', *Hindustan Times*, 26 January 1950, New Delhi, p. 1.

46   'The Republican Ideal: CP Ramaswamy Iyer', *Hindustan Times, Republic Day Special*, 26 January 1950, New Delhi, p. 5.

47   'Nation's Crowning Achievement: K.M. Munshi', *Times of India, Republic Day Special*, 26 January 1950, Bombay, p. A1.

48   Ibid.

49   'Constitution Acclaimed by All Sections', *Times of India*, 26 January 1950, Bombay, p. B18.

50   'People's Will Prevails: K. Santhanam', *Hindustan Times, Republic Day Special*, 26 January 1950, New Delhi, p. 15.

51   'Hail, Our Sovereign Republic: A Day of Great Significance and Fulfilment', *Hindustan Times*, 26 January 1950, New Delhi, p. 1.

52   'Constitution of India Analysed', *Times of India*, 26 January 1950, Bombay, p. B8.

53 'Biggest Liberal Experiment in Democratic Government: Kenneth C. Wheare', *Hindustan Times*, 26 January 1950, New Delhi, p. 1.

54 'Nehru, Syama Prasad clash led to first Constitution amendment: Jaitley', *India Today*, 6 July 2018, https://www.indiatoday.in/india/story/nehru-syama-prasad-clash-led-to-first-constitution-amendment-jaitley-1279078-2018-07-06 (accessed on 12 November 2018).

55 *The Indian Express*, 31 October 2022. https://indianexpress.com/article/india/sc-plea-constitution-first-amendment-8239228/ (accessed on 15 November 2022).

56 It is a sad testament to the state of knowledge on Indian constitutional history that not a single book – neither popular nor academic – and not even a handful of academic papers have ever been written about this most defining moment in Indian political and constitutional history.

57 Maya Sharma, '"We Are Here To Change The Constitution," Says Union Minister In New Controversy', NDTV, 26 December 2017, https://www.ndtv.com/india-news/we-are-here-to-change-the-constitution-says-union-minister-anant-kumar-hegde-in-new-controversy-1792197 (accessed on 15 February 2019); Rajeev Dikshit, 'Seers Moot Constitutional Amendment for Early Disposal of Ram Mandir Issue', *The Times of India*, 29 November 2018, https://timesofindia.indiatimes.com/city/varanasi/seers-moot-constitutional-amendment-for-early-disposal-of-ram-mandir-issue/articleshow/66860449.cms (accessed on 15 February 2019).

58 'Indian Civilization Is Purely under Threat: Shashi Tharoor', United News of India, 10 February 2018, http://www.uniindia.com/indian-civilization-is-purely-under-threat-shashi-tharoor/states/news/1134101.html (accessed on 15 February 2019).

59 'Climate for Free Speech Severely Deteriorated Under Modi Govt: PEN International', The Wire, 30 September 2018, https://thewire.in/rights/india-freedom-speech-modi-govt-pen-international-abuse; Parul Abrol, 'In India, Constitutional Secularism Comes Under Threat', The Diplomat, 31 August 2018, https://thediplomat.com/2018/08/in-india-constitutional-secularism-comes-under-threat/ (accessed on 15 February 2019).

60 Gyan Prakash, *Emergency Chronicles: Indira Gandhi and Democracy's Turning Point* (New Delhi: Penguin, 2019), pp. 104, 19, 75–6.]

61 'Indian Civilization Is Purely under Threat: Shashi Tharoor', United News of India, 10 February 2018, http://www.uniindia.com/indian-civilization-is-purely-under-threat-shashi-tharoor/states/news/1134101.html (accessed on 15 February 2019).

62 E.g.: Kanishk Tharoor, 'Why the Battle for India's Past Is a Fight for Its Future', *The Nation*, 15 August 2017 (https://www.thenation.com/article/archive/why-the-battle-for-indias-past-is-a-fight-for-its-future/)

63 See: Samuel Moyn, *Human Rights and the Uses of History* (London: Verso, 2014) pp. xi–xiii.

64 David Armitage, 'In Defense of Presentism', in Darrin M. MacMahon, ed., *History and Human Flourishing* (Oxford: Oxford University Press, forthcoming 2023) p. 68.

65 Granville Austin, *The Indian Constitution: Cornerstone of a Nation* (New Delhi: Oxford University Press, 1999).

66 See Gautam Bhatia, 'The Conservative Constitution: Freedom of Speech and Constituent Assembly Debates', in Udit Bhatia, ed., *The Indian Constituent Assembly: Deliberations on Democracy* (Abingdon: Routledge, 2020), pp. 255–318.

67 See, for example, Gyan Prakash, *Emergency Chronicles: Indira Gandhi and Democracy's Turning Point* (New Delhi: Penguin, 2019); Madhav Khosla, *India's Founding Moment: The Constitution of a Most Surprising Democracy* (Cambridge, MA: Harvard University Press, 2020); Gautam Bhatia, *The Transformative Constitution* (New Delhi: Harper Collins, 2019); Uday Mehta 'Indian Constitutionalism: Crisis, Unity and History', in Sujit Chaudhary et al., eds, *The Oxford Handbook of the Indian Constitution* (Oxford: Oxford University Press, 2016), pp. 38–54.

68 For a succinct examination of the idea of critical junctures, see Giovanni Capoccia, 2007. 'The Study of Critical Junctures: Theory, Narrative and Counterfactuals in Historical Institutionalism', *World Politics*, 59 (3): 341–69.

69 Upendra Baxi, 'The Judiciary as a Resource for Indian Democracy', http://www.india-seminar.com/2010/615/615_upendra_baxi.htm (accessed on 20 November 2018).

Chapter 1: The Build-up

1 *Constituent Assembly Debates*, Vol. I, 11 December 1946.

2 A. G. Noorani, *Challenges to Civil Rights Guarantees in India* (New Delhi: Oxford University Press, 2012), p. 5; Sarbani Sen, *The Constitution of India: Popular Sovereignty and Democratic Transformations* (New Delhi: Oxford University Press, 2007).

3 *Constituent Assembly Debates*, Vol. V, 22 August 1947.

4   Arudra Burra, *Arguments from Colonial Continuity: The Constitution (First Amendment) Act, 1951*, (7 December 2008), pp. 27–8. Available at https://dx.doi.org/10.2139/ssrn.2052659 (accessed on 15 July 2019).

5   Member from Madras. Wife of the future finance minister in the Nehru Cabinet, C. D. Deshmukh.

6   *Constituent Assembly Debates*, Vol. IX, 16 September 1949.

7   See B. Shiva Rao, ed., *The Framing of India's Constitution: Select Documents*, Vol. II (New Delhi: Indian Institute of Public Administration, 1967), pp. 21–304.

8   *Constituent Assembly Debates*, Vol. III, 29 April 1947.

9   Ibid.

10 *Constituent Assembly Debates*, Vol. III, 30 April 1947.

11 'Nation's Crowning Achievement: K.M. Munshi', *Times of India, Republic Day Special*, 26 January 1950, Bombay, p. A1.

12 'Highlights of Our Constitution', *Times of India, Republic Day Special*, 26 January 1950, Bombay, p. B14.

13 Ibid.

14 'No Infringement on Fundamental Rights: K. Santhanam', *Hindustan Times, Republic Day Special*, 26 January 1950, New Delhi, p. 3.

15 'Protection of Liberties', *Times of India*, 25 January 1950, Bombay, p. 5.

16 'The Republic of India', *Times of India, Republic Day Special*, 26 January 1950, Bombay, p. 8.

17 'Constitution of India Analysed', *Times of India*, 26 January 1950, Bombay, p. B8.

18 'Hail, Our Sovereign Republic: A Day of Great Significance and Fulfilment', *Hindustan Times*, 26 January 1950, New Delhi, p. 1.

19 'People's Pledge Fulfilled After 20 Years', *Hindustan Times*, 26 January 1950, New Delhi, p. 1.

20 'Biggest Liberal Experiment in Democratic Government: Kenneth C. Wheare', *Hindustan Times*, 26 January 1950, New Delhi, p. 1.

21 Jawaharlal Nehru to Chief Ministers, 18 January 1950, G. Parthasarathi, ed., *Letters to Chief Ministers, 1947–1964*, Vol. 2 (New Delhi: Jawaharlal Nehru Memorial Fund, 1986), p. 3.

22 Jawaharlal Nehru to Lord Mountbatten, 16 January 1950, S. Gopal, ed., *Selected Works of Jawaharlal Nehru*, Vol. 14/1 (New Delhi: Jawaharlal Nehru Memorial Fund, 1992), p. 458.

23 *Constituent Assembly Debates*, Vol. XI, 25 November 1949.

24 'People's Pledge Fulfilled After 20 Years', *Hindustan Times*, 26 January 1950, New Delhi, p. 1.

25 'No Infringement on Fundamental Rights: K. Santhanam', *Hindustan Times – Republic Day Special*, 26 January 1950, New Delhi, p. 3.

26 'Reverence for the State: C. Rajagopalachari', *Hindustan Times, Republic Day Special*, 26 January 1950, New Delhi, p. 6.

27 See Rohit De, *A People's Constitution* (Princeton: Princeton University Press, 2018).

28 'Bombay Security Measures Act: Validity Challenged', *Times of India*, 7 February 1950, Bombay, p. 3.

29 And declared by the Supreme Court – *State of Madras v. V.G. Row*, AIR 1950 SC 27.

30 'Police Detention of Alleged Communists: Orders Set Aside by High Court', *Times of India*, 9 February 1950, Bombay, p. 3.

31 'Security Act Repeal: Socialist's Move', *Times of India*, 9 February 1950, Bombay, p. 3.

32 'Externment Order: Government's Powers Restricted', *Times of India*, 11 February 1950, Bombay, p. 8.

33 'Bihar Safety Ordinance: Validity Upheld', *Times of India*, 20 January 1950, Bombay, p. 11.

34 'Bihar Act Declared Void', *Times of India*, 16 February 1950, Bombay, p. 5.

35 'Parliament Passes Detention Bill: Measures to Deal with Emergencies', *Times of India*, 26 February 1950, Bombay, p. 1.

36 Member from Assam.

37 'Parliament Passes Detention Bill: Measures to Deal with Emergencies', *Times of India*, 26 February 1950, Bombay, p. 1.

38 'Parliament Passes Preventive Detention Bill: Measure Necessary for Security of State', *Times of India*, 27 February 1950, Bombay, p. 9.

39 Within a few months, the Supreme Court would extend the power of judicial review over preventive detention cases through its judgment in the case of the communist detainee A. K. Gopalan. See also, *A.K. Gopalan v. State of Madras*, AIR 1950 SC 27.

40 Jawaharlal Nehru to Sardar Patel, 4 March 1950, S. Gopal, ed., *Selected Works of Jawaharlal Nehru*, Vol. 14/1 (New Delhi: Jawaharlal Nehru Memorial Fund, 1992), p. 462.

41 Madhava Menon to Sardar Patel, 17 February 1950, Durga Das, ed., *Sardar Patel's Correspondence*, Vol. IX (Ahmedabad: Navajivan Publishing House, 1973), p. 296.

42 'Rioting in Salem Jail', *Times of India*, 13 February 1950, Bombay, p. 1.

43 'Survivor of Salem Prison Massacre Recalls the Black Day', *The Hindu*, 13 February 2006, Chennai, https://www.thehindu.com/todays-paper/tp-national/tp-tamilnadu/survivor-of-salem-prison-

massacre-recalls-the-black-day/article18408295.ece (accessed on 25 November 2018). Amazingly enough, the inquiry commission found the firing justified.

44 Sardar Patel to Madhava Menon, Minister for Education, Law and Jails, 16 February 1950, Durga Das, ed., *Sardar Patel's Correspondence*, Vol. IX (Ahmedabad: Navajivan Publishing House, 1973), pp. 295–6.

45 Jawaharlal Nehru to Sardar Patel, 15 February 1950, S. Gopal, ed., *Selected Works of Jawaharlal Nehru*, Vol. 14/1 (New Delhi: Jawaharlal Nehru Memorial Fund, 1994), p. 458.

46 Jawaharlal Nehru to Sardar Patel, 4 March 1950, S. Gopal, ed., *Selected Works of Jawaharlal Nehru*, Vol. 14/1 (New Delhi: Jawaharlal Nehru Memorial Fund, 1994), p. 462.

47 Brother of Romila Thapar, the distinguished historian.

48 Arudra Burra, 'Civil Liberties in the Early Constitution: *CrossRoads* and *Organiser* cases', 2017, pp. 9–11, http://www.academia. edu/37231132/Civil_Liberties_in_the_Early_Constitution_the_ CrossRoads_and_Organiser_cases (accessed on 25 November 2018).

49 See *Cross Roads*, 17 March 1950.

50 See *Cross Roads*, 7 April 1950.

51 Arudra Burra, 'Civil Liberties in the Early Constitution: *CrossRoads* and *Organiser* Cases', 2017, http://www.academia.edu/37231132/ Civil_Liberties_in_the_Early_Constitution_the_CrossRoads_and_ Organiser_cases (accessed on 25 November 2018).

52 See *Organiser*, 27 February 1950.

53 For example, Myron Weiner, *Party Politics in India: The Development of a Multi-Party System* (Princeton: Princeton University Press, 1957), p. 77.

54 Jawaharlal Nehru to Sardar Patel, 20 February 1950, S. Gopal, ed., *Selected Works of Jawaharlal Nehru*, Vol. 14/1 (New Delhi: Jawaharlal Nehru Memorial Fund, 1992), p. 48.

55 Head of the Gorakhnath mutt. Digvijainath would later be elected to Parliament from Gorakhpur, inaugurating a political tradition continued by his successors Mahant Avaidyanath and Mahant Adityanath.

56 Jawaharlal Nehru to Chief Ministers, 2 February 1950, G. Parthasarathi, ed., *Letters to Chief Ministers, 1947–1964*, Vol. 2 (New Delhi: Jawaharlal Nehru Memorial Fund, 1986), p. 6; Pattabhi Sitaramayya's statement to Congress Working Committee, S. Gopal, ed., *Selected Works of Jawaharlal Nehru*, Vol. 14/1 (New Delhi: Jawaharlal Nehru Memorial Fund, 1992), p. 76.

57 Jawaharlal Nehru to Jayaprakash Narayan, 23 March 1950, S. Gopal, ed., *Selected Works of Jawaharlal Nehru*, Vol. 14/1 (New Delhi: Jawaharlal Nehru Memorial Fund, 1992), p. 141.

58 Jawaharlal Nehru to B. C. Roy, 16 March 1950, S. Gopal, ed., *Selected Works of Jawaharlal Nehru*, Vol. 14/1 (New Delhi: Jawaharlal Nehru Memorial Fund, 1992), p. 124.

59 'Nehru Condemns Distortion of Facts', *Hindustan Times*, 27 April 1950, New Delhi, p. 9; Statement to the press, 26 April 1950, S. Gopal, ed., *Selected Works of Jawaharlal Nehru*, Vol. 14/2 (New Delhi: Jawaharlal Nehru Memorial Fund, 1993), p. 73.

60 Jawaharlal Nehru to Sardar Patel, 26 March 1950, S. Gopal, ed., *Selected Works of Jawaharlal Nehru*, Vol. 14/1 (New Delhi: Jawaharlal Nehru Memorial Fund, 1992), pp. 148–9.

61 Jawaharlal Nehru to C. Rajagopalachari, 16 March 1950, S. Gopal, ed., *Selected Works of Jawaharlal Nehru*, Vol. 14/1 (New Delhi: Jawaharlal Nehru Memorial Fund, 1992), p. 126.

62 Jawaharlal Nehru to Chief Ministers, 1 March 1950, G. Parthasarathi, ed., *Letters to Chief Ministers, 1947–1964*, Vol. 2 (New Delhi: Jawaharlal Nehru Memorial Fund, 1986), p. 41.

63 'Validity of Order Challenged: Delhi Editor's Petition', *Times of India*, 11 April 1950, Bombay, p. 5; see also, *Brij Bhushan v. State of Delhi*, AIR 1950 SC 129.

64 Malkani was the first and longest-serving chief editor of *Organiser*. He was a Nieman Fellow at Harvard and the first man to be arrested when the Emergency was declared by Nehru's daughter Indira. He was later elected as an MP to the Rajya Sabha and served as the governor of Puducherry.

65 *Organiser*, 6 March 1950.

66 For an excellent overview of the journey to the courts and the substantive arguments the two cases raise in the context of India's early constitutional history, see: Arudra Burra, 'Civil Liberties in the Early Constitution: The *Cross Roads* and *Organiser* Cases', in Satvinder Juss, ed., *Human Rights in India* (Abingdon: Routledge, 2020), pp. 3–36.

67 *Organiser*, 13 March 1950.

68 Interestingly, N. C. Chatterjee's son Somnath Chatterjee became a prominent communist leader and was Speaker of Parliament from 2004 to 2009.

69 'Right to Freedom of Speech and Expression: Editor's Plea in Supreme Court', *Times of India*, 26 April 1950, Bombay, p. 9.

70 See Arudra Burra, 'What Self-Styled Nationalists Could Learn from the Hindu Right's Own Past Record on Free Speech', *Scroll. in*, 27 January 2016, https://scroll.in/article/802327/what-self-styled-nationalists-could-learn-from-the-hindu-rights-own-past-record-

on-free-speech (accessed on 22 November 2018). More recently and substantively, see Arudra Burra 'Civil Liberties in the Early Constitution: The *Cross Roads* and Organiser Cases' in Satvinder Juss ed., *Human Rights in India* (Abingdon: Routledge, 2020), esp. pp. 22–7.

71   *Brij Bhushan v. State of Delhi*, AIR 1950 SC 129.
72   *Romesh Thappar v. State of Madras*, AIR 1950 SC 124.
73   'Apathy Towards Civil Rights Deplored: Socialist Leader's Warning', *Times of India*, 17 April 1950, Bombay, p. 5.
74   'Personal Liberty in a Democracy: Mr. M.C. Chagla Emphasizes Supreme Importance', *Times of India*, 2 May 1950, Bombay, p. 5.
75   Brother of the nationalist leader C. R. Das, a Congress stalwart popularly known as Deshbandhu. C.R. was a prominent figure in the non-cooperation movement and defended Aurobindo Ghosh during the Alipore Conspiracy Case.
76   'One Party State Cannot Be Democratic: Criticism at UP Convention', *Times of India*, 15 May 1950, Bombay, p. 9.
77   Interestingly, K. N. Katju's grandson is the outspoken Justice Markandey Katju, and his sometime grandson-in-law was the Congress leader Shashi Tharoor.
78   'Care for Democracy Needed While Maintaining Law: Dr. Katju Wants Utmost Liberty of Expression', *Hindustan Times*, 20 May 1950, New Delhi.
79   *Romesh Thappar v. State of Madras*, AIR 1950 SC 124.
80   'Madras Ban on Bombay Paper: Order Quashed', *Times of India*, 27 May 1950, Bombay, p. 11.
81   *Romesh Thappar v. State of Madras*, AIR 1950 SC 124.
82   Sardar Patel to Jawaharlal Nehru, 3 July 1950, Durga Das, ed., *Sardar Patel's Correspondence*, Vol. X (Ahmedabad: Navajivan Publishing House, 1974), p. 358.
83   'Supreme Court's Judgements: Freedom of the Press', *Times of India*, 5 June 1950, Bombay, p. 6.
84   'Apathy Towards Civil Rights Deplored: Socialist Leader's Warning', *Times of India*, 17 April 1950, Bombay, p. 5.

Chapter 2: Will the People Wait?

1   In present-day Jharkhand.
2   The state was only taking over the power to manage properties – collect rent and arrears, appoint employees, let out properties and evict tenants – rather than acquiring the property itself. Thus, the state would have no power to sell, distribute or otherwise alienate

property, but would simply control it and pay the proprietor 20 per cent of its revenue.

3   'Alleged Contempt by Bihar Govt.: Injunction Order Violated', *Times of India*, 20 January 1950, Bombay, p. 8.

4   Ibid.

5   *State of Bihar v. Kamakhya Narain Singh*, AIR 1950 Pat. 366.

6   *Kameshwar Singh v. State of Bihar*, AIR 1950 Pat. 392.

7   See Jawaharlal Nehru to V. K. Krishna Menon, 20 March 1950, S. Gopal, ed., *Selected Works of Jawaharlal Nehru*, Vol. 14/1 (New Delhi: Jawaharlal Nehru Memorial Fund, 1992), p. 129; Jawaharlal Nehru to Rajendra Prasad, 20 March 1950, S. Gopal, ed., *Selected Works of Jawaharlal Nehru*, Vol. 14/1 (New Delhi: Jawaharlal Nehru Memorial Fund, 1992), p. 130; Jawaharlal Nehru to Vijaya Lakshmi Pandit, 20 March 1950, S. Gopal, ed., *Selected Works of Jawaharlal Nehru*, Vol. 14/1 (New Delhi: Jawaharlal Nehru Memorial Fund, 1992), p. 132; Jawaharlal Nehru to Vijaya Lakshmi Pandit, 12 April 1950, S. Gopal, ed., *Selected Works of Jawaharlal Nehru*, Vol. 14/2 (New Delhi: Jawaharlal Nehru Memorial Fund, 1993), p. 27.

8   Sardar Patel to Jawaharlal Nehru, 28 March 1950, Durga Das, ed., *Sardar Patel's Correspondence*, Vol. X (Ahmedabad: Navajivan Publishing House, 1974), p. 19. Like many of Nehru's critics, Patel believed that ignoring what was happening in Pakistan and its effects in India meant relying solely on coercion and suppression to deal with prejudices against Pakistan and Indian Muslims. 'Our secular ideals impose a responsibility on our Muslim citizens in India – a responsibility to remove the doubts and misgivings entertained by a large section of the people about their loyalty founded largely on their past association with the demand for Pakistan and the unfortunate activities of some of them,' he stated to Nehru.

9   See a condensed report of the *Hindustan Times* on how the Bengali press had presented Nehru: 'Calcutta's Mixed Reception to Nehru-Liaquat Pact', *Hindustan Times*, 12 April 1950, Bombay, p. 12. The Bengali press remained almost universally critical of the prime minister and his approach to Pakistan.

10   Jawaharlal Nehru to Sardar Patel, 26 March 1950, S. Gopal, ed., *Selected Works of Jawaharlal Nehru*, Vol. 14/1 (New Delhi: Jawaharlal Nehru Memorial Fund, 1992), p. 148.

11   Sardar Patel to Jawaharlal Nehru, 28 March 1950, Durga Das, ed., *Sardar Patel's Correspondence*, Vol. X (Ahmedabad: Navajivan Publishing House, 1974), p. 20.

12   Ibid.

13   Sardar Patel to Jawaharlal Nehru, 3 July 1950, Durga Das, ed.,
      Sardar Patel's Correspondence, Vol. X (Ahmedabad: Navajivan
      Publishing House, 1974), p. 358.
14   The Pakistani government had complained that despite the Nehru–
      Liaquat Pact and the creation of a new editorial consultative
      mechanism, the tone of the West Bengal press had not improved;
      that they continued to print material doubting the bona fides of
      the East Bengal and Pakistani governments and indulged in anti-
      Pakistan propaganda.
15   Jawaharlal Nehru to Zafarullah Khan, 20 May 1950, S. Gopal,
      ed., *Selected Works of Jawaharlal Nehru*, Vol. 14/2 (New Delhi:
      Jawaharlal Nehru Memorial Fund, 1993), p. 111. Nehru even
      assured Zafarullah Khan that every effort was being made to
      improve the tone of the West Bengal press.
16   'Amendment to UP Zamindari Abolition Bill Rejected', *Hindustan
      Times*, 1 April 1950, New Delhi, p. 3.
17   Ibid.
18   'Amendment to UP Zamindari Bill: Proposal to Limit Debate',
      Times of India, 8 April 1950, Bombay, p. 5.
19   'UP Land Bill Changes', *Times of India*, 28 July 1950, Bombay,
      p. 6.
20   'Time Limit on Discussion of Bills: Debate in UP Assembly',
      Hindustan Times, 23 April 1950, New Delhi, p. 12; 'Battle Royal in
      UP Assembly', *Hindustan Times*, 24 April 1950, New Delhi, p. 6.
      There were, after all, several rajas ranged against the Congress in
      the assembly.
21   Purushottam Das Tandon, a senior Congress leader and future
      Congress president.
22   'Deadline for Passing Zamindari Bill: 40 Days Allotted for Further
      Discussion', *Hindustan Times*, 26 April 1950, New Delhi, p. 6.
23   'UP Assembly Debates Zamindari Bill', *Hindustan Times*, 6 May
      1950, New Delhi, p. 8; 'Zamindars Entitled to Compensation:
      Socialist Amendment Lost in UP Assembly', *Hindustan Times*, 9
      May 1950, New Delhi, p. 8.
24   'Zamindars' Vain Bid for Higher Compensation Rate', *Hindustan
      Times*, 13 May 1950, New Delhi, p. 8.
25   'UP Land Bill Changes', *Times of India*, 28 July 1950, Bombay,
      p. 6; 'Cash Compensation for Big Zamindars Doubtful', *Hindustan
      Times*, 14 June 1950, New Delhi, p. 8.
26   For representative examples, see 'Benefits of Zamindari Abolition:
      Cultivators Urged to Become Bhumidars', *Hindustan Times*, 30
      April 1950, New Delhi, p. 12; 'Contribution to ZAF Urged: UP
      Minister's Call', *Hindustan Times*, 1 June 1950, New Delhi, p. 6.

27   'Zamindari Abolition in UP: Kisans Urged to Acquire Bhumidari
      Rights Soon', *Hindustan Times*, 15 April 1950, New Delhi, p. 8.
28   Farmer willing to buy the land at ten times his annual rent.
29   'End of ZA Fund Drive on June 30th', *Hindustan Times*, 19 April
      1950, New Delhi, p. 8.
30   'Educating Peasants on Agrarian Reforms: Congress Committees to
      Launch Campaign', *Hindustan Times*, 29 April 1950, New Delhi, p. 5.
31   'Zamindari Abolition: A Great Reform', *Hindustan Times*, 26 April
      1950, New Delhi, p. 6.
32   'UP Newsletter: ZAF Drive', *Hindustan Times*, 10 July 1950, New
      Delhi, p. 6; Walter Crocker called this nationalist propaganda
      about a new heaven as soon as the British had gone: Walter
      Crocker, *Nehru: A Contemporary's Estimate* (New Delhi: Random
      House, 2011).
33   'More Clauses of Bihar Land Reforms Bill Passed', *Hindustan
      Times*, 14 April 1950, New Delhi, p. 8.
34   'Bihar Land Reforms Bill: 8 More Clauses Passed', *Hindustan
      Times*, 20 April 1950, New Delhi, p. 6.
35   'Bihar Land Reforms Bill Passed', *Hindustan Times*, 23 April 1950,
      New Delhi, p. 1.
36   'Bihar Newsletter: Land Reforms', *Hindustan Times*, 28 April 1950,
      New Delhi, p. 5.
37   'Zamindar Walk-Out in UP Assembly: Land Reforms Bill', *Times of
      India*, 15 May 1950, Bombay, p. 3.
38   *Kameshwar Singh v. State of Bihar*, AIR 1950 Pat. 392.
39   'Bihar Management of Estates Act Invalid: Interim Injunctions
      against Government Made Permanent', *Hindustan Times*, 7 June
      1950, p. 3.
40   *Kameshwar Singh v. State of Bihar*, AIR 1950 Pat. 392; 'Bihar Land
      Act Held Invalid: Decision by Patna High Court', *Times of India*,
      7 June 1950, Bombay, p. 5; Gopal Sankaranarayanan, 'The Fading
      Right to Property in India', *Law and Politics in Africa, Asia and
      Latin America*, 44 (2): 225.
41   'Right to Spread Disaffection against Party Govt.: Allahabad High
      Court's Ruling', *Hindustan Times*, 3 June 1950, New Delhi, p. 8.
42   Ibid.
43   Interestingly, Matthai was the uncle of Verghese Kurien, the
      man responsible for Amul and the White Revolution. His son,
      Ravi Matthai, was the founder director of the Indian Institute of
      Management, Ahmedabad.
44   'Matthai's Statement on Resignation', *Hindustan Times*, 3 June
      1950, New Delhi, p. 4; 'Grave Misgivings on Delhi Pact: Dr.
      Matthai's Reasons for Resignation', *Times of India*, 3 June 1950,
      Bombay, p. 1.

45 'Pandit Nehru Refutes Charge of Authoritarianism', *Times of India*, 2 June 1950, Bombay, p. 1.

46 'Cause of Dr. Matthai's Exit from the Cabinet: Resignation "Demanded" by Prime Minister', *Times of India*, 6 June 1950, Bombay, p. 1.

47 Diary entry, 17 September 1946, Penderel Moon, ed., *Wavell: The Viceroy's Journal* (Oxford: Oxford University Press, 1973), p. 351.

48 'Cause of Dr. Matthai's Exit from the Cabinet: Resignation "Demanded" by Prime Minister', *Times of India*, 6 June 1950, Bombay, p. 1.

49 Ibid.

50 The fact that Matthai shunned political office and rejoined the Tata group lent him further credence in the public eye.

51 See Jawaharlal Nehru to John Matthai, 4 June 1950, p. 234; Jawaharlal Nehru to Vijaya Lakshmi Pandit, 5 June 1950, S. Gopal, ed., *Selected Works of Jawaharlal Nehru*, Vol. 14/2 (New Delhi: Jawaharlal Nehru Memorial Fund, 1993), p. 234, p. 246; Jawaharlal Nehru to Sardar Patel, 5 June 1950, p. 244; Jawaharlal Nehru to Vijaya Lakshmi Pandit, 5 June 1950, S. Gopal, ed., *Selected Works of Jawaharlal Nehru*, Vol. 14/2 (New Delhi: Jawaharlal Nehru Memorial Fund, 1993), p. 246.

52 Jawaharlal Nehru to C. Rajagopalachari, 4 June 1950, S. Gopal, ed., *Selected Works of Jawaharlal Nehru*, Vol. 14/2 (New Delhi: Jawaharlal Nehru Memorial Fund,1993), p. 239. Interestingly, Nehru took some newspapermen along for a holiday aboard the naval ship as well. See also Jawaharlal Nehru to Vijaya Lakshmi Pandit, 5 June 1950, S. Gopal, ed., *Selected Works of Jawaharlal Nehru*, Vol. 14/2 (New Delhi: Jawaharlal Nehru Memorial Fund, 1993), p. 246.

53 'Unabated Hostility to Pact', *Times of India*, 15 June 1950, Bombay, p. 6.

54 Jawaharlal Nehru to Vijaya Lakshmi Pandit, 12 April 1950, S. Gopal, ed., *Selected Works of Jawaharlal Nehru*, Vol. 14/2 (New Delhi: Jawaharlal Nehru Memorial Fund, 1993), p. 27; Jawaharlal Nehru to Vijaya Lakshmi Pandit, 15 April 1950, S. Gopal, ed., *Selected Works of Jawaharlal Nehru*, Vol. 14/2 (New Delhi: Jawaharlal Nehru Memorial Fund, 1993), p. 44; Jawaharlal Nehru to V. K. Krishna Menon, 4 June 1950, S. Gopal, ed., *Selected Works of Jawaharlal Nehru*, Vol. 14/2 (New Delhi: Jawaharlal Nehru Memorial Fund, 1993), p. 241; Jawaharlal Nehru to Vijaya Lakshmi Pandit, 5 June 1950, S. Gopal, ed., *Selected Works of Jawaharlal Nehru*, Vol. 14/2 (New Delhi: Jawaharlal Nehru Memorial Fund, 1993), p. 245.

55   See B. Shiva Rao, ed., *The Framing of India's Constitution: Select Documents*, Vol. II (New Delhi: N. M. Tripathi, 1967), pp. 231–40; Gopal Sankaranarayanan, 'The Fading Right to Property in India', *Law and Politics in Africa, Asia and Latin America*, 44 (2): 225.

56   For example, see 'Contribution to ZAF Urged: UP Minister's Call', *Hindustan Times*, 1 June 1950, New Delhi, p. 6. C. B. Gupta would become chief minister of UP three times in the 1960s.

57   Sahay also had his own axe to grind. He had an accident with a truck, which he alleged had been ordered by Maharaja Kameshwar Singh of Darbhanga to kill him. See 'Land Reforms: Loop Full of Holes', *Hindustan Times*, 26 July 2004, https://www. hindustantimes.com/india/land-reforms-loop-full-of-holes/story-aesBOfmlsJ3IAKnwjGJq6J.html (accessed on 1 May 2019).

58   'Another Estate Plan for Bihar', *Times of India*, 10 June 1950, Bombay, p. 7.

59   Ibid.

60   'Observance of Constitutional Morality: Dr. Ambedkar's Views', *Times of India*, 11 June 1950, Bombay, p. 14.

61   'Land Reform in Bihar: Zamindars Anxious to Cooperate', *Hindustan Times*, 12 June 1950, New Delhi, p. 5.

62   'Unconstitutional Laws', *Times of India*, 22 June 1950, Bombay, p. 6.

63   'Bihar Estates', *Times of India*, 13 July 1950, Bombay, p. 8.

64   'Land Reforms', *Times of India*, 6 July 1950, Bombay, p. 1.

65   The committee consisted of C. Rajagopalachari, C. D. Deshmukh, K. M. Munshi, Jagjivan Ram, B. R. Ambedkar and N. V. Gadgil.

66   'UP Zamindari Abolition Bill: Compensation Issue', *Times of India*, 12 June 1950, Bombay, p. 1.

67   'Zamindari Abolition to Cost Rs. 414 Crores', *Hindustan Times*, 15 July 1950, New Delhi, p. 5.

68   '72 Clauses of UP Zamindari Abolition Bill Passed', *Hindustan Times*, 5 July 1950, New Delhi, p. 7.

69   'Indian Constitution a Clumsy Document: Criticism by Socialist Party Conference', *Times of India*, 11 July 1950, Bombay, p. 3.

70   Ibid.

71   Note to the home minister, 25 July 1950, S. Gopal, ed., *Selected Works of Jawaharlal Nehru*, Vol. 14/2 (New Delhi: Jawaharlal Nehru Memorial Fund, 1993), p. 223.

72   Ibid.

73   For a good overview of communal representation and Justice Party politics, see P. Maran, 'The Evolution of Communal Representation in Tamil Nadu', Unpublished PhD Dissertation (Madurai Kamaraj University, 2012), especially Chapter 3.

74   See K. Veeramani, *The History of the Struggle for Social Justice in Tamil Nadu* (Chennai: Dravidar Kazagham Publications, 1998), p. 25, 26; P. Maran, 'The Evolution of Communal Representation in Tamil Nadu', Unpublished PhD Dissertation (Madurai Kamraj University, 2012), pp. 124–40.

75   'Admission to Colleges: Validity of Madras Order Questioned', *Times of India*, 8 June 1950, Bombay, p. 3.

76   'Madras Order on Colleges Again Challenged: Student's Petition', *Times of India*, 15 June 1950, Bombay, p. 3.

77   *Champakam Dorairajan v. State of Madras*, AIR 1950 Mad. 120.

78   Ibid.

79   'Appeal against Madras Order: Student's Petition', *Times of India*, 14 June 1950, Bombay, p. 7.

80   Ibid.

81   'Penalty for Talent', *Times of India*, 12 June 1950, Bombay, p. 6.

82   'Communal Rule: To the Editor', *Times of India*, 6 June 1950, Bombay, p. 6.

83   Ibid.

84   'Letters from Our Readers', *Hindustan Times*, 17 June 1950, New Delhi, p. 7.

85   'Communal Rule: To the Editor', *Times of India*, 16 June 1950, Bombay, p. 6.

86   'Penalty for Talent', *Times of India*, 12 June 1950, Bombay, p. 6.

87   Ibid.

88   'Communal Basis for Admissions Invalid: Madras High Court Upholds Petitions', *Hindustan Times*, 28 July 1950, New Delhi, p. 1.

89   *Champakam Dorairajan v. State of Madras*, AIR 1950 Mad. 120.

90   Ibid.; 'Madras Govt. to Appeal to Supreme Court', *Hindustan Times*, 29 July 1950, New Delhi, p. 5.

91   *Champakam Dorairajan v. State of Madras*, AIR 1950 Mad. 120.

92   Ibid.; 'Madras Govt. to Appeal to Supreme Court', *Hindustan Times*, 29 July 1950, New Delhi, p. 5.

93   'Minister Warns Madras Students: Strikes in Colleges Deplored', *Times of India*, 6 August 1950, Bombay, p. 13.

94   'A Dangerous Portent', *Times of India*, 11 August 1950, Bombay, p. 6.

95   'Minister Warns Madras Students: Strikes in Colleges Deplored', *Times of India*, 6 August 1950, Bombay, p. 13.

96   'Invalidation of Communal G.O.', *Times of India*, 11 August 1950, Bombay, p. 7.

97   *Champakam Dorairajan v. State of Madras*, AIR 1950 Mad. 120.

98   'A Dangerous Portent', *Times of India*, 11 August 1950, Bombay, p. 6.

99   Note to the Home Minister, 25 July 1950, S. Gopal, ed., *Selected Works of Jawaharlal Nehru*, Vol. 14/2 (New Delhi: Jawaharlal Nehru Memorial Fund, 1993), p. 223.

100 Jawaharlal Nehru to Chief Ministers, 3 August 1950, G. Parthasarathi, ed., *Letters to Chief Ministers, 1947–1964*, Vol. 2 (New Delhi: Jawaharlal Nehru Memorial Fund, 1986), p. 162.

101 'A Dangerous Portent', *Times of India*, 11 August 1950, Bombay, p. 6.

102 'Rehabilitation Grants to Smaller Landholders: Schedule to UP Zamindari Abolition Bill Passed', *Hindustan Times*, 28 July 1950, New Delhi, p. 8.

103 'UP Zamindari Abolition Bill', *Times of India*, 5 August 1950, Bombay, p. 7; 'UP Land Bill Changes', *Times of India*, 28 July 1950, Bombay, p. 6.

104 'Bhumidari Zindabad: UP Zamindari Abolition Bill Passed', *Hindustan Times*, 5 August 1950, New Delhi, p. 1.

105 'UP's Feudal Order Being Changed: Intermediary Rights Acquired', *Hindustan Times*, 5 August 1950, New Delhi, p. 9.

106 'Zamindari Abolition', *Times of India*, 30 June 1950, Bombay, p. 6.

Chapter 3: The Deepening Crisis

1   'Year of Deepening Gloom: Unsolved Problems, Demoralised People', *Times of India*, 15 August 1950, Bombay, p. 6.

2   Ibid.

3   Rohit De, *A People's Constitution* (Princeton: Princeton University Press, 2018), p. 2.

4   'Indian Political Notes: Issues for Congress Presidential Election', *Times of India*, 10 August 1950, Bombay, p. 6.

5   Ibid.

6   An independent country composed of the current states of Andhra Pradesh, Telangana, Tamil Nadu, Kerala and Karnataka.

7   'The Indian Background: Befuddled Communists', *Times of India*, 23 August 1950, Bombay, p. 6.

8   Ibid.

9   Ibid.

10   'Zamindari Abolition in Bihar: Talks in Delhi Concluded', *Times of India*, 21 August 1950, Bombay, p. 1.

11   See B. Shiva Rao, ed., *The Framing of India's Constitution: Select Documents*, Vol. II (New Delhi: Indian Institute of Public Administration, 1967), pp. 231–40; Gopal Sankaranarayanan, 'The

Fading Right to Property in India', *Law and Politics in Africa, Asia and Latin America*, 44, 2: 225.

12   Ibid., p. 226; Granville Austin, *The Indian Constitution: Cornerstone of a Nation* (Oxford: Oxford University Press, 1972), pp. 87–99.

13   Jawaharlal Nehru to Sardar Patel, 26 August 1950; Jawaharlal Nehru to Sardar Patel, 28 August 1950, S. Gopal, ed., *Selected Works of Jawaharlal Nehru*, Vol. 15/1 (New Delhi: Jawaharlal Nehru Memorial Fund, 1993), pp. 104–5; Rajmohan Gandhi, *Patel: A Life* (Ahmedabad: Navajivan Publishing House, 1990), pp. 520–26.

14   'Tandon Elected Congress President: Outright Victory Over Rivals', *Hindustan Times*, 3 September 1950, New Delhi, p. 1.

15   Rajmohan Gandhi, *Patel: A Life* (Ahmedabad: Navajivan Publishing House 1990), pp. 504–06, 520–6, particularly p. 526.

16   'Fears of Crisis in Congress Discounted: Election of Mr. Tandon Hailed', *Times of India*, 4 September 1950, Bombay, p. 5. Funnily enough, Tandon only lasted a year of his supposed three-year term. He gave way to Nehru, who then held the office of prime minister and Congress president for the remainder of the term.

17   Kripalani was a former Congress president, who had been associated with Congress for close to three decades, and had been its general secretary for twelve years.

18   'Bihar Land Reforms Bill to be Amended: President's Assent Expected Soon', *Times of India*, 7 September 1950, Bombay, p. 1.

19   'Decision on Compensation', *Times of India*, 8 September 1950, Bombay, p. 6.

20   Ibid.

21   See Jawaharlal Nehru to Rajendra Prasad, 11 September 1950, S. Gopal, ed., *Selected Works of Jawaharlal Nehru*, Vol. 15/1 (New Delhi: Jawaharlal Nehru Memorial Fund, 1993), p. 51; Sardar Patel to Jawaharlal Nehru, 11 September 1950, Durga Das, ed., *Sardar Patel's Correspondence*, Vol. IX (Ahmedabad: Navajivan Publishing House, 1974), p. 274.

22   See G. P. Sharma, 'Nationalist Response to Agrarian Conflict: Dr. Rajendra Prasad and Peasant Politics in Bihar in the 1930s', *Studies in People's History*, 2 (2): 216–24.

23   Sardar Patel to Jawaharlal Nehru, 11 September 1950, Durga Das, ed., *Sardar Patel's Correspondence*, Vol. IX (Ahmedabad: Navajivan Publishing House, 1974), p. 274.

24   See Jawaharlal Nehru to Rajendra Prasad, 11 September 1950, S. Gopal, ed., *Selected Works of Jawaharlal Nehru*, Vol. 15/1 (New Delhi: Jawaharlal Nehru Memorial Fund, 1993), p. 51.

25 Sardar Patel to Jawaharlal Nehru, 11 September 1950, Durga Das, ed., *Sardar Patel's Correspondence*, Vol. IX (Ahmedabad: Navajivan Publishing House, 1974), p. 274.

26 Nehru would complain bitterly to Patel about his having masterminded Tandon's election, and accused him of pressuring and bullying people into voting for his preferred candidate. Jawaharlal Nehru to Sardar Patel, 28 September 1950 (Draft Letter), S. Gopal, ed., *Selected Works of Jawaharlal Nehru*, Vol. 15/1 (New Delhi: Jawaharlal Nehru Memorial Fund, 1993), p. 107.

27 Jawaharlal Nehru to Rajendra Prasad, 11 September 1950, S. Gopal, ed., *Selected Works of Jawaharlal Nehru*, Vol. 15/1 (New Delhi: Jawaharlal Nehru Memorial Fund, 1993), p. 51.

28 Ibid.

29 Jawaharlal Nehru to Sardar Patel, 12 September 1950, S. Gopal, ed., *Selected Works of Jawaharlal Nehru*, Vol. 15/1 (New Delhi: Jawaharlal Nehru Memorial Fund, 1993), p. 52.

30 Statement to the Press, 12 September 1950, S. Gopal, ed., *Selected Works of Jawaharlal Nehru*, Vol. 15/1 (New Delhi: Jawaharlal Nehru Memorial Fund, 1993), p. 114.

31 'Estates Should Not Be Taken Over: Bihar Zamindar's Notices', *Times of India*, 20 September 1950, Bombay, p. 8.

32 Ibid.

33 'Communal Reservations in UP End', *Hindustan Times*, 11 September 1950, New Delhi, p. 1.

34 Jawaharlal Nehru to Vijaya Lakshmi Pandit, 12 September 1950, S. Gopal, ed., *Selected Works of Jawaharlal Nehru*, Vol. 15/1 (New Delhi: Jawaharlal Nehru Memorial Fund, 1993), p. 117.

35 Ibid.

36 'Nehru Deplores Craze for Office: Congressmen Reminded of Gandhiji's Teachings', *Hindustan Times*, 18 September 1950, New Delhi, p. 4.

37 Ibid.

38 See Jawaharlal Nehru to Sardar Patel, 28 September 1950 (Draft Letter), S. Gopal, ed., *Selected Works of Jawaharlal Nehru*, Vol. 15/1 (New Delhi: Jawaharlal Nehru Memorial Fund, 1993), p. 107.

39 Jawaharlal Nehru to Vijaya Lakshmi Pandit, 19 September, S. Gopal, ed., *Selected Works of Jawaharlal Nehru*, Vol. 15/1 (New Delhi: Jawaharlal Nehru Memorial Fund, 1993), p. 136.

40 'Indo-Pakistan Issues to Be Solved Amicably: Nehru Condemns Loose Talk of War, Subjects Body Adopts Motion on Communalism', *Hindustan Times*, 20 September 1950, New Delhi, p. 6; Rajmohan Gandhi, *Patel: A Life* (Ahmedabad: Navajivan Publishing House, 1990), p. 526.

41 'Unqualified Support to the Constitution: Clear Exposition of Secular State Ideal', *Hindustan Times*, 21 September 1950, New Delhi, p. 1.

42 'Economic Plan Adopted', *Hindustan Times*, 21 September 1950, New Delhi, p. 1; 'Congress Favours Continuation of Controls: Economic Policy Motion Passed', *Hindustan Times*, 22 September 1950, New Delhi, p. 1.

43 'Tandon Approves Government's Foreign and Home Policies: Firm Attitude Towards Pakistan Urged', *Hindustan Times*, 21 September 1950, New Delhi, p. 5.

44 See Myron Weiner, *Party Politics in India: The Development of a Multi-Party System* (Princeton: Princeton University Press, 1957), pp. 70–8.

45 'Nasik Session: Control of Election Machinery', *Times of India*, 22 September 1950, Bombay, p. 6.

46 Jawaharlal Nehru to Vijaya Lakshmi Pandit, 19 September, S. Gopal, ed., *Selected Works of Jawaharlal Nehru*, Vol. 15/1 (New Delhi: Jawaharlal Nehru Memorial Fund, 1993), p. 136.

47 Harshan Kumarasingham, 'The Indian Version of First Among Equals: Executive Power during the First Decade of Independence', *Modern Asian Studies*, 44 (4): 715.

48 'Confidence Vote in Pandit Nehru: C.R.'s Comment', *Times of India*, 23 September 1950, Bombay, p. 8.

49 'Unqualified Support to the Constitution: Clear Exposition of Secular State Ideal', *Hindustan Times*, 21 September 1950, New Delhi, p. 1.

50 Jawaharlal Nehru to Chief Ministers, 1 October 1950, G. Parthasarathi, ed., *Letters to Chief Ministers, 1947–1964*, Vol. 2 (New Delhi: Jawaharlal Nehru Memorial Fund, 1986), p. 209.

51 Jawaharlal Nehru to Chief Ministers, 27 September 1950, G. Parthasarathi, ed., *Letters to Chief Ministers, 1947–1964*, Vol. 2 (New Delhi: Jawaharlal Nehru Memorial Fund, 1986), p. 205.

52 *VG Row v. State of Madras*, AIR 1951 Mad. 147.

53 Ibid.

54 Ibid.

55 'Right of Association Cannot be Denied', *Times of India*, 15 September 1950, Bombay, p. 1.

56 Jawaharlal Nehru to Chief Ministers, 14 September 1950, S. Gopal, ed., *Selected Works of Jawaharlal Nehru*, Vol. 15/1 (New Delhi: Jawaharlal Nehru Memorial Fund, 1993), p. 540.

57 *Kameshwar Singh v. State of Bihar*, AIR 1951 Pat. 91.

58 Jawaharlal Nehru to Sri Krishna Sinha, 19 October 1950, S. Gopal, ed., *Selected Works of Jawaharlal Nehru*, Vol. 15/1 (New Delhi: Jawaharlal Nehru Memorial Fund, 1993), p. 52.

59 Statutory agriculturalists had been a category created in colonial Punjab to address what was considered a major cause of the rebellion in 1857 by preventing agricultural land from passing on to or being transferred to the hands of auction purchasers or urban mercantile communities.

60 'Current Topics: Reservation of Posts', *Times of India*, 11 October 1950, Bombay, p. 6.

61 Ibid.

62 Ibid.

63 *Bharati Press, Smt. Shaila Bala Devi v. The Chief Secretary, Government of Bihar*, AIR 1951 CriLJ 309 (Patna)

64 Ibid.; Abhinav Chandrachud, 'Freedom of Expression Was Once Wide-Ranging in India. Then Jawaharlal Nehru Asked for Changes', *Scroll.in*, 5 September 2017, https://scroll.in/ article/849499/freedom-of-expression-was-once-absolute-in-india-then-jawaharlal-nehru-asked-for-changes (accessed on 1 June 2019).

65 *Bharati Press, Smt. Shaila Bala Devi v. The Chief Secretary, Government of Bihar*, AIR 1951 CriLJ 309 (Patna).

66 'Bombay State Road Transport Organisation Illegal: Decision by High Court', *Times of India*, 17 October 1950, Bombay, p. 7.

67 'UP Bus Drivers Move High Court: Full Bench to Hear Writ Petitions', *Hindustan Times*, 8 April 1950, New Delhi, p. 8; 'Nationalisation of Road Transport in UP Challenged: Case Before High Court', *Hindustan Times*, 13 April 1950, New Delhi, p. 7; 'Right to Ply Private Buses: Further Hearing in Transport Nationalisation Challenge Case', *Hindustan Times*, 15 April 1950, New Delhi, p. 8; 'Restrictions on Use of Bus Routes Unconstitutional: Further Arguments in Allahabad High Court', *Hindustan Times*, 17 April 1950, New Delhi, p. 8.

68 *Moti Lal and Others v. State of Uttar Pradesh*, AIR 1951 All. 257.

69 'Failure to Consider Permit Applications on Merit: High Court Judgement in UP Bus Owners Case', *Hindustan Times*, 14 May 1950, New Delhi, p. 12.

70 'Nationalisation of Transport: UP Cabinet Approves Draft Bill', *Hindustan Times*, 29 July 1950, New Delhi, p. 8.

71 'Bombay State Road Transport Body: Bill to Enlarge Powers', *Times of India*, 3 April 1950, Bombay, p. 3; 'Procedure About State Road Transport Body Criticised: Debate on Official Bill in Bombay Assembly', *Times of India*, 11 April 1950, Bombay, p. 5; 'Wide Powers of Decision for State Road Transport Body', *Times of India*, 12 April 1950, Bombay, p. 3.

72   'Bombay State Road Transport Organisation Illegal: Decision by
      High Court', *Times of India*, 17 October 1950, Bombay, p. 7.
73   Ibid.
74   'Parliament Approves Road Transport Bill: Establishment of
      Bombay State Organisation Validated', *Times of India*, 30
      November 1950, Bombay, p. 9.
75   Granville Austin, *Working a Democratic Constitution: The Indian
      Experience* (New Delhi: Oxford University Press, 2003), p. 42.
76   Ministry of Law, File No. F34/51-C – National Archives of India,
      quoted in Ibid.
77   Munsif literally means a judge or magistrate. A munsif court is the
      lowest court handling civil matters in India.
78   *B. Venkataramana v. State of Tamil Nadu*, AIR 1951 SC 229.
79   'PM Fixes General Election Deadline: Caretaker Government
      Cannot Have Indefinite Lease of Life', *Hindustan Times*, 1
      November 1950, New Delhi, p. 1.
80   For a succinct account of the situation in Punjab, see J. S. Grewal,
      *Master Tara Singh in Indian History: Colonialism, Nationalism,
      and the Politics of Sikh Identity* (New Delhi: Oxford University
      Press, 2018), pp. 454–62.
81   'General Election Likely to be Put Off: Autumn Suggested as New
      Date', *Hindustan Times*, 11 November 1950, New Delhi, p. 1.
82   'General Elections Next October: Decision Made by Delhi', *Times
      of India*, 12 November 1950, Bombay, p. 1.
83   'General Elections in November 1951', *Hindustan Times*, 15
      November 1950, New Delhi, p. 1.
84   'Sudden Postponement of General Elections: Socialists' Concern',
      Times of India, 12 November 1950, Bombay, p. 1.
85   Ibid.
86   'Pandit Nehru Now "Shri Jawaharlal"', *Times of India*, 7
      November 1950, Bombay, p. 7.
87   'Ensuring Rights and Liberties of Citizens: Bombay Judge's Views',
      Times of India, 16 November 1950, Bombay, p. 5.
88   'Zamindars Plan to Fight New Law: Legal Action Proposed', *Times
      of India*, 22 November 1950, Bombay, p. 3.
89   Ibid.
90   'Master Tara Singh Released', *Times of India*, 30 November 1950,
      Bombay, p. 3.
91   *Tara Singh v. State of Punjab*, AIR 1951 Punj. 27.
92   'Fundamental Rights', *Times of India*, 5 December 1950, Bombay,
      p. 4.
93   'Government and State', *Times of India*, 30 November 1950,
      Bombay, p. 6.

94 'Fundamental Rights', *Times of India*, 5 December 1950, Bombay, p. 4.
95 'Master Tara Singh Released', *Times of India*, 30 November 1950, Bombay, p. 3.
96 'Government and State', *Times of India*, 30 November 1950, Bombay, p. 6.
97 'Civil Liberties in Peril Says N.M. Joshi', *Times of India*, 3 December 1950, Bombay, p. 4.
98 Ibid.
99 Ibid.
100 'Fundamental Rights', *Times of India*, 5 December 1950, Bombay, p. 4.
101 Jawaharlal Nehru to Chief Ministers, 18 December 1950, G. Parthasarathi, ed., *Letters to Chief Ministers, 1947–1964*, Vol. 2 (New Delhi: Jawaharlal Nehru Memorial Fund, 1986), p. 291.
102 Ibid.
103 Ibid.
104 Ibid.
105 See Rajmohan Gandhi, *Patel: A Life* (Ahmedabad: Navajivan Publishing House, 1990), pp. 520–4.
106 Sardar Patel to Jawaharlal Nehru, 3 July 1950, Durga Das, ed., *Sardar Patel's Correspondence*, Vol. X (Ahmedabad: Navajivan Publishing House, 1974), p. 358.
107 Ibid.

Chapter 4: The Gathering Storm

1 Freedom of the Press/Speech at the All India Newspaper Editors Conference, 3 December 1950, S. Gopal, ed., *Selected Works of Jawaharlal Nehru*, Vol. 15/2 (New Delhi: Jawaharlal Nehru Memorial Fund, 1993), pp. 250–1.
2 'Nehru Not Visiting Washington: AINEC Plea for Liaison Machinery Accepted', *Hindustan Times*, 4 December 1950, New Delhi, p. 1.
3 'Nehru's Address to AINEC', *Hindustan Times*, 4 December 1950, New Delhi, p. 10.
4 Jawaharlal Nehru to B. C. Roy, 16 December 1950, S. Gopal, ed., *Selected Works of Jawaharlal Nehru*, Vol. 15/2 (New Delhi: Jawaharlal Nehru Memorial Fund, 1993), p. 257.
5 'Validity of Bihar Estate Act: Govt. Challenges High Court Order', *Hindustan Times*, 9 December 1950, New Delhi, p. 5.

6   Jawaharlal Nehru to G. V. Mavalankar, 13 December, S. Gopal,
      ed., *Selected Works of Jawaharlal Nehru*, Vol. 15/2 (New Delhi:
      Jawaharlal Nehru Memorial Fund, 1993), p. 233.
7   Ibid.
8   Harshan Kumarasingham, 'The Indian Version of First among
      Equals: Executive Power during the First Decade of Independence',
      Modern Asian Studies, 44 (4): 718–27.
9   Jawaharlal Nehru to Chief Ministers, 18 December 1950, G.
      Parthasarathi, ed., *Letters to Chief Ministers, 1947–1964*, Vol. 2
      (New Delhi: Jawaharlal Nehru Memorial Fund, 1986), p. 291.
10   Sardar Patel's Note to Mahatma Gandhi, 12 January 1948, Durga
      Das, ed., *Sardar Patel's Correspondence*, Vol. VI (Ahmedabad:
      1973), pp. 21–2.
11   Nirad C. Chaudhuri, *Three Horsemen of the New Apocalypse*
      (New Delhi: Oxford University Press, 1997), p. 114.
12   Walter Crocker, *Nehru: A Contemporary's Estimate* (New Delhi:
      Random House, 2009), pp. 222, 231.
13   S. Gopal and Uma Iyengar, eds, *The Essential Writings of
      Jawaharlal Nehru* (New Delhi: Oxford University Press, 2003),
      pp. 644–5.
14   Jawaharlal Nehru to Chief Ministers, 31 December 1950, G.
      Parthasarathi, ed., *Letters to Chief Ministers, 1947–1964*, Vol. 2
      (New Delhi: Jawaharlal Nehru Memorial Fund, 1986), p. 309.
15   'Zamindari Bill', *Times of India*, 23 December 1950, Bombay, p. 6.
16   Ibid.
17   'UP Zamindari Bill: Passage in Assembly May be Delayed',
      Hindustan Times, 30 December 1950, New Delhi, p. 6.
18   Ibid.
19   Literally meaning 'victory to Mother India'.
20   'Zamindari Abolition Bill Passed: Act May Be Enforced on Republic
      Day', *Hindustan Times*, 11 January 1951, New Delhi, p. 1.
21   'Council Passes UP Zamindari Bill', *Hindustan Times*, 17 January
      1951, New Delhi, p. 1.
22   *Kameshwar Singh v. State of Bihar*, AIR 1951 Pat. 91.
23   'Land Reforms Act Essential: Bihar Govt's Plea in High Court',
      Hindustan Times, 18 January 1951, New Delhi, p. 4.
24   Ibid.
25   Law Ministry Note, 6 January 1951, quoted in Granville Austin,
      Working a Democratic Constitution: The Indian Experience (New
      Delhi: Oxford University Press, 2003), p. 43.
26   Granville Austin, *Working a Democratic Constitution: The Indian
      Experience* (New Delhi: Oxford University Press, 2003), p. 43.

27   Law Ministry Note, 15 January 1951, quoted in Granville Austin, *Working a Democratic Constitution: The Indian Experience* (New Delhi: Oxford University Press, 2003), p. 43.

28   Ibid. Also see Granville Austin, *Working a Democratic Constitution: The Indian Experience* (New Delhi: Oxford University Press, 2003), p. 81.

29   Granville Austin, *Working a Democratic Constitution: The Indian Experience* (New Delhi: Oxford University Press, 2003), p. 43.

30   Article 226 of the Constitution governed the rights and powers of the high courts.

31   'UP Zamindars Move', *Times of India*, 18 January 1951, Bombay, p. 9.

32   'President's Assent to UP Zamindari Abolition Bill: Fabric of a New Order Complete Says Pant', *Hindustan Times*, 25 January 1951, New Delhi, p. 1.

33   Ibid.

34   'Injunction on UP Government', *Hindustan Times*, 26 January 1951, New Delhi, p. 12.

35   Ibid.

36   'Zamindari Abolition in UP Stayed: Allahabad High Court Issues Injunctions', *Hindustan Times*, 26 January 1951, New Delhi, p. 1; *Raja Suryapal Singh and Others v. State of Uttar Pradesh*, AIR 1951 All. 674.

37   Ibid.

38   'Zamindari Abolition in UP Stayed: Allahabad High Court Issues Injunctions', Hindustan Times, 26 January 1951, New Delhi, p. 1.

39   'Congress Hold Over People Discussed', *Hindustan Times*, 26 January 1951, New Delhi, p. 1.

40   For example, 'Opposition from Within: Democrats Crusade Against Corruption', *Times of India*, 23 December 1950, Bombay, p. 6; See also Myron Weiner, *Party Politics in India: The Development of a Multi-Party System* (Princeton: Princeton University Press, 1957), pp. 71–74.

41   'Congress Hold Over People Discussed', *Hindustan Times*, 26 January 1951, New Delhi, p. 1.

42   Ibid.

43   Jawaharlal Nehru to Chief Ministers, 1 February 1951, G. Parthasarathi, ed., *Letters to Chief Ministers, 1947–1964*, Vol. 2 (New Delhi: Jawaharlal Nehru Memorial Fund, 1986), p. 325.

44   See, for example, Harshan Kumarasingham, 'The Indian Version of First among Equals: Executive Power during the First Decade of Independence', *Modern Asian Studies*, 44: (4): 719.

45   'Amending the Constitution: Committee's Call, MPs Asked for Suggestions', *Times of India*, 14 February 1951, Bombay, p. 1.

46   Mohan Lal Gautam's daughter, Sheela, was a noted BJP leader, who was elected several times as MP from Aligarh. She also founded the Sleepwell mattress brand.

47   Granville Austin, *Working a Democratic Constitution: The Indian Experience* (New Delhi: Oxford University Press, 2003), p. 43.

48   'Amending the Constitution: Committee's Call, MPs Asked for Suggestions', *Times of India*, 14 February 1951, Bombay, p. 1.

49   Ibid.

50   Statement in Parliament, 16 February 1951, S. Gopal, ed., *Selected Works of Jawaharlal Nehru*, Vol. 15/2 (New Delhi: Jawaharlal Nehru Memorial Fund, 1993), p. 235.

51   Jawaharlal Nehru to Chief Ministers, 18 February 1951, G. Parthasarathi, ed., *Letters to Chief Ministers, 1947–1964*, Vol. 2 (New Delhi: Jawaharlal Nehru Memorial Fund, 1986), p. 337.

52   Ibid.

53   G. B. Pant to Jawaharlal Nehru, 5 March 1951, File 3, Pant–Nehru Correspondence, G. B. Pant Collection, National Archives of India; Granville Austin, *Working a Democratic Constitution: The Indian Experience* (New Delhi: Oxford University Press, 2003), pp. 43, 81, 93.

54   Ibid.

55   Granville Austin, *Working a Democratic Constitution: The Indian Experience* (New Delhi: Oxford University Press, 2003), pp. 43, 84</PG>.

56   'Bihar Land Reform Act Held "Ultra Vires": High Court Ruling in Favour of Zamindars', *Times of India*, 13 March 1951, Bombay, p. 1.

57   *Kameshwar Singh v. State of Bihar*, AIR 1951 Pat. 91.

58   Granville Austin, *Working a Democratic Constitution: The Indian Experience* (New Delhi: Oxford University Press, 2003), p. 84.

59   Remarks at a Press Conference, 13 March 1951, S. Gopal, ed., *Selected Works of Jawaharlal Nehru*, Vol. 16/1 (New Delhi: Jawaharlal Nehru Memorial Fund, 1994), p. 153.

60   Memorandum, 14 March 1951, Law Ministry File F34/51-C, National Archives of India; quoted in Granville Austin, *Working a Democratic Constitution: The Indian Experience* (New Delhi: Oxford University Press, 2003), pp. 43–4.

61   Ibid.

62   Memorandum, 14 March 1951, Law Ministry File F34/51-C, National Archives of India; quoted in Granville Austin, *Working a Democratic Constitution: The Indian Experience* (New Delhi: Oxford University Press, 2003), p. 84.

63   In one of the many quirks of fate, in 1952, Ambedkar would find himself out of the government and arguing in the Supreme

Court against zamindari abolition legislation in Madhya Pradesh alongside P. R. Das. *Vishweshwar Rao v. State of Madhya Pradesh*, AIR 1952 SC 252. He would also appear for Maharaja Kameshwar Singh in the state's appeal against the Patna High Court judgment.

64   Harshan Kumarasingham, 'The Indian Version of First Among Equals: Executive Power during the First Decade of Independence', *Modern Asian Studies*, 44 (4): 711.

65   Memorandum, 14 March 1951, Law Ministry File F34/51-C, National Archives of India; quoted in Granville Austin, *Working a Democratic Constitution: The Indian Experience* (New Delhi: Oxford University Press, 2003), p. 44.

66   Ibid.

67   'SC Verdict in Priyanka Sharma's Case Is a Classic Example of the Half Loaf of Freedom: Meghnad Desai', *The Indian Express*, 19 May 2019, New Delhi; https://indianexpress.com/article/ opinion/columns/independence-british-rule-women-safety- sexual-harrassment-waiting-for-freedom-democracy-5735394/ (accessed on 25 June 2019).

68   Granville Austin, *Working a Democratic Constitution: The Indian Experience* (New Delhi: Oxford University Press, 2003), p. 44.

69   Jawaharlal Nehru to Chief Ministers, 21 March 1951, G. Parthasarathi, ed., *Letters to Chief Ministers, 1947–1964*, Vol. 2 (New Delhi: Jawaharlal Nehru Memorial Fund, 1986), p. 363.

70   V. K. T. Chari to K. V. K. Sundaram, 14 March 1951, Law Ministry File F34/51-C, National Archives of India; quoted in Granville Austin, *Working a Democratic Constitution: The Indian Experience* (New Delhi: Oxford University Press, 2003), p. 84.

71   Quoted from Upendra Baxi, 'Constitution contains a kindred concept of justice, asks a citizen to be responsive to sufferings of co-citizens', *Indian Express*, 6 June 2019, https://indianexpress. com/ article/opinion/columns/the-constitutional-citizen-rights- freedom-india-5767375/ (accessed on 16 December 2019). In certain cases, Chief Justice Gajendragadkar of the Bombay High Court is said to be the source of this quote.

72   *Kameshwar Singh v. State of Bihar*, AIR 1951 Pat. 91.

73   Ibid.

74   Ibid.

75   Ibid.

76   'Zamindari Abolition', *Times of India*, 14 March 1951, Bombay, p. 4.

77   Ibid.

78   Sarbani Sen, *The Constitution of India: Popular Sovereignty and Democratic Transformations* (New Delhi: Oxford University Press, 2007), p. 160.

79   *West Bengal Settlement Kanungo Cooperative Society v. Bela Banerjee & Others*, AIR 1951 Cal. 111.

80   Ibid.

81   'Report of the Cabinet Committee (Amendment to the Constitution)', 9 April 1951, Law Ministry File No. 34/1951-C, National Archives of India.

82   Ibid.

83   Ibid.

84   Ibid.

85   Granville Austin, *Working a Democratic Constitution: The Indian Experience* (New Delhi: Oxford University Press, 2003), p. 45.

86   'Reverence for the State: C. Rajagopalachari', *Hindustan Times, Republic Day Special*, 26 January 1950, New Delhi, p. 6.

87   'Biggest Liberal Experiment in Democratic Government: Kenneth C. Wheare', *Hindustan Times*, 26 January 1950, New Delhi, p. 1.

88   The article was penned under the pseudonym 'Chanakya'. It was first printed in a publication titled *Rashtrapati* in November 1937, and again in *The Modern Review* of Calcutta in November 1947. See S. Gopal and Uma Iyengar, eds, *The Essential Writings of Jawaharlal Nehru* (New Delhi: 2003), pp. 644–5. See also Harshan Kumarasingham, 'The Indian Version of First among Equals: Executive Power during the First Decade of Independence', *Modern Asian Studies*, 44 (4): 709–11.

Chapter 5: The Clouds Burst

1   *State of Madras v. Champakam Dorairajan*, AIR 1951 SC 226.

2   *B. Venkataramana v. State of Tamil Nadu*, AIR 1951 SC 229.

3   'Communal GO Not Constitutional: Madras Case in Supreme Court', *Times of India*, 27 March 1951, Bombay, p. 5.

4   Granville Austin, *Working a Democratic Constitution: The Indian Experience* (New Delhi: Oxford University Press, 2003), p. 43.

5   Sarvepalli Gopal, *Jawaharlal Nehru: A Biography Volume Two: 1947–1956* (London: Cape, 1979), p. 312.

6   Harshan Kumarasingham, 2009. 'The Indian Version of First among Equals: Executive Power during the First Decade of Independence', *Modern Asian Studies*, 44 (4): 719.

7   Gopal was the son of India's first vice-president, Sarvepalli Radhakrishnan. He served as director of the Historical Division in the external affairs ministry, as reader in Indian history at

the University of Oxford and a founding figure and professor at the Centre of Historical Studies, Jawaharlal Nehru University.

8   Sarvepalli Gopal, *Jawaharlal Nehru: A Biography Volume Two: 1947–1956* (London: Cape, 1979), p. 304.

9   Ibid., p. 313.

10 'Removing Lacunae in Constitution: Amendments Proposed', *Times of India*, 9 April 1951, Bombay, p. 5.

11 'Proposed Amendments to Constitution: Move to Abridge Fundamental Rights of Citizens', *The Statesman*, 9 April 1951, Calcutta, p. 5.

12 *State of Madras v. Champakam Dorairajan*, AIR 1951 SC 226.

13 *B. Venkataramana v. State of Tamil Nadu*, AIR 1951 SC 229.

14 Ibid.

15 'Communal Ratio in Madras Public Services: Government Order Invalid', *Times of India*, 10 April 1951, Bombay, p. 5; 'Madras Communal GO Declared Void: Repugnant to Fundamental Rights says Supreme Court', *The Statesman*, 10 April 1951, Calcutta, p. 5.

16 Ibid.

17 Jawaharlal Nehru to P. S. Kumaraswamy Raja, 11 April 1951, S. Gopal, ed., *Selected Works of Jawaharlal Nehru*, Vol. 16/1 (New Delhi: Jawaharlal Nehru Memorial Fund, 1994), p. 153.

18 Ibid.

19 'Communal GO', *Times of India*, 10 April 1951, Bombay, p. 4.

20 'Fundamental Rights', *Times of India*, 12 April 1951, Bombay, p. 6.

21 'The Rule of Law', *Times of India*, 18 April 1951, Bombay, p. 4.

22 Ibid.

23 'Alterations in Constitution: Defer Action till After Elections', *Times of India*, 14 April 1951, Bombay, p. 5.

24 'Curtailment of the Right of Speech: Mr. P.N. Mehta's Views', *Times of India*, 20 April 1951, Bombay, p. 8.

25 'Proposed Changes in Constitution: Mr. P.R. Das's Protest', *Times of India*, 23 April 1951, Bombay, p. 7.

26 'Amending Articles in Constitution: Move Unwise says Dr. M.R. Jayakar', *Times of India*, 22 April 1951, Bombay, p. 1.

27 Ibid.

28 Ibid.

29 'Proposed Changes in Constitution: Lawyers' Protest', *Times of India*, 24 April 1951, Bombay, p. 6.

30 'Revision of Indian Constitution: Opposition by Merchants', *Times of India*, 30 April 1951, Bombay, p. 5.

31 'Reader's Views: Amendment of the Constitution', *Times of India*, 14 April 1951, Bombay, p. 4.

32 Ibid.

33 'Unreasonable Move: To the Editor', *Times of India*, 30 April 1951, Bombay, p. 4.
34 Ibid.
35 Rajindar Sachar, 'Credibility is Crucial', *PUCL Bulletin*, 36, 2, February 2016, p. 12.
36 Granville Austin, *Working a Democratic Constitution: The Indian Experience* (New Delhi: Oxford University Press, 2003), p. 85.
37 Ibid., p. 94.
38 Ibid., p. 97.
39 'Ministry of Law: Supplementary Report to the Cabinet Committee', 19 April 1951, Law Ministry File No. 34/1951-C, National Archives of India.
40 'Amending Constitution', *Times of India*, 20 April 1951, Bombay, p. 7.
41 'Bill to Amend the Constitution: Changes to be Limited in Number and Scope', *Times of India*, 19 April 1951, Bombay, p. 1.
42 Ibid.
43 For example, see: K. V. K. Sundaram (Secretary, Ministry of Law) to Chief Secretaries of States, 20 April 1951, Law Ministry File No. 34/1951-C, National Archives of India.
44 'Madras Ministers Meet Mr. Nehru: Communal GO Issue', *Times of India*, 28 April 1951, Bombay, p. 7.
45 'Communal GO', *Times of India*, 10 May 1951, Bombay, p. 6.
46 Ibid.
47 Note on Amendments to the Constitution, 30 April 1951, Valmiki Chaudhary, ed., *Dr. Rajendra Prasad: Correspondence and Selected Documents*, Vol. 14 (New Delhi: Allied Publishers, 1991), p. 273.
48 Ibid.
49 Ibid., p. 275. Interestingly, a similar point was made by the West Bengal government when asked for its opinion. See: S. N. Ray (Chief Secretary, West Bengal) to K. V. K. Sundaram (Secretary, Law Ministry), 30 April 1951, Law Ministry File No. 34/1951-C, National Archives of India.
50 Note on Amendments to the Constitution, 30 April 1951, Valmiki Chaudhary, ed., *Dr. Rajendra Prasad: Correspondence and Selected Documents*, Vol. 14 (New Delhi: Allied Publishers, 1991), p. 274.
51 Ibid., p. 273.
52 Ibid.
53 Ibid., p. 274.
54 Note on Amendments to the Constitution, 30 April 1951, Valmiki Chaudhary, ed., *Dr. Rajendra Prasad: Correspondence and Selected Documents*, Vol. 14 (New Delhi: Allied Publishers, 1991), p. 277; Granville Austin, *Working a Democratic Constitution: The Indian Experience* (New Delhi: Oxford University Press, 2003), p. 86.

55 See Harshan Kumarasingham, 'The Indian Version of First among Equals: Executive Power during the First Decade of Independence', *Modern Asian Studies*, 44 (4): 719.

56 Records of the subsequent Cabinet meeting do not even mention Prasad's note being considered. See: 'Meeting of the Cabinet held on 2 May 1951, 3 pm: Amendment of the Constitution', Law Ministry File No. 34/1951-C, National Archives of India.

57 Jawaharlal Nehru to Chief Ministers, 2 May 1951, G. Parthasarathi, ed., *Letters to Chief Ministers, 1947–1964*, Vol. 2 (New Delhi: Jawaharlal Nehru Memorial Fund, 1986), p. 387.

58 'Meeting of the Cabinet held on 2 May 1951, 3 pm: Amendment of the Constitution', Law Ministry File No. 34/1951-C, National Archives of India; Meeting of the Cabinet held on 7 May 1951, 5 pm: Amendment of the Constitution, Law Ministry File No. 34/1951-C, National Archives of India.

59 'UP Zamindari Abolition Act Declared Valid', *The Statesman*, 11 May 1951, Calcutta, p. 1; *Raja Suryapal Singh and Others v. State of Uttar Pradesh*, AIR 1951 All. 674.

60 Sunil Khilnani, *The Idea of India* (New Delhi: Penguin Books India, 2012), p. 24.

61 'Freedoms of the Press', *Times of India*, 21 May 1951, Bombay, p. 4.

62 See Harshan Kumarasingham, 'The Indian Version of First Among Equals: Executive Power during the First Decade of Independence', *Modern Asian Studies*, 44 (4): 712.

63 Ibid.

64 For more, see: Harshan Kumarasingham, *A Political Legacy of the British Empire: Power and the Parliamentary System in Post-Colonial India and Sri Lanka* (London: I.B. Tauris, 2013), Chapter 1.

65 'Provision against Sedition to Be Made in Constitution: Mr. Nehru Might Introduce Bill This Week', *The Statesman*, 11 May 1951, Calcutta, p. 1.

66 Ibid.

67 Granville Austin, *Working a Democratic Constitution: The Indian Experience* (New Delhi: Oxford University Press, 2003), p. 86.

68 Hussain Imam, 12 May 1951, *Parliamentary Debates*, Part II, Vol. XII (New Delhi: 1951), p. 8584.

69 Speaker, 12 May 1951, *Parliamentary Debates*, Part II, Vol. XII (New Delhi: 1951), p. 8584.

70 'Nehru Introduces Bill to Amend Constitution: Further Curbs on Freedom', *The Statesman*, 13 May 1951, Calcutta, p. 1.

71 'Amendment of Constitution: Mr. P.N. Mehta's Views', *Times of India*, 16 May 1951, Bombay, p. 5.

72 Ibid.

73 'Amendment to Constitution Not Right Now: Lawyers Urged to Protest', *Times of India*, 17 May 1951, Bombay, p. 7; 'Lawyers Criticise Proposed Measure', *The Statesman*, 17 May 1951, Calcutta, p. 5.

74 'Fundamental Rights', *Times of India*, 15 May 1951, Bombay, p. 4.

75 Ibid.

76 'Early Action on Constitution Amendment Bill: Mr. Nehru to Serve on Select Committee', *Times of India*, 16 May 1951, Bombay, p. 4.

77 Ibid.

78 Ibid.; 'Constitution Amendment Bill', *The Statesman*, 13 May 1951, Calcutta, p. 1.

79 Jawaharlal Nehru, 16 May 1951, *Parliamentary Debates*, Part II, Vol. XII (New Delhi: 1951), p. 8815.

80 Ibid.

81 Ibid.

82 Ibid., p. 8818.

83 Ibid., p. 8826.

84 Ibid., p. 8828.

85 Ibid., p. 8823.

86 Ibid., p. 8824.

87 Ibid., p. 8816.

88 Ibid., p. 8821.

89 Ibid., p. 8831.

90 Ibid., p. 8832.

91 Dr. S. P. Mookerji, 16 May 1951, *Parliamentary Debates*, Part II, Vol. XII (New Delhi: 1951), p. 8836.

92 Ibid., p. 8838.

93 Ibid., pp. 8841–3.

94 Ibid., p. 8838.

95 Ibid., p. 8855.

96 Ibid., p. 8846.

97 Ibid., pp. 8849–50.

98 Ibid., p. 8850.

99 Ibid., pp. 8851–2.

100 Ibid., p. 8851.

101 Ibid., p. 8856.

102 Prof. N. G. Ranga, 16 May 1951, *Parliamentary Debates*, Part II, Vol. XII (New Delhi: 1951), p. 8857.

103 Ibid.

104 'Proposed Changes in Constitution: Mr. Nehru's Assurances in Parliament', *Times of India*, 17 May 1951, Bombay, p. 1.

105 *Parliamentary Debates*, Part II, Vol. XII (New Delhi: 1951), pp. 8856–80.

106 Kameshwar Singh, 16 May 1951, *Parliamentary Debates*, Part II, Vol. XII (New Delhi: 1951), p. 8865.

107 See: *Parliamentary Debates*, Part II, Vol. XII (New Delhi: 1951), p. 8890.

108 Ibid., p. 8867.

109 'Nehru is Adamant on Curbing Press: Defends His Bill', *New York Times*, 17 May 1951, New York, p. 8.

110 Jawaharlal Nehru to Chief Ministers, 17 May 1951, G. Parthasarathi, ed., *Letters to Chief Ministers, 1947–1964*, Vol. 2 (New Delhi: Jawaharlal Nehru Memorial Fund, 1986), p. 397.

Chapter 6: The Battle Rages

1 Jawaharlal Nehru to G.V. Mavalankar, 16 May 1951, S. Gopal, ed., *Selected Works of Jawaharlal Nehru*, Vol. 16/1 (New Delhi: Jawaharlal Nehru Memorial Fund, 1994), p. 171. Also see footnote to the letter.

2 Ibid., p. 172.

3 Ibid.

4 Vir Sanghvi, 'Karanjia and His Blitz', *Hindustan Times*, 2 February 2008.

5 See: 'Nehru Denies Aim Is a Gagged Press', *New York Times*, 19 May 1951, New York, p. 2.

6 Ibid.

7 'Right of Freedom of Speech Being Curtailed: Further Criticism of Bill to Amend Constitution', *Times of India*, 18 May 1951, Bombay, p. 5.

8 M. P. Mishra, 17 May 1951, *Parliamentary Debates*, Part II, Vol. XII (New Delhi: 1951), p. 8989.

9 'Amendment Bill Referred to Select Committee', *Times of India*, 19 May 1951, Bombay, p. 1.

10 'Right of Freedom of Speech Being Curtailed: Further Criticism of Bill to Amend Constitution', *Times of India*, 18 May 1951, Bombay, p. 5.

11 H. N. Kunzru, 17 May 1951, *Parliamentary Debates*, Part II, Vol. XII (New Delhi: 1951), p. 8902.

12 'Right of Freedom of Speech Being Curtailed: Further Criticism of Bill to Amend Constitution', *Times of India*, 18 May 1951, Bombay, p. 5.

13 Ibid.

14 'Inherent police powers' or 'implied police powers' refers to the US Supreme Court reading into the bare-bones US Constitution,

through a process of interpretation, certain limited grounds for the state to restrict the otherwise expansive right to freedom of speech and expression to protect its own security. Since the US Constitution only enumerated certain freedoms without mentioning the grounds on which they could be restricted, the doctrine of 'police powers' was progressively evolved by the Supreme Court to deal with major threats to state security. In contrast, in India, the grounds on which rights may be restricted are written into the Constitution, precluding the need or the ability of the Supreme Court to read any 'police powers' into the fundamental rights provisions.

15 'Amendment Bill Referred to Select Committee', *Times of India*, 19 May 1951, Bombay, p. 1.

16 B. R. Ambedkar, 18 May 1951, *Parliamentary Debates*, Part II, Vol. XII (New Delhi: 1951), p. 9028.

17 Jawaharlal Nehru, 18 May 1951, Ibid., p. 9083.

18 'Nehru's Bill Sent to Select Committee', *The Statesman*, 19 May 1951, Calcutta, p. 1.

19 See, for example, 'Mr. Kripalani Resigns from Congress', *Times of India*, 18 May 1951, Bombay, p. 1; 'Kripalani Resigns from Congress: 1500 word Letter to Tandon', *The Leader*, 18 May 1951, Allahabad, p. 1.

20 'All Opposition Forces to be Gathered into One Fold: Acharya Kripalani's Aim', *Times of India*, 19 May 1951, Bombay, p. 1.

21 'Amendment Bill: Congress Parliamentary Party Meeting', *Times of India*, 21 May 1951, Bombay, p. 5.

22 Jawaharlal Nehru to Chief Ministers, 17 May 1951, G. Parthasarathi, ed., *Letters to Chief Ministers, 1947–1964*, Vol. 2 (New Delhi: Jawaharlal Nehru Memorial Fund, 1986), p. 397; see also, 'Nehru Denies Aim Is a Gagged Press', *New York Times*, 19 May 1951, New York, p. 2.

23 'Editors Meet Mr. Nehru', *Times of India*, 21 May 1951, Bombay, p. 5.

24 'Indian Editors Score Nehru's Press Curb', *New York Times*, 20 May 1951, New York, p. 33.

25 'Amendment of Constitution Not Right Now: Lawyers Urged to Protest', *Times of India*, 17 May 1951, Bombay, p. 7.

26 'Lawyers Criticise Proposed Measure', *The Statesman*, 17 May 1951, Calcutta, p. 5.

27 Ibid.

28 'Amendments to Constitution: Time Inopportune', *Times of India*, 18 May 1951, Bombay, p. 7.

29 See: 'Indian Editors Score Nehru's Press Curb', *New York Times*, 20 May 1951, New York, p. 33.

30   'Press Privileges in Constitution: Amendment Uncalled For', *Times of India*, 22 May 1951, Bombay, p. 5.

31   Jawaharlal Nehru to Deshbandhu Gupta, 20 May 1951, S. Gopal, ed., *Selected Works of Jawaharlal Nehru*, Vol. 16/1 (New Delhi: Jawaharlal Nehru Memorial Fund, 1994), p. 188.

32   Ibid.

33   'Guarding Press Liberties', *Times of India*, 24 May 1951, Bombay, p. 1.

34   'Inept, Ill Advised and Ill Timed', *The Statesman*, 19 May 1951, Calcutta, p. 5.

35   'Freedoms of the Press', *Times of India*, 21 May 1951, Bombay, p. 4.

36   Ibid.

37   Ibid.

38   'Fundamental Changes: Government's Undignified Haste, By Vivek', *Times of India*, 23 May 1951, Bombay, p. 4.

39   Ibid.

40   Ibid.

41   'The Great Debate: Amendments to Constitution', *Times of India*, 22 May 1951, Bombay, p. 4.

42   'Reader's Views: The Constitution', *Times of India*, 24 May 1951, Bombay, p. 6.

43   This point is also noted by Arudra Burra. See: *Arudra Burra, Arguments from Colonial Continuity: The Constitution (First Amendment) Act, 1951* (7 December 2008), p. 28. Available at https://dx.doi.org/10.2139/ssrn.2052659 (accessed on 15 July 2019).

44   Jawaharlal Nehru to T. T. Krishnamachari, 22 May 1951, S. Gopal, ed., *Selected Works of Jawaharlal Nehru*, Vol. 16/1 (New Delhi: Jawaharlal Nehru Memorial Fund, 1994), p. 189.

45   Ibid.

46   'Constitution Amendment Bill to Be Modified: Bid to Meet Criticism', *Times of India*, 25 May 1951, Bombay, p. 1.

47   Granville Austin, *Working a Democratic Constitution: The Indian Experience* (New Delhi: Oxford University Press, 2003), p. 47.

48   'Constitution Amendment Bill to Be Modified: Bid to Meet Criticism', *Times of India*, 25 May 1951, Bombay, p. 1.

49   Jawaharlal Nehru to B. C. Roy, 25 May 1951, S. Gopal, ed., *Selected Works of Jawaharlal Nehru*, Vol. 16/1 (New Delhi: Jawaharlal Nehru Memorial Fund, 1994), p. 191.

50   'Guarding Press Liberties: Editors' Body to Meet', *Times of India*, 24 May 1951, Bombay, p. 1.

51   Granville Austin, *Working a Democratic Constitution: The Indian Experience* (New Delhi: Oxford University Press, 2003), p. 97.

52   'Changes in Bill to Amend Constitution', *The Leader*, 26 May
      1951, Allahabad, p. 1.
53   Ibid.
54   Ibid., p. 95.
55   Jawaharlal Nehru to Rajendra Prasad, 25 May 1951, S. Gopal,
      ed., *Selected Works of Jawaharlal Nehru*, Vol. 16/1 (New Delhi:
      Jawaharlal Nehru Memorial Fund, 1994), p. 191. See footnote to
      letter.
56   Ibid.
57   Ibid., p. 192.
58   Ibid.
59   *The Constitution (First Amendment) Bill, 1951: Report of the
      Select Committee*, Parliament Library, New Delhi.
60   'No Major Alteration in Bill to Amend Constitution: Report of
      Select Committee, Five Notes of Dissent', *Times of India*, 26 May
      1951, Bombay, p. 1.
61   See: *The Constitution (First Amendment) Bill, 1951: Report of the
      Select Committee*, Parliament Secretariat, New Delhi, pp. 6–7.
62   'Report on Bill to Amend Constitution', *The Statesman*, 26 May
      1951, Calcutta, p. 5.
63   Ibid.
64   'No Major Alteration in Bill to Amend Constitution: Report of
      Select Committee, Five Notes of Dissent', *Times of India*, 26 May
      1951, Bombay, p. 1.
65   Ibid., p. 8.
66   Ibid.
67   'Report on Bill to Amend Constitution', *The Statesman*, 26 May
      1951, Calcutta, p. 5.
68   Ibid.
69   'No Major Alteration in Bill to Amend Constitution: Report of
      Select Committee, Five Notes of Dissent', *Times of India*, 26 May
      1951, Bombay, p. 1.
70   *The Constitution (First Amendment) Bill, 1951: Report of the
      Select Committee*, Parliament Secretariat, New Delhi, pp. 10–12.
71   Ibid., p. 11.
72   Sarvepalli Gopal, *Jawaharlal Nehru: A Biography Volume Two:
      1947–1956* (London: Cape, 1979), p. 312.
73   'No Major Alteration in Bill to Amend Constitution: Report of
      Select Committee, Five Notes of Dissent', *Times of India*, 26 May
      1951, Bombay, p. 1.
74   'Not Enough', *Times of India*, 28 May 1951, Bombay, p. 1.
75   Ibid.
76   Ibid.
77   Ibid.

78   Ibid.
79   'Today's Debate on Amendment Bill: Opposition Forces Gather
     Strength', *Times of India*, 29 May 1951, Bombay, p. 1.
80   H. V. Kamath, 29 May 1951, *Parliamentary Debates*, Part II, Vol.
     XII (New Delhi: 1951), p. 9,612.
81   Jawaharlal Nehru, 29 May 1951; Ibid., p. 9,627.
82   Ibid., p. 9,623.
83   Ibid., p. 9,624.
84   Ibid., p. 9,628.
85   Ibid., p. 9,629.
86   Ibid., p. 9,630.
87   'Government Armed to Fight Disruptive Forces: Mr. Nehru on
     Need for a Flexible Constitution', *Times of India*, 30 May 1951,
     Bombay, p. 1.
88   Ibid.
89   Ibid.
90   Ibid.
91   Ibid.
92   'Storm Affects Parliament', *Times of India*, 30 May 1951, Bombay,
     p. 1.
93   'Case for Amending Constitution Challenged', *The Statesman*, 31
     May 1951, Calcutta, p. 5.
94   Rev. D'Souza, 30 May 1951, *Parliamentary Debates*, Part II, Vol.
     XII (New Delhi: 1951), p. 9,691.
95   Ibid., p. 9,693.
96   'Restrictive Provisions Contained in Amendment Bill: Mookerji–
     Kripalani Attack in Parliament', *Times of India*, 31 May 1951,
     Bombay, p. 7.
97   Frank Anthony, 31 May 1951, *Parliamentary Debates*, Part II, Vol.
     XII (New Delhi: 1951), p. 9,789.
98   Ibid.
99   Ibid., p. 9,788.
100 'Restrictive Provisions Contained in Amendment Bill: Mookerji–
     Kripalani Attack in Parliament', *Times of India*, 31 May 1951,
     Bombay, p. 7.
101 S. P. Mookerji, 30 May 1951, *Parliamentary Debates*, Part II, Vol.
     XII (New Delhi: 1951), p. 9,685.
102 Ibid., p. 9,711.
103 Ibid., p. 9,702.
104 Ibid., p. 9,711.
105 'Restrictive Provisions Contained in Amendment Bill: Mookerji–
     Kripalani Attack in Parliament', *Times of India*, 31 May 1951,
     Bombay, p. 7.
106 Ibid.

107   Ibid.
108   Acharya Kripalani, 30 May 1951, *Parliamentary Debates*, Part II, Vol. XII (New Delhi: 1951), p. 9,721.
109   Ibid., p. 9,725.
110   Ibid., p. 9,728.
111   'Unconvincing', *Times of India*, 31 May 1951, Bombay, p. 6.
112   'Curves of Life', *Times of India*, 1 June 1951, Bombay, p. 4.
113   'Fundamental Rights: To the Editor', *Times of India*, 1 June 1951, Bombay, p. 4.
114   Constitutional Amendment: A Denial of Democracy, 31 May 1951, Bimal Prasad, ed., *Jayaprakash Narayan: Selected Works*, Vol. 6 (New Delhi: Manohar Books, 2005), p. 135.
115   Jawaharlal Nehru, 31 May 1951, *Parliamentary Debates*, Part II, Vol. XII (New Delhi: 1951), p. 9,796.
116   Jawaharlal Nehru, 31 May 1951, *Parliamentary Debates*, Part II, Vol. XII (New Delhi: 1951), pp. 9791–800.
117   'Parliament to Consider Bill to Amend Constitution', *Times of India*, 1 June 1951, Bombay, p. 5.
118   'Parliament to Consider Constitution Bill: Big Majority for Nehru Motion', *The Statesman*, 1 June 1951, Calcutta, p. 1.
119   'Restrictive Provisions Contained in Amendment Bill: Mookerji–Kripalani Attack in Parliament', *Times of India*, 31 May 1951, Bombay, p. 7.
120   'Freedom of Vote on Bill: MP Seeks Permission', *Times of India*, 1 June 1951, Bombay, p. 5.
121   H.V. Kamath, 1 June 1951, *Parliamentary Debates*, Part II, Vol. XII (New Delhi: 1951), p. 9814, p. 9827.
122   S. L. Saksena, 1 June 1951, *Parliamentary Debates*, Part II, Vol. XII (New Delhi: 1951), pp. 9,814, 9,819.
123   M. A. Ayyangar, 1 June 1951, *Parliamentary Debates*, Part II, Vol. XII (New Delhi: 1951), p. 9,816.
124   S. P. Mookerji, 1 June 1951, *Parliamentary Debates*, Part II, Vol. XII (New Delhi: 1951), pp. 9,852, 9,853.
125   Ibid.
126   Jawaharlal Nehru, 1 June 1951, *Parliamentary Debates*, Part II, Vol. XII (New Delhi: 1951), p. 9,876.
127   Shyamnandan Sahay, 1 June 1951, *Parliamentary Debates*, Part II, Vol. XII (New Delhi: 1951), p. 9,911.
128   'Controversial Clauses Adopted: Discussion on Constitution Amendment Bill', *Times of India*, 2 June 1951, Bombay, p. 5.
129   Ibid.
130   S. L. Saksena, 2 June 1951, *Parliamentary Debates*, Part II, Vol. XII (New Delhi: 1951), p. 10,039.
131   Ibid., p. 10,043.

132   S. P. Mookerji, 2 June 1951, *Parliamentary Debates*, Part II, Vol. XII
      (New Delhi: 1951), pp. 10,084, 10,085.
133   Ibid., pp. 10,086, 10,089.
134   Ibid., p. 10,091.
135   Jawaharlal Nehru to Chief Ministers, 15 June, G. Parthasarathi,
      ed., *Letters to Chief Ministers, 1947–1964*, Vol. 2 (New Delhi:
      Jawaharlal Nehru Memorial Fund, 1986), p. 417.
136   Jawaharlal Nehru, 2 June 1951, *Parliamentary Debates*, Part II, Vol.
      XII (New Delhi: 1951), p. 10,092.
137   S. P. Mookerji, 2 June 1951, *Parliamentary Debates*, Part II, Vol. XII
      (New Delhi: 1951), p. 10,092.
138   'First Amendment to 17 Month Old Constitution Passed', *Times of
      India*, 2 June 1951, Bombay, p. 5.
139   Ibid.
140   For the back and forth between Nehru and Mookerji, see
      Parliamentary Debates, Part II, Vol. XII (New Delhi: 1951),
      pp. 10,092, 10,093.
141   Ibid.
142   Jawaharlal Nehru, 2 June 1951, *Parliamentary Debates*, Part II,
      Vol. XII (New Delhi: 1951), p. 10,094.
143   Ibid., p. 10,096.
144   'First Amendment to 17 Month Old Constitution Passed', *Times of
      India*, 2 June 1951, Bombay, p. 5.
145   Deputy Speaker, 2 June 1951, *Parliamentary Debates*, Part II,
      Vol. XII (New Delhi: 1951), p. 10,107.

Chapter 7: The Aftermath

1   'Fundamental Rights Restricted: Parliament Approves
    Amendments', *The Leader*, 2 June 1951, Allahabad, p. 1.
2   Jawaharlal Nehru to Chief Ministers, 2 June 1951, G.
    Parthasarathi, ed., *Letters to Chief Ministers, 1947–1964*, Vol. 2
    (New Delhi: Jawaharlal Nehru Memorial Fund, 1986), p. 405.
3   'Respective Roles of Judiciary, Executive and Legislature:
    Independence of Each Must be Preserved', *Times of India*, 6 June
    1951, Bombay, p. 1.
4   Ibid.
5   'Reader's Views: Freedom of the Press', *Times of India*, 7 June
    1951, Bombay, p. 6.
6   Remarks at a Press Conference: The Press and the Constitution
    (First Amendment) Bill, S.Gopal, ed., *Selected Works of Jawaharlal*

Nehru, Vol. 16/1 (New Delhi: Jawaharlal Nehru Memorial Fund, 1994), p. 247.

7 Rajendra Prasad to Alladi Krishnaswamy Aiyyar, 14 June 1951, Valmiki Chaudhary, ed., *Dr. Rajendra Prasad: Correspondence and Selected Documents*, Vol. 14 (New Delhi: Allied Publishers, 1991), pp. 69–71.

8 Ibid., p. 70.

9 Granville Austin, *Working a Democratic Constitution: The Indian Experience* (New Delhi: Oxford University Press, 2003), p. 90.

10 Record of Meeting with Deshbandhu Gupta, 19 June 1951, Valmiki Chaudhary, ed., *Dr. Rajendra Prasad: Correspondence and Selected Documents*, Vol. 14 (New Delhi: Allied Publishers, 1991), p. 220.

11 'Editors Retort to Mr. Nehru: Day Without Newspapers', *Manchester Guardian*, 25 June 1951, Manchester, p. 8.

12 Ibid.

13 'Papers in India Will Close for a Day to Protest Curbs', *New York Times*, 25 June 1951, New York, p. 4.

14 'Editors Retort to Mr. Nehru: Day Without Newspapers', *Manchester Guardian*, 25 June 1951, Manchester, p. 8.

15 'Papers of India to Strike Over Curbs', *Chicago Daily Tribune*, 25 June 1951, p. 16.

16 'India's Newsmen Plan Suspension to Protest Curbs', *Washington Post*, 25 June 1951, p. 6.

17 Tilak (1856–1920) was a prominent nationalist leader who belonged to the extremist faction of the Congress and was tried for sedition three times. His slogan, 'Swaraj (freedom) is my birth-right and I shall have it', is still famous.

18 'Postpone Hartal by Newspapers: Nagpur Editors' Plea', *Times of India*, 7 July 1951, Bombay, p. 5.

19 'Postponement of Press Hartal', *Times of India*, 11 July 1951, Bombay, p. 7.

20 See: 'Appeal to Postpone Press Hartal: AINEC President's Statement', *Times of India*, 10 July 1951, Bombay, p. 4; 'Postponement of Hartal: Grave Step', *Times of India*, 10 July 1951, Bombay, p. 4.

21 *Sankari Prasad Singh Deo v. Union of India*, AIR 1951 SC 458; see also Granville Austin, *Working a Democratic Constitution: The Indian Experience* (New Delhi: Oxford University Press, 2003), p. 91.

22 Upendra Baxi, *The Judiciary as a Resource for Indian Democracy*, http://www.india-seminar.com/2010/615/615_upendra_baxi.htm (accessed on 20 November 2018).

23 'Protecting Civil Liberties in India', *Times of India*, 27 August 1951, Bombay, p. 7.

24   Record of Meeting with Deshbandhu Gupta, 19 June 1951, Valmiki
     Chaudhary, ed., *Dr. Rajendra Prasad: Correspondence and Selected
     Documents*, Vol. 14 (New Delhi: Allied Publishers, 1991), p. 221.
25   O. Chinappa Reddy, *The Court and the Constitution of India*
     (Oxford: Oxford University Press, 2008), p. 43.
26   Purvi Gharia Pokhariyal, 'Critical Evaluation of the Functioning
     of Judicial Review in India' (Unpublished PhD Thesis, Maharaja
     Sayajirao University of Baroda: 2006), p. 243.
27   O. Chinappa Reddy, *The Court and the Constitution of India*
     (Oxford: Oxford University Press, 2008), p. 43.
28   Granville Austin, *Working a Democratic Constitution: The Indian
     Experience* (New Delhi: Oxford University Press, 2003), p. 50.
29   Jawaharlal Nehru to Chief Ministers, 2 June 1951, G.
     Parthasarathi, ed., *Letters to Chief Ministers, 1947–1964*, Vol. 2
     (New Delhi: Jawaharlal Nehru Memorial Fund 1986), p. 405.
30   Jawaharlal Nehru to Chief Ministers, 15 June 1951, G.
     Parthasarathi, ed., *Letters to Chief Ministers, 1947–1964*, Vol. 2
     (New Delhi: Jawaharlal Nehru Memorial Fund, 1986), p. 419.
31   Sarbani Sen, *The Constitution of India: Popular Sovereignty and
     Democratic Transformations* (New Delhi: Oxford University Press,
     2007), p. 141.
32   Harshan Kumarasingham, *A Political Legacy of the British Empire:
     Power and the Parliamentary System in Post-Colonial India and Sri
     Lanka* (London: I.B. Tauris, 2013), p. 229.
33   Ibid., p. ix, pp. 4–6, 47–9.
34   Granville Austin, *Working a Democratic Constitution: The Indian
     Experience* (New Delhi: Oxford University Press, 2003), p. 97.
35   Jawaharlal Nehru to Chief Ministers, 15 June 1951, G.
     Parthasarathi, ed., *Letters to Chief Ministers, 1947–1964*, Vol. 2
     (New Delhi: Jawaharlal Nehru Memorial Fund, 1986), p. 418.
36   Arudra Burra, *Arguments from Colonial Continuity: The
     Constitution (First Amendment) Act, 1951* (7 December, 2008),
     p. 28. Available at https://dx.doi.org/10.2139/ssrn.2052659
     (accessed on 15 July 2019).
37   *Sajjan Singh v. State of Rajasthan*, AIR 1965 SC 845; see also
     Madhav Khosla, 'Constitutional Amendment' in Madhav Khosla,
     Sujit Chaudhary and Pratap Bhanu Mehta, eds, *The Oxford
     Handbook of the Indian Constitution* (New Delhi: Oxford
     University Press, 2016), p. 236.
38   Nivedita Menon, 'Citizenship and the Passive Revolution:
     Interpreting the First Amendment', *Economic and Political Weekly*,
     39(18): 1813.
39   Sunil Khilnani, *The Idea of India* (New Delhi: Penguin Books,
     2012), p. 35.

40 K. V. K. Sundaram (Secretary, Ministry of Law) to Chief Secretaries of States, 20 April 1951, Law Ministry File No. 34/1951-C, National Archives of India.

41 Granville Austin, *Working a Democratic Constitution: The Indian Experience* (New Delhi: Oxford University Press, 2003), p. 98.

42 Gopal Sankaranarayanan, 'The Fading Right to Property in India', *Law and Politics in Africa, Asia and Latin America*, 44, (2): 217.

43 A. G. Noorani, 'Ninth Schedule and the Supreme Court', *Economic and Political Weekly*, 42 (9): 732.

44 *Kesavananda Bharati v. State of Kerala*, AIR 1973 SC 1461.

45 *I.R. Coelho v. State of Tamil Nadu*, AIR 2007 SC 197.

46 For example: *AG v Amritlal Prajivandas*, AIR 1994 SC 2179, upheld draconian Emergency-era laws like the Conservation of Foreign Exchange and Prevention of Smuggling Activities Act and the Smugglers and Foreign Exchange Manipulators Act by partially relying on their inclusion in the Ninth Schedule.

47 *I.C. Golaknath v State of Punjab*, AIR 1967 SC 1643.

48 For a brief overview of the 42nd Amendment, please see: O. Chinappa Reddy, *The Court and the Constitution of India* (Oxford: Oxford University Press, 2008) pp. 65–72.

49 For example, look at the Statement of Objects and Reasons in Constitution (Twenty-Fifth) Amendment Act, 1971 and Constitution (Forty-Second) Amendment Act, 1976.

50 Gyan Prakash, *Emergency Chronicles: Indira Gandhi and Democracy's Turning Point* (New Delhi: Penguin, 2019), p. 680.] It was a commitment that Nehru and his successors found difficult to live up to.

51 'Parliamentary Trends', *Times of India*, 11 June 1951, Bombay, p. 4.

52 *State of Bihar v. Maharaja Kameshwar Singh*, AIR 1952 SC 252.

53 Ibid.

54 'Parliamentary Trends', *Times of India*, 11 June 1951, Bombay, p. 4.

55 A term used by Gyan Prakash. See Gyan Prakash, *Emergency Chronicles: Indira Gandhi and Democracy's Turning Point* (New Delhi: Penguin, 2019), p. 679.

56 Sunil Khilnani, *The Idea of India* (New Delhi: Penguin Books, 2012), p. 27.

57 Ibid., p. 28.

58 Speech at Mathura: Slanderous Gossips, 23 September 1949, B. R. Nanda, ed., *Selected Works of Govind Ballabh Pant*, Vol. 13 (New Delhi: Oxford University Press, 2000), p. 173.

59 Sunil Khilnani, *The Idea of India* (New Delhi: Penguin Books, 2012), p. 26.

60 Ibid.

61 Ibid., p. 34.

INDEX

Ahmed, Naziruddin 5, 143, 146, 156, 162–3, 170, 172
Aiyyar, Alladi Krishnaswamy 53, 128, 154, 177–9
'Akhand Bharat' 27–8, 37
Ali, Ahmad, release of 44
Ali, Saiyid Fazal (J) 113
Allahabad District Zamindars' Association 82
Allahabad High Court 2, 22, 43, 92–3, 126–7, 147
All India Civil Liberties Conference 30–1, 179
All India Congress Committee 94
All India Newspaper Editors Conference (AINEC) 5, 87, 145–7, 152, 176, 178–9
  Nehru at 129
  Standing Committee of 147
All India Trade Union Congress 84
Alva, Joachim 170
Ambedkar, B.R. 19, 63, 77–8, 97, 100–2, 108, 149, 169–70, 175, 190
  chairman of Drafting Committee 8
  on Constitutional amendment 143–4
  and Nehru 92
amendments to Constitution 78, 84, 91, 113, 115, 176, 188.
  see also Constitution of India

Annadurai, C.N. 62
Anthony, Frank 164
Armitage, David 13
Austin, Granville 13, 153, 178, 183, 187
authoritarianism 83, 90, 185, 189, 193
Ayyangar, M.A. 169
Azad, Maulana 78, 97

backward caste assertion 50
backward classes 50–2, 54, 113–14, 122, 152–3, 156, 158, 161, 163, 169, 181–2
  reservations for 1
backward communities 4, 56
balance of power 13, 88
bar associations 5–6, 119, 130, 192
Barooah, Dev Kant 132
Baxi, Upendra 4, 179
Bengal 27, 32, 44–5, 62, 66, 69, 94
  communal strife in 36
  public opinion in 46
  refugee influx in 61
'bhakti' or political 'hero worship' 19
Bharati, Kesavananda 188
Bhargava, Thakurdas 97, 138–9
Bhattacharya, K.K. 10, 172
  to Nehru 169
  resignation of 169
Bhushan, Brij 29

Bihar
   government 36, 39, 41–3,
      47–8, 63, 72–3, 88, 190
   zamindari abolition law 107
Bihar Land Reforms Act 42, 67,
   88, 91, 98–9, 104, 124, 139
Bihar Land Reforms Bill 47–8, 60,
   63, 66
Bihar Legislative Assembly 35, 38
Bihar State Management of
   Estates and Tenures Act 2,
   43, 46, 88
Bihar Congress 48, 65
Bihar Public Safety Ordinance 22
BJP 11
Bombay High Court 26, 31, 76–7,
   82, 118
   and communist detainees 21–2,
      24
Bombay Public Safety Measures
   Act 21–2
Bombay State Lawyers Conference
   118
Bombay State Road Transport
   Corporation (BSRTC) 76
   nationalization 76
Bose, Vivian (J) 113
Brij Bhushan v. The State of Delhi
   30
Burra, Arudra 184

Cabinet Committee 97, 100–1,
   107, 112, 114, 121–3
Calcutta High Court 107, 147
caste 51–6, 58, 79, 81, 106, 114,
   123, 153, 156, 162–3, 181–2
caste-based reservations 4, 112,
   122
   in educational institutions 3
Central Press Advisory Committee
   28
Central Provinces and Berar
   Regulation of Manufacture
   of Bidis Act 2

Chagla, M.C. (CJ) 10, 18, 31–2,
   118
Chari, V.K.T. 103
Chatterjee, N.C. (J) 30, 104, 130,
   147
Chatterjee, Somnath 30
Chaudhary, Rohini Kumar 23
Chaudhuri, Nirad C. 89
Christians 51, 54, 114, 163
   Backward Class 164
civil liberties 10, 12, 15–16, 22–5,
   29–30, 33–4, 71, 139, 142,
   146, 156, 186, 188, 190,
   193
   attempts to curtail 2
   and freedoms 11
   Maitra on 16
   oppose amendments to 5
Civil Liberties Conference 118
class discrimination 153, 162
coercive
   legislation 11
   powers 23, 180, 190
collective policymaking 112,
   131
colonialism 12, 187
Commonwealth of India Bill
   (1925) 8
communal
   conflict 61
   policy 54
   representation 51, 67, 111
   situation in Bengal 44, 68,
      see also Bengal
Communal Government Order
   (GO) 3, 51–7, 79, 111,
   113–15, 122–3, 128,
   143, 163
Communist Party of India 26, 71,
   79, 84
   on transfer of power 25
communists 23, 29
   detention of 21
communitarianism 191

compensation 39–43, 48, 60,
63–5, 91, 99–100, 104–7,
139, 180, 190
Calcutta High Court on 107
inadequacy of 105
Zamindars and 42
compensatory discrimination,
Austin on 153
Congress Parliamentary Party 97,
125, 144–5, 151–2
Constitutional Changes
Committee 122
Congress Working Committee
(CWC) 94–5
Constituent Assembly 8, 10, 15,
17–19, 23, 58–9, 63, 65,
103–4, 123, 128, 131–2,
149–50
Constitution (Amendment) Act
179
Constitution (First Amendment)
Bill 1951 1, 3, 7, 10–13,
129, 131, 146, 149, 155,
169, 173, 175, 183–6, 188,
193
Select Committee 146
Constitution (Removal of
Difficulties) Order 177
constitutional
amendments 9, 59, 78–9, 82,
84, 86–8, 96–7, 106–7,
119, 125, 137, 154–5, 159,
184–5, 187, 189
freedoms 47, 84, 93, 98, 101,
159
guarantees 116–17, 119
history 12–13
liberties 115, 118
morality 8, 23, 48, 116, 121
subversion 132, 185, 193
constitutionalism 11, 62, 89, 183
Constitution Amendment Bill 129,
166, 190

Constitution of India 8, 12, 15,
30, 35, 52–3, 59, 116, 119,
129–30, 143
24th Amendment 188
25th Amendment 188
26 January 1950 9
42nd Amendment 189
103rd Amendment 182
Article 13 18, 93, 98
Article 13 (2) 177
Article 14 2, 98–9, 104, 107–8,
113, 122, 180
Article 15 3, 52–3, 112–13,
122, 128, 144, 152, 156–8,
161, 169–70, 181
Article 15 (1) 3, 53, 55, 57–8
Article 16 54, 114–15
Article 19 30, 32, 71, 91–3,
100–1, 108, 120, 122, 145,
147, 150–2, 157, 160
Article 19 (2) 92, 151–2, 164
Article 22 21–2
Article 29 52, 55, 114, 153, 181
Article 29 (2) 53, 55, 111, 113,
128, 152, 157
Article 31 63–4, 66, 91, 93,
99–100, 103–4, 121–2, 139,
141, 155, 157, 170–1
Article 31A 121, 124, 180
Article 31B 143, 170, 180
Article 32 113
Article 39(B & C) 188
Article 46 54–5
Article 226 92
Article 368 117, 177, 183
Article 372 162
Article 392 177–8
fundamental principles of 4,
136
Nehru on 134
Prasad on sanctity of 123
promulgation of 13, 18, 21
Sachar on sovereignty of 121

Constitution of India Bill (Swaraj Bill), Tilak 8
Constitution of India Society 117, 129
contempt of court 4, 32, 36, 75
Criminal Law Amendment (Madras) Act 71
criticism 3–5, 25, 27–9, 32–3, 45, 85, 97, 106, 108, 119–21, 126–7, 145–6, 148–9, 151, 163
Crocker, Walter 89
Cross Roads 25, 29, 75
    ban on 26
    verdict on 32

Das, C.R. 31
Das, P.R. (J) 31–2, 90, 93, 104, 118
Das, Sarangadhar 172
Das, Seth Govind 170
Das, Sudhi Ranjan (J) 113
De, Rohit 21
de-Brahminization 51
defamation 4, 32, 75, 161
Defence of India Rules 156
democracy 20–1, 30, 102, 104, 116, 117–18, 152, 162, 164–5, 167, 172–3, 191–3
Democratic Convention in Lucknow 31
Democratic Front 94, 144, 159
Democratic Party 31, 39, 91
Deshmukh, C.D. 63
Deshmukh, Durgabai 16
Deshmukh, Punjabrao 97
detention, preventive 16, 23–4, 85
Deva, Narendra 81
Devi, Shaila Bala 74–5
Digvijainath, Mahant 27
Directive Principles of State Policy 1, 3, 7, 9, 54, 56, 113–14, 134, 143–4, 185, 188–9
    Part IV 56

discrimination, prohibiting 112–13, 128
dissidents 21, 94, 151
Dorairajan, Champakam 50, 52
Dravida Munnetra Kazhagam (DMK) 50, 62
Dravidar Kazhagam (DK) 50
Dravidistan 62, *see also* Tamil Nadu
D'Souza, Jerome 163

East Pakistan 107
    communal riots in 27
East Punjab Public Safety Act 2, 30, 32
    'pre-censorship order' 28–9
economically weaker sections 153, 182
educational institutions 51, 53, 79, 111, 113–14, 128
    reservations 3, 114
Election Commission 80
elections 3, 8, 46, 64, 66–7, 72, 79–82, 133, 168, 188, 190
emergency 189

fake news 133
Federation of Indian Chambers of Commerce and Industry (FICCI) 5, 119
foreign relations 128–9
foreign states 4, 92, 108, 136, 151, 161, 186
fourth estate 38, 116, 145, 148
freedom of individual 24, 134
freedom of speech and expression 4, 11–12, 30, 32–3, 37, 83–4, 87, 91–2, 98, 100–1, 128–30, 143–52, 164–5, 168–70, 178, 180
    Kamath on 163
    Mookerji and 155

freedom of Press 33, 87, 147,
    176–8, 182
free speech 7, 12, 24–6, 32–3, 38,
    133, 139, 141, 143, 150,
    155, 186
  confrontation over 24–34
fundamental rights 1–3, 7–16, 21–3,
    29–31, 56, 82, 84, 91–3, 114,
    116–19, 125–6, 129–31, 134,
    137, 149–52, 155–6, 160–2,
    164–5, 167, 184–9
  Ambedkar on 175
  amendments 113, 185
  Chagla on 18–19
  and execution of government
    policies 113
  Mookerji on 165
  Munshi on 18
  Paten on 19
  permanent guarantees 17–19,
    184
  Subcommittee on 46, 63

Gadgil, N.V. 85
Gandhi, Devadas 147
Gandhi, Father of Nation 68
Gandhi, Indira 188
Gautam, Mohan Lal 97, 171
Gautam, Sheela 97
general elections 72, 79, 81, 101,
    119, 121, 124, 142, 147, 157
Goenka, Ramnath 147
Gopal, Sarvepalli 112, 157, 189
Government of India Act, 1935 16
Gupta, C.B. 46
Gupta, Deshbandhu 87, 142–3,
    145, 147, 152, 178, 180

Hidayatullah (CJ) 103, 184
high courts 36–7, 49, 60–1, 75–6,
    85, 87–9, 95–6, 124, 126,
    193
  Nehru on 59

Hindu Code Bill 190
Hindu Mahasabha 27–8, 30, 37,
    45, 68, 70, 84
Hindu refugees, migration of 27
Hindu revivalism 69
human rights 9, 19

Imam, Hussain 129, 142–3, 172
Indian Criminal Law Amendment
    (Madras) Act 71
Indian National Congress 1, 9, 11,
    29, 31, 33, 40, 46, 48, 67–8,
    71–3, 96–9, 121, 169, 187,
    192
Indian Penal Code (IPC) 124, 156,
    180, 182, 186
  Section 124A 12, 82–3, 124,
    156, 180, 186
  Section 153A 82–3, 124, 156,
    180, 182, 186
  Section 295A 182, 186
Indian Press (Emergency Powers)
    Act 75
individual freedom 1, 10–11, 15,
    17, 24, 33, 56, 116, 123,
    156, 179
  Ambedkar on 19–20
  Patel on 19
individual liberty 1, 13, 134, 191
  Santhanam on 19
individual rights 10–11, 16, 20,
    116, 130, 178, 181, 185,
    191
  Ambedkar on 8, 19
Information Technology Act
    186

jagirdari 67, *see also* zamindari
    systems
Jaitley, Arun 11
Jayakar, M.R. 10, 118
Joshi, N.M. 84
Justice Party 50–1

Kamath, H.V. 10, 5, 142–3, 159–60, 162–3, 169–70, 172, 193
Kania, Harilal (CJ) 113, 175–6
Katju, Kailash Nath 32
Khaliquzzaman, Chaudhary 129
Khan, Jamshed Ali, Nawab 91
Khan, Liaquat Ali 27
Khan, Zafarullah 38
Khilnani, Sunil 185–6, 192
Kidwai, Rafi Ahmed 94, 144
Kripalani, Jivatram (Acharya Kripalani) 5, 10, 64, 68–9, 144, 164–6, 172, 193
    resignation of 144
Kripalani, Sucheta 172
Krishnamachari, T.T. 150
Krishnaswamy, S. 54
Kumarasingham, Harshan 100, 128, 183
Kumaraswamy Raja, P.S. 79, 114–15, 123
Kunzru, Gopi Nath 130
Kunzru, H.N. 5–6, 9, 132, 142, 146, 155–6, 168, 170, 172, 193
Kurien, Verghese 45

landlordism 41, 90
land redistribution 3, 35, 42, 73, 80, 99
Land Reform Bill, in Bihar 39, 41–2, 64, 70; in Uttar Pradesh (UP) 39, 42–3, 48, 62, 90, 92, 124
land reform: legislation 35, 38–9, 143, 183, 188; programme 1, 34–5, 39, 41, 43, 46, 57–9, 62, 69, 74, 77–8, 81, 91, 94–6, 105–6
Land Reforms Act, Bihar 72–3
Legislative or Executive Act or Order 7, 114

libel 4, 32, 75, 100
liberalism 5, 10, 20, 101, 129, 175, 185, 190, 192–3
liberties
    constitutional 115, 118
    personal 7, 37, see also civil liberties
    Santhanam on 18

Madhya Pradesh, Central Provinces and Berar Regulation of Manufacture of Bidis Act 2
Madras, 'zamindars' 2, see also Allahabad District Zamindars' Association; zamindari system
Madras Communal General Order (GO) 7, 51, 78
Madras government 25, 54–5, 71, 79, 113–14
    banning Cross Roads 25
    and Salem jail incident 25
Madras High Court 52, 55, 58, 71, 79, 113, 115
    Article 15 (1) preventing discrimination 3, 55, 58
    and Communal GO 54, 57, 62
Madras Legislative Assembly 57
Madras Maintenance of Public Order Act 2, 25, 32
Mahajan, Mehr Chand (J) 113
Mahtab, Hare Krishna 98
Maintenance of Internal Security Act 186
Maitra, P.L.K. 16
majoritarianism 185
Malkani, K.R. 29, 193
Malviya, Govind 172
Malviya, Madan Mohan 172
Management of Estates and Tenures Act 35–6
Masani, Minocher 'Minoo' 148

Matthai, John 44–6, 101
  resignation of 45
  Wavell on 45
Mavalankar, G.V. 88, 170
  to Nehru 141
Mehta, Pran Nath 10, 117
Menon, K. Madhava 57
  and police fracas 24–5
Menon, Nivedita 185
Mishra, M.P. 142
Mookerji, Shyama Prasad, 4–6,
  10–11, 44–5, 132, 135–9,
  146, 155, 164–5, 169–72,
  184, 187, 193
  encountering Nehru 135–8
  on freedom of speech 155, 169
  on fundamental rights 187
  for individual freedom 11, 139
  on Nehru 6–7, 171–2, 193
  and Partition 27
  resignation of 44–5
Moraes, Frank 26
Motilal Nehru Report in 1928 8
Mukherjee, B.K. (J) 113
Mukherjee, S.N. 91–2
Munshi, K.M. 9, 18, 63, 97, 101
Muslims 51, 54, 114, 147
  evacuee property 27

Nagpur 124
Nagpur High Court Bar
  Association 4, 147
Narain, Guru 82
Narayan, Jayaprakash 10, 32, 34,
  81, 116
  on Constitution 49
  on dictatorship 84–5, 167
  on freedom of individual 30
Nasik Congress 69–70
nationalization 1, 72, 77, 81, 98,
  116, 188
  of industry 1, 122
  of road transport in Bombay 2,
  76, 78

Nationalization of Transport Bill,
  UP 76
National Planning Committee,
  first (1938) 1
National Security Act 186
Nehru, Jawaharlal 1, 3, 6, 8–9,
  19, 24, 67–70, 126–8, 145,
  159, 164
  to Ambedkar 77
  Anthony on 164
  to Bidhan Roy 88
  confidence-building measures
  27
  Gopal on 112
  to his chief ministers 102
  his message to nation 8
  and news on China 169
  and press 38, 97–8
  'soft' Hindu nationalism 64
  and Tara Singh 85
Nehru–Liaquat Pact 44–5
Nehruvian:
  revolution 175
  secularism 69
  socialism 191
  statism 13
Neogy, K.C. 44–5, 101
  resignation of 45
Ninth Schedule 92, 103, 137,
  143, 156–7, 170–1, 180–1,
  187–8
non-Brahmins 51, 54, 114
Noorani, A.G. 4, 188

Organiser 2, 27, 30, 75
  ban on 26

Pakistan 27–9, 36–7, 44–5, 61, 68,
  70, 108, 120, 129, 136, 179
Palkhivala, Nani 77
Pandit, Vijaya Lakshmi 68–9
Pant, Govind Ballabh 39, 60,
  91–2, 94, 98, 126, 192
Partition 13, 27–8, 136

Patanjali Shastri, M. (J) 113
Patel, Vallabhbhai 23–5, 28, 34,
    36–8, 64, 67–9, 78, 85–6,
    94, 101
  death of 88–9
  on fundamental rights 16–17, 19
  interim report 17
  to Nehru 33, 37, 66
Patna High Court 22, 31, 36, 43,
    46, 73–5, 98–9, 102–3, 118,
    124, 144
  and violation of Articles 14
    and 31 2
  Mookerji on judgment by 136
Peasants and Workers Party 22
People's Education Society 71
Permanent Settlement, abolishing
    104
personal freedoms 16, 20, 34, 38,
    86, 128
police powers 80, 149
Prakash, Gyan 189
Prasad, Rajendra 8, 15, 17, 65–6,
    92, 99, 122–6, 136, 153–4,
    177–9
  to Nehru 154
  and freedom of Press 178
  and zamindari abolition 136
Prasad, Sarjoo (J) 75
pre-censorship order 28, 30, 32
Press 3, 5–6, 28–9, 33, 37–8,
    65–7, 75, 87–8, 97, 113,
    115–16, 121–2, 129–33,
    147–8, 151–2, 154–5,
    157–8, 161–2, 175, 177–8,
    see also sedition law
  curbing 88, 108, 139
  Nehru and 28, 66–7, 87, 97,
    99, 167
  regulation of 2
The Press (Objectionable Matter)
    Act 75, 180, 182
Preventive Detention Bill, Patel
    on 23

private property 64, 113, 170, 190
Provincial Congress Committees
    41
public criticism 25, 108
public opinion 45–6, 141–2,
    145–6, 164, 171
'public order' 2, 4, 32–3, 116,
    120, 129–30, 148, 151, 155,
    158, 180, 186
'public safety' 2, 7, 32–3, 180
Punjab High Court, and release of
    Tara Singh 82
Punjab Legislative Assembly 74
Punjab State Civil Liberties
    Conference 85
purna swaraj 19
  resolution of 1930 8

Radhakrishnan, Sarvepalli 112
Rajagopalachari, Chakravarti
    (Rajaji) 20, 28, 63, 69, 78,
    97, 101, 108–9, 169
  on fundamental rights 189–90
Ram, Jagjivan 63, 78, 97
Ramasamy Periyar, E.V. 50, 62
Ramaswamy Iyer, C.P. 9
Ramaswamy Reddiyar, O.P. 51
Ranga, N.G. 138
Rao, Shiva 147
Rashtriya Swayamsevak Sangh
    (RSS) 2, 11, 26, 28–9, 37,
    68
Ray, Renuka 97, 142, 170
'reasonable restrictions' 91, 98,
    150–1, 158
Representation of the People Bill
    6, 128
Republic, anniversary of 89–94
reservations 32, 51, 53, 55–8, 62,
    72, 74, 80–1, 106, 111, 114,
    152–3, 181–2
  as administrative tool 51
  in educational institutions 79,
    114

rights
    of association 37
    bearing citizens 22
    to dissent 11–12
    to equality, Article 14 2
    of free movement 37
    to free speech 101, 155
    with obligations 87
    to property 2, 4, 34, 39, 43, 46,
        63, 65, 86, 98, 100, 190,
        193
Road Transport Corporation Act,
    Bombay 76
*Romesh Thappar v. The State of
    Madras* 30
Roy, Bidhan Chandra 6, 28, 88,
    152

Sabavala, S.A. 176
Sachar, Rajinder 5, 120
Sahay, K.B. 39, 47, 63
Sahay, Syamnandan 10, 142–3,
    170
Saksena, Shibban Lal 10, 68, 170,
    172
Salem Central Jail, communist
    prisoners strike at 24
Sankaranarayanan, Gopal 187
Santhanam, K. 9, 18–19, 77
Sayeed, Basheer Ahmed (J) 53
Scheduled Classes 122, 164, 169,
    181
Scheduled Tribes 122, 181
security of State 4, 7, 12, 23, 30,
    32–3, 75, 83, 92, 100–1,
    186–7
    Nehru and 167
sedition law 7, 11–12, 78, 80,
    82–3, 85, 128, 178, 180,
    182–3, 186–7
Select Committee 132, 144, 146,
    149–50, 153–5, 157, 159,
    166

Sen, Sarbani 106
Setalvad, M.C. 66, 108
Seth, Damodar Swarup 172
Shah, K.T. 132, 146, 156, 162,
    172
Shahi, Virendra, Raja 39
Sharma, Krishna Chandra 142
Shastri, Algu Rai 68
Shiromani Akali Dal 80
Singh, Arjun 153
Singh, Chaudhary Charan 41
Singh, Hukam 39, 146, 156, 172
Singh, Jaipal 172
Singh, Kamakhya Narain, Raja
    35–6, 73
Singh, Kameshwar, Sir 36, 43, 48,
    73, 139
Singh, Raghubir 41, 46
Singh, Ramnarain 142, 172
Singh, Tribhuvan Narayan 170
Singh, Vishweshwar, Raja 73
Singh, V.P. 153
Sinha, Krishna 47, 63, 77, 80, 92
    to Nehru 73
Sinha, S.P. 147
slander 4, 32, 75, 100
social
    agenda 46, 48, 57–8, 73, 77,
        79, 81, 95–7, 99, 102, 131,
        134
    engineering 1, 35
    justice 50, 53–4, 56–7, 134
    reforms 1, 13, 35, 39, 50, 95
    revolution 13, 46, 72–3, 79,
        81, 125, 127, 135, 181, 187,
        189
Socialist Party 22, 40
Sovereign Democratic Republic of
    India 9
sovereign democratic State 83
sovereignty 22, 117
Srinivasan, C.R. 52
Srivastava, Jwala Prasad, Sir 147

State Management of Estates and Tenures Act, in Bihar 2
Suhrawardy, Hussain Shaikh 129
Sundaram, K.V.K. 92, 103, 128
Supreme Court 2–3, 29–30, 32–3, 42–3, 57–8, 60–2, 75, 78–9, 82–3, 87–8, 100, 106, 111, 113–15, 124–5, 137, 143, 149, 179, 188
Supreme Court Bar Association 131, 146
Swatantra Party 35, 138, 148, 190

Tamil Nadu 50, 111, 122
Tandon, Purushottam Das 64, 67–70
Tara Singh, Master 80, 82, 84
Telangana, armed communist rebellion in 23
Tendolkar, S.R. (J) 82
Thapar, P.N. Gen. 26
Thapar, Romesh 25–6, 29
Thapar, Romila 26
Tharoor, Shashi 11
Tilak, Bal Gangadhar 8, 178–9
transfer of power 25
Tyagi, Mahavir 8

Uniform Civil Code 134
Unlawful Activities Prevention Act 186
utilitarianism 192
Uttar Pradesh (UP) 2, 34, 38, 42, 190
    nationalize bus routes 76
Uttar Pradesh (UP) legislative assembly 38, 40, 42, 60, 90
Uttar Pradesh (UP) Legislative Council 90

Uttar Pradesh (UP) Public Safety Act 22
Uttar Pradesh (UP) Zamindari Abolition and Land Reform Act 126
Uttar Pradesh (UP) Zamindari Abolition and Land Reform Bill 39, 60, 62, 90, 92
Uttar Pradesh (UP) Zamindars Conference 31

Venkataramana, B. 78, 111

Wavell, Viceroy 45
West Bengal 6, 16, 27, 38, 107
Wheare, Kenneth, Sir 9
white sahibs and brown sahibs 15

Zamindari Abolition Acts 2, 82, 120, 126, 141, 190
Zamindari Abolition Bill 60, 90, 92
    Bank of India estimating 49
Zamindari Abolition Fund 41
Zamindari Abolition Publicity Board 41
zamindari system 2, 39, 41–3, 48–9, 60, 63, 65, 67, 82, 91–3, 102, 104–5, 126
    abolition of 1–2, 35, 38–9, 41–2, 46–8, 59–60, 64–5, 69–70, 72–3, 80–1, 90–2, 94–6, 98–100, 126–7, 136–7, 139
    associations 119
    compensation 39–43, 48, 60, 63–4, 65, 67, 91, 99–100, 104–7, 136, 139
    properties 2, 35–6, 39
    Nehru on 49, 102